Bill Miner at age sixty-four after his capture near Gainesville, Georgia, for train robbery in February 1911. The picture was taken by photographer W. J. Ramsey of Gainesville. From Mark Dugan's collection.

The Grey Fox

The Grey Fox

THE TRUE STORY OF BILL MINER—
LAST OF THE OLD-TIME BANDITS

By
Mark Dugan
and
John Boessenecker

UNIVERSITY OF OKLAHOMA PRESS
NORMAN AND LONDON

Library of Congress Cataloging-in-Publication Data

Dugan, Mark, 1939–
　　The Grey Fox : the true story of Bill Miner, last of the old time bandits / by Mark Dugan and John Boessenecker.
　　　　p.　cm.
　　Includes bibliographical references and index.
　　ISBN 0-8061-2435-0 (alk. paper)
　　1. Miner, William A., 1847?–1919.　2. Outlaws—United States—Biography.　3. Fugitives from justice—United States—Biography. 4. Aged offenders—United States—Biography.　5. Train robberies—West (U.S.)—History—19th century.　6. Train robberies—British Columbia—History—20th century.　7. Train robberies—Georgia—History—20th century. I. Boessenecker, John, 1953–　. II. Title.
HV6248.M57D85　1992
364.1′552′092—dc20
[B]　　　　　　　　　　　　　　　　　　　　　　　　　　91–50860

All maps were drawn by Mark Dugan with the exception of the one on page 116, which was drawn by William B. Secrest.

The paper in this book meets the guidelines for permanence and durability of the Committee on Production Guidelines for Book Longevity of the Council on Library Resources, Inc. ∞

Copyright ©1992 by the University of Oklahoma Press, Norman, Publishing Division of the University. All rights reserved. Manufactured in the U.S.A. First edition.

Dedicated to the Memory of Frank T. Dugan
A Good Father and Friend

—Mark Dugan

Contents

List of Illustrations	*page* ix
Preface	xi
Acknowledgments	xv
Introduction: "A Kindly, Lovable Old Man"	xix
Prologue: The Grey Fox	xxiii
1. Birth of a Bandit	3
2. "I'm on the Rob"	11
3. "Hello, Stranger, Stop a Minute"	24
4. The Old Con	35
5. Old Tricks—New Turf	44
6. "Oh, But It Was Great Fun"	49
7. On the Road Again	54
8. "The Drivers on This Line Are All Damned Fine Fellows"	65
9. Home Again, San Quentin	78
10. No More Stages to Rob	93
11. Canada's First Train Robbery	105
12. Fifteen-Dollar Fiasco	118
13. "No Prison Walls Can Hold Me"	135
14. A Gentleman of Wealth and Leisure	149
15. Last of the Old-Time Bandits	155
16. "It Was No Harm to Rob an Express Car That Was Robbing the People"	165
17. "He Will Go Hurtling through Georgia History"	176
18. Final Escape	191
Epilogue: Folk Hero or Social Bandit?	200
Chronology	213
Appendix	219
Notes	225
Bibliography	243
Index	251

Illustrations

Bill Miner, age sixty-four	frontispiece
Union School, Clinton, Michigan	*page* 6
Land holdings of Joseph Miner	7
Yankee Jims, California, 1857	9
Bill Miner, age seventeen	14
Stockton, California, jail	19
Alkali Jim Harrington and Charlie Cooper	27
One of eleven letters written by Bill Miner requesting early release from San Quentin during his second term, 1871–80	38
Billy LeRoy, 1881	46
Bill Miner, 1881	50
Grave of Jennie Willis Boucher in Onondaga, Michigan	52
James East prison photograph and identification card, 1881	58
Map of Bill Miner's criminal career in Colorado, 1880–81	62
James Crum, 1881	67
Bill Miller, 1881	67
California law officers A. W. Stone, John Thacker, Tom Cunningham, Ben K. Thorn, and Harry N. Morse	70
Outlaw Ben Frazee	71
Wells, Fargo reward circular for the 1881 Sonora, California, stage robbers	74
Map of Bill Miner's criminal career in California, 1866–81	76
Bill Miner and Bill Miller, 1888	80
San Quentin Prison, 1890	87
Convict Bill Hicks	87
Headline announcing the shooting of Miner and Marshall	89
Convict Joseph Marshall	90
Charles Hoehn and Gay Harshman	96
Map of Bill Miner's criminal career in Oregon, 1903	100
Reward poster for the arrest of Bill Miner for the Portland train robbery on September 23, 1903	102
Prison photographs of Charles Hoehn and Gay Harshman	103
San Quentin mug photo of Jake Terry	107
Princeton, British Columbia, 1900	108
Mission Junction and CPR train in 1909	115

Map of Bill Miner's criminal career in Washington, 1905	116
Bill Miner, 1906	120
Shorty Dunn and Louis Colquhoun, 1906	120
Full-length photo of Bill Miner, 1906	122
British Columbia Provincial Police, 1906	123
Royal North West Mounted Policemen, 1906	124
Site of Bill Miner's capture in May 1906	125
Handguns taken by the Canadian Mounties from Miner's gang in 1906	127
Mug shots of Shorty Dunn and Louis Colquhoun, 1906	127
Reward poster issued by the Canadian Pacific Railway for the Ducks train robbery of May 9, 1906	129
Kamloops, British Columbia, 1906	130
Royal Canadian Mounted Police and their prisoners: Miner, Dunn, and Colquhoun	131
Two views of courtroom during trial of Miner, Dunn, and Colquhoun in Kamloops, British Columbia, 1906	132
Map of Bill Miner's criminal career in Canada, 1904–6	133
Penitentiary at New Westminster, British Columbia, 1900	136
Reward poster issued for Bill Miner by the Dominion Police, Ottawa, Ontario, after his escape in 1907	139
Mug shots of Bill Miner, 1906	152
Charley Hunter, Bill Miner, and Jim Handford, 1911	157
Bill Miner's meerschaum pipe	167
Railroad employees David Fant, C. H. Shirley, and W. T. Mooney, 1911	168
Bill Miner and his captors, 1911	169
Sheriff John F. Sargent, Bill Miner, and Detective Tom N. Hanie, 1911	170
Jim Handford and Charley Hunter, 1911	178
Mug shots of Bill Miner, 1911	180
Old Georgia State Prison Farm at Milledgeville	192
Map of Bill Miner's criminal career in Georgia, 1911–13	195
Last photograph taken of Bill Miner, 1913	197
Bill Miner's tombstone in Memory Hill Cemetery, Milledgeville, Georgia	198
Poster advertising the movie *The Grey Fox*	222

Preface

THE image of the western outlaw is etched into our national consciousness. Thousands of novels, films, and television programs have portrayed the frontier badman. He has captured the imagination of generations of Americans, from dime novels of the nineteenth century to such sophisticated modern films as *Butch Cassidy and the Sundance Kid*. Whether a powerful symbol of freedom or rebelliousness or simply a fictional vehicle for adventure, the myth of the western outlaw occupies a special niche in our culture.

The genesis of this myth is the real badmen of the Old West, such men as Jesse and Frank James, the Younger brothers, Butch Cassidy, and the Dalton boys. Bill Miner ranks among them as one of the West's most notorious. If historians were to rate western bandits (excluding Billy the Kid, who was not a highwayman) in terms of contemporary notoriety, they would probably place the James-Younger band at the top of the list and would follow with the Dalton brothers, Butch Cassidy's Wild Bunch, and then Bill Miner.

Bill Miner was better known in his day than such western bandits as Sam Bass, Bill Doolin, Henry Starr, Bill Cook, and Black Jack Ketchum. Each of these was notorious regionally—Doolin, Cook, and Starr in Oklahoma and Indian territories, Sam Bass in Texas, Black Jack Ketchum in New Mexico and Arizona—and in the ensuing years they have become better known as a result of their treatment in books and magazines.

Bill Miner, on the other hand, has been largely neglected by historians and writers of Western Americana. This is strange: Miner, during a criminal career spanning some fifty years, achieved notoriety throughout the western United States, as well as in Canada and the Deep South. No other Old West bandit accumulated such a lengthy and wide-ranging record. Even Jesse James's career lasted only one-third as long as Bill Miner's. Bill Miner robbed more stagecoaches and only one less train than did the James-Younger band.

It is surprising that no full-length biography of Bill Miner has yet appeared. Countless books have been published about other bandits and badmen of the Old West, but comparatively little has been written about Bill Miner. Even after the release of the charming 1983 film *The Grey Fox*, which dramatized Miner's exploits as an aging train robber during the early years of this century and made him known to the modern public, no factual studies have appeared, with the exception of a chapter on Miner's Colorado career in *Bandit Years: A Gathering Of Wolves* (1987) by Mark Dugan and a chapter on his California exploits in *Badge and Buckshot: Lawlessness in Old California* (1988) by John Boessenecker.

The main reason for this lack of attention by historians is that Bill Miner was a shadowy, elusive character in life and remained so long after his death. Just as he spent his lifetime evading the law, after death he long succeeded in eluding those who sought to track down his true story.

In writing a conventional biography there are many potential research tools: personal interviews, public records, diaries, memoirs, and personal correspondence. Such sources exist if the subject is a statesman, soldier, entertainment personality, or other public figure. But what if he is an outlaw, a bandit from the distant past? Where does one find relevant records? An outlaw does not leave a diary or write open correspondence. His desire for anonymity erases the clues which guide the researcher. The biographer must become sleuth as well as historian to unearth the man and his story.

Bill Miner is a perfect example of what one might expect from a habitual criminal. He deliberately fabricated as much personal information as he could and presented it to all who dealt with him. Most articles and books that have touched on Miner's life treat this misinformation as fact.

Even something as simple as Bill Miner's date and place of birth have long remained a mystery. At different times during his career, Miner claimed to have been born in four separate locations, with Kentucky being the most widely accepted. During his first term in the California state prison at San Quentin, he claimed Michigan as his birthplace, but he never again made that claim. In tracing his life history, the authors ran across the story of his trip to Onondaga, Michigan, where he hoodwinked the natives into believing that he was a wealthy California mining man. Why would Bill Miner pick a tiny village like Onondaga to visit instead of Chicago, Kansas City,

PREFACE   xiii

or even New York? Knowing from the San Quentin records that he claimed Michigan as his birthplace, author Mark Dugan checked the Miner name through the Michigan State Library and the records from Ingham County and found our man. All the records were there: census returns, land transactions, and county histories. Bill Miner had been born just outside the small village of Onondaga.

Miner's criminal history in California was also suspect. The San Quentin prison records reported only the county in which Miner was convicted and the date he entered prison. Therefore, we researched the newspapers in each of the areas he had been convicted. Again we were lucky: the newspapers reported all his earlier crimes in detail.

The real break concerning Miner's life history came from newspaper articles in the state of Georgia. This information was particularly important because it offered much insight into Miner's personality, beliefs, and psychological makeup. Much of this was in Miner's own words. After his 1911 capture and conviction for train robbery in Georgia, Bill Miner became a great favorite of the Georgia press. Several newspapers repeatedly interviewed him and then flattered him with their press releases. As the old bandit openly granted more interviews and talked freely to reporters, he inadvertently allowed glimpses into his character. The rapport that developed between the outlaw and the Georgia press afforded rare insights into Bill Miner the bandit and Bill Miner the man.

Tracing the history of this mysterious, charming, and curious yet conniving old badman has been a delight. Our only wish is that the reader will derive from this book half the enjoyment we had compiling it.

Banner Elk, North Carolina

San Francisco, California

Mark Dugan

John Boessenecker

Acknowledgments

THE authors have taken great pains to ensure the accuracy of this book. Years were spent in researching and hunting down leads, shreds of data, old records, and photographs. In every phase of this endeavor we received the kind help of many individuals and to each of them we would like to offer our sincere gratitude. Without the special help from two outstanding California researchers and writers, William B. Secrest and Robert Olson, many essential portions and keynotes throughout the book could never have been included. These two men, who are extremely knowledgeable in the history of lawlessness in early California, unselfishly shared their findings with the authors. Over a period of many years, we made a multitude of calls and requests for information to Joseph P. Samora, archivist at the California State Archives in Sacramento. No matter how many requests he received, Joe ungrudgingly uncovered these bits of information and immediately replied with his findings.

James M. Whalen, at the Archives Branch of the Public Archives Canada in Ottawa, was more than helpful. Mr. Whalen made various searches for material not only in Ottawa but also in other branch areas in British Columbia. In addition, he searched out and provided vital information previously unknown. Mr. Whalen's diligence and persistence were invaluable.

Most of the Georgia material came from the diligent work of Bob Davis of Jasper, Georgia. Mr. Davis is a professional researcher of Georgia history and without a doubt is preeminent in his field. He left nothing to chance and furnished some of the most vital material needed for this book.

Many photographs in the book had to be reproduced in one form or another. Everything was turned over to photographer Bill White of Raleigh, North Carolina, who often had to improve the quality of the photos. His excellent work allowed the use of many photographs that otherwise would have been excluded.

Sincere thanks also go to the following people, state by state, in the order the events take place in this book. *Michigan:* Mary Jane Trout, Michigan State Library, Lansing; Paula Johnson, Register of Deeds, Ingham County, Mason; Dawn M. Kemroy, Deputy Register, Judge of Probates Office, Mason; Vikki Marr, Lenawee County Probate Court, Adrian; Ruth Hoover, Clinton; Lucille Williams, Dimondale; Dr. William Mulligan, Central Michigan University, Mount Pleasant; Isabelle Moyer, Onondaga; Nadine Bodell, Onondaga; Joseph Boucher, Jackson; Robert Corwin, Jackson. *California:* Penny Doss, Deputy Clerk, Office of Clerk and Recorder of Calaveras County, San Andreas; Doris Parker-Coons, Assistant Curator at the Placer County Historical Museum, Auburn; Ruth Marshak, Deputy Clerk, Placer County Clerks Office, Auburn; Dr. Robert Chandler and Elaine Gilleran, Wells Fargo Bank History Department, San Francisco; Roger McGrath, University of California at Los Angeles; George Ellis, San Diego; Thelen Blum, Pinkerton's Inc., Van Nuys. *Colorado:* Theresa Falagrady, Catherine Engel, and Amy Vigil, Colorado Historical Society, Denver; Billie Ward, Clerk of the Court, Saguache County Courthouse, Saguache; R. E. Pittman, Records Supervisor, Colorado Department of Corrections, Colorado Springs. *New Mexico:* Margaret Costales, Silver City Public Library. *Ohio:* Janet Thompson, Ohio Historical Society, Columbus. *Oregon:* Walter Kurth, Multnomah County Library, Portland; Wayne Baker, Oregon State Penitentiary, Salem. *Washington:* Joyce Justice, Federal Archives and Records Center, Seattle; Dave Hastings, Division of Archives and Records Management, Olympia; Jean Engerman, Washington State Historical Society, Tacoma; Janet Lowery, Bellingham Public Library, Bellingham; Eunice W. Darvill, Skagit County Historical Museum, LaConner; Dean DeBoer, Manager of Bay View Cemetery, Bellingham. *Canada:* Les Mobbs, Provincial Archives of British Columbia, Victoria, British Columbia; Paul Yee, City of Vancouver Archives, Vancouver, British Columbia; Art Downs, Heritage House Publishing Company Ltd., Surrey, British Columbia. *Georgia:* Dr. Thomas F. Armstrong, Professor of History, Georgia College, Milledgeville; Dr. Janice Fennell, Nancy Davis, and Roger McLeod, Georgia College Library, Milledgeville; Louis Andrews, historian, Milledgeville; Mickey Couey, Moore's Funeral Home, Milledgeville; Robert Rice, Atlanta; Mr. and Mrs. Otto Ramsey, Gainesville; Sybil McRay, Chestatee Regional Library, Gainesville; James C. Bonner Jr., Decatur; Marvin E. Joyce,

Forstmann & Company, Milledgeville. *North Carolina:* Bobby Y. Emory, Raleigh; Dick Martin, Peat Marwick Mitchell and Company, Raleigh; Ray Steckenrider, Raleigh; Krista Ayscue and Mark Underwood, Raleigh; Mike Romanger and Bob Nussle, Appalachian State University, Boone.

There is not space enough to list all the many kinds of help received from Mark Dugan's wife, Sarah, but without her invaluable assistance this book would never have been completed.

Introduction:
"A Kindly, Lovable Old Man"

ON September 2, 1913, in Milledgeville, Georgia, a wizened sixty-six-year-old relic of a man died. The next day, one of the largest newspapers in the Southeast ran a four-column photograph and two stories extolling him, all on the front page. One of these articles described him as "a kindly, lovable old man, whose thoughts were humorous, whose manner was that of one who was a friend to all humankind . . . the most courtly, the most kindly spoken, the most venerable man . . . one whom they all regard with affection and something of esteem."[1] These words do not portray a great philanthropist, a well-known religious leader, or even a benevolent old southern statesman, but rather a stagecoach bandit and train robber, a criminal who from the age of eighteen had spent more than thirty-seven years behind bars. The words describe Old Bill Miner.

Why would a major newspaper print such statements about a notorious criminal? Bill Miner was blessed, or maybe cursed, with the uncanny ability to charm and influence nearly everyone with whom he came in contact. His deftness in mesmerizing others allowed him to lure many younger men into crime. It is evident that he had the same success with the Georgia press. His many years in prison seemed to mellow him and to give him an image of trustworthiness and kindness instead of making him appear sinister or dangerous. Wherever Miner went, he was viewed as a gentle, good-natured man.

These characteristics set him apart from the stereotypical western badman, but they did not make him unique in the annals of the Old West. What made him unique was that he was one of the first, and most certainly the last, of the old-time bandits, successfully continuing his career into the second decade of the twentieth century. His criminal career seems to have begun in 1863, several years before Jesse James reportedly committed his first robbery at Liberty, Missouri, in February 1866. It ended in 1913, thirty-one years after Jesse James's death.

Miner's career began with stealing horses and then escalated to stagecoach holdups. After the turn of the century, when the stagecoach had become obsolete, he turned to train robbery, using the method pioneered by A. J. ("Big Jack") Davis in the Old West's first train robbery, near Reno, Nevada, in 1870. By holding up a train in the state of Georgia in 1911, Miner earned himself the title "Last of the Old Time Bandits."

Miner circumscribed his criminal escapades with two rules of conduct. He never killed anyone (though in his younger days he had been dangerous in a tight spot), and he robbed only corporations, justifying these crimes on the basis that corporations robbed the common man. Thus the public related to Bill Miner and he became a folk hero in two countries. Once he was even cheered by crowds while being returned to prison following an escape attempt. Few criminals have made this kind of impact on the public.

Bill Miner was a paradox. He was not an exceptional or extraordinary bandit like Jesse James, who plied his criminal trade for sixteen years and was never captured. As Miner's time in prison attests, he was good at being caught. He was neither original nor a mastermind. Miner's two most sensational and profitable robberies, the first train robbery ever committed in Canada, in 1904, and a train robbery in Washington state in 1905, evidently were devised by a friend and confederate, but Miner got the credit and the blame. Legend has it that Miner was the first to use the term "Hands up!" but detailed accounts of his first robberies provide no evidence to support this assertion.

Politically, Miner claimed he was a socialist, but when he had money, he thoroughly enjoyed living a fashionable life in high society, dressing in the latest style, and spending his money freely.

Intellectually, he had a keen mind, and even though he had no formal schooling he was highly literate and had a good command of speech. This he owed to his mother, a schoolteacher who seems to have ensured that he receive a decent education.

Throughout Miner's life he pursued women and engaged in numerous love affairs. He even became engaged to a socially prominent young woman in Michigan in 1880. But there was another side to his sexual life. There is strong evidence that Miner was homosexual when imprisoned and bisexual outside prison walls. This was a subject not openly discussed during that era, but in 1903, after Miner had attempted to rob a train in Oregon, the Pinkerton Detective

Agency brought out the fact. By the time he was fifty-four years old, he had spent more than thirty-three years in San Quentin, a prison notorious for sexual brutality when Miner first entered it in 1866. After so many years behind bars, apparently sodomy became second nature to the old bandit. And during his criminal escapades, he always enlisted the aid of younger men, who may have provided outlets for his sexual urges. Thus Bill Miner appears to be the first known homosexual outlaw of the Old West.

Much mystery surrounds Miner's life as a result of his habitual lying and misleading statements. Over the years he used at least seven aliases and could spin a tale so convincing that to this day many are accepted as fact. Fanciful tales were as much a part of Bill Miner as was his ability to influence everyone around him. As he grew older the tales seemed to become truth to him. Bill Miner, like the people who extolled and idolized him, came to believe the legend he created.

Prologue:
The Grey Fox

EVERY bump, lurch, and sway of the automobile was painful to the old man. He was fortunate that the ride would be short, for just a few years earlier he would have been forced to make the trip by buckboard or buggy. To take his mind off the racking pains in his stomach and the discomfort of restrictive shackles on his wrists, the old man reflected on the past six days, the most agonizing period he had spent in his life.

The ill-conceived escape from the Georgia prison farm at Milledgeville had been doomed to failure from the beginning. The old man had given them fair warning, but he hadn't bargained on the severe price he would pay for that warning. He and his two companions made little headway through the unknown swamps that even the native residents avoided. It caused the death of one of the escapees and the old man himself nearly drowned, swallowing a bellyful of the rancid water, which caused the gastric attacks that now made him writhe in pain. At age sixty-five, the old man figured he was lucky to be alive.

After staggering out of the treacherous morass six days later into the humid, early morning heat of July 3, 1912, their clothes torn to shreds and their bodies covered with insect bites and lacerations, the old man and his companion were actually relieved to be returning to the more hospitable confines of the prison farm. During their ordeal, the two fugitives had traveled in circles, emerging at Toomsboro, only twenty miles from the prison.

The automobile, which had been quickly dispatched to Toomsboro, picked up the escapees soon after their capture and by midmorning approached Milledgeville. Dozing fitfully, the old man awoke to a sound not unlike the buzzing of bees. As the automobile entered the town, the sound became more discernible, that of many human voices. Reaching the center of town, the automobile was forced to stop by a huge mob that blocked the road.

The old man's eyes quickly turned from fear to surprise to pleasure as he realized the sounds from the throng were not shouts of anger but cheers of welcome. These people had taken the old man into their hearts, not for what he was, but for what he represented to them: a symbol of resistance to and defiance of a political and economic system riddled with corporate corruption. Thus the old man inadvertently had become a Jesse James–type folk hero in the Deep South.

Reacting to the crowd's exuberance, the old man, although in pain, acknowledged his noisy reception. Money and cigars were liberally thrust upon him, which he gratefully accepted. When the excitement finally began to die down, the crowd slowly parted and allowed the automobile to proceed to the prison farm. As a final gesture, with a true emotion he rarely exhibited, the old man waved his hat to the still-cheering crowd until they were out of sight. Surely he appreciated this unexpected show of feeling by these people of Georgia, for he realized that his time was short and his career nearly over.

During the last few minutes before reaching the prison farm, the old man's thoughts returned to reality and he reverted into habits that had dominated his life for nearly fifty years—a life of deceit, lies, and falsehoods. Before his escape, the old man had been dictating his autobiography to a prison guard who had befriended him and now he could look forward to completing it. The autobiography would be an excellent representation of his character, but not his true life history. Old Bill Miner, the Grey Fox, would continue to spread his lies and fanciful tales unto death, for by now not even the old bandit could separate the lies from the truth. He furrowed his brow as his mind strained to remember.

The Grey Fox

CHAPTER I

Birth of a Bandit

ALTHOUGH his true surname was Miner, he had used many aliases throughout his career: California Bill, William A. Morgan, George Morgan, Jim James, George Edwards, William Anderson, George Anderson, John Luck, and George Budd. More often, however, he was known as William A. Miner, which, with age, evolved into Old Bill Miner.

All accounts to date have stated that he was born in Jackson or Bowling Green, Kentucky, in either 1843 or 1847, that he was the son of a prosperous farmer named McDonald or Anderson, and that he ran away to Texas in 1859. Other records in which Miner himself gave direct information variously state his birthplace as Canada, Ohio, and California. In newspaper accounts, in which reporters took the information that Miner dictated to prison officials in Georgia, his father was a ne'er-do-well miner in Bowling Green, Kentucky, who abandoned his schoolteacher wife and children.

Miner also claimed he ran away to Texas at age thirteen and by 1863 was in San Diego, California, with Brig. Gen. George Wright of the Department of the Pacific. According to Miner's claim, the army was offering a one-hundred-dollar reward to anyone who would make a dangerous ride through Apache territory to deliver a message to Colonel Corner on the Gila River in Arizona Territory. Miner said he accepted and, except for a temporary stop at Tejon Ranch near Salt Lake, rode all night and returned to Wright's headquarters the next morning. As a result of this incident, Miner claimed, he was offered a contract to run a mail service in the area. He accepted and ran the service at rates of five, ten, or twenty-five dollars per letter until he spent all his money and turned to crime.[1]

But there were a few things wrong with Bill's story. There were no Apache Indians in Southern California. Rancho El Tejon is located in the Tehachapi Mountains north of Los Angeles, more than a hundred miles from San Diego and far off his purported route. The Salton Sea is the only salt lake in Southern California and did not form until 1905. The distance from San Diego to the Gila River and back is 350 miles; no horse could make this ride in one day. This yarn was simply one of the inventive ramblings that Miner loved to spin in his later life.[2]

Bill Miner's early life was vastly different from that which he wanted the public to believe. He was born Ezra Allen Miner in Vevay Township, an outskirt of the town of Onondaga, in Ingham County, Michigan, the son of Joseph and Harriet Miner.[3] He was named after his grandfather Ezra Miner, (for clarity, he will be referred to as Bill Miner throughout the text).[4]

Joseph Miner, one of ten children, was born in New London, Connecticut, in 1810, the son of Ezra (b. 1781) and Mary Miner (b. 1782). Bill Miner's mother, Harriet Jane, was born in New York in 1816 and married Joseph Miner about 1833. While living in Connecticut, the Miners had one daughter, Harriet R., who was born in 1834. In 1836 the Miners moved to Vevay Township, Ingham County, Michigan, where Joseph began farming.[5] On November 21, 1840, their first son, Henry Clay, was born, followed by a daughter, Mary Jane, on May 17, 1843. Ezra Allen (Bill), called Allen by his family, was born on December 27, 1846.[6]

The first record of Joseph Miner's obtaining land in Ingham County was in July 1836 when he purchased property in Section 16 of Vevay Township. His Ingham County holdings were extensive as evidenced by his many land transactions. It is probable that he obtained these holdings through the bounty land laws by proving that an ancestor had served either in the Revolutionary War or the War of 1812. In 1841 the Miners began selling their property.

On February 22, 1841, Joseph and Harriet Miner sold a parcel of land in Aurelius Township to Burton Robinson, followed by a sale of land in Delhi Township on January 9, 1843, to Isaac Butler. The Miners then sold three sections of land in Vevay Township: the first to Freeman Spauldin on June 21, 1848; the second to Russel Brewster on April 10, 1850; and the last to Levi Chapin on June 20, 1850.[7]

The 1850 census, enumerated on August 14, recorded that the Miners still had real estate in Ingham County which was valued at one thousand dollars. Apparently other members of the Miner family migrated to Michigan as the 1850 census shows Joseph's father, Ezra, and sons Ezra A. and William living in Conway Township,

Livingston County, Orrin in Vevay Township, and Lyman in Bunker Hill Township in Ingham County.

Moving approximately forty-five miles southeast to Clinton, Michigan, in 1852, the Miners sold their remaining land in Vevay Township to Waldo May, Jr., on February 15, 1853, and to Allen Hathaway on February 25, 1853.[8]

The Miners' last child, a son they named Joseph Benjamin, was born on April 1, 1853, in Clinton. He was called Benjamin to distinguish him from his father.[9]

The village of Clinton is located in the extreme northeast portion of Lenawee County, the heartland of Michigan agriculture. First settled in 1825, Clinton developed along the old Sauk Indian trail and was a direct link between Detroit and Chicago. After arriving in Clinton, the Miner children, Henry, Mary Jane, and Allen (Bill), attended school in classes held in a house across from the woolen mill office. In 1858, Union School was completed and classes were first held in January 1859 under the tutelage of Professor and Mrs. O. C. Williams. Here the Miner children attended school, at least through the year 1859.[10]

Bill Miner was almost ten years old when tragedy struck the family: Joseph Miner died of brain disease on November 1, 1856. Of the sons, only Henry was old enough to help support the family. From January 1, 1858, through 1860, Henry was employed as a clerk in the J. S. Kies and Co. hardware store in Clinton. Although his entire salary went to support the family, help also came from town charity. To keep fuel in the home, Henry borrowed a team of horses and cut wood himself from the surrounding forest. By 1859 the Miners' situation had become so desperate that Harriet Miner decided to sell their small house and plots of land in Clinton.[11]

Apparently Joseph Miner left no will and his estate went to his four children. His eldest daughter, Harriet, had left home and no longer needed his support. On July 25 and 30, 1859, the widowed Harriet Miner petitioned the Lenawee Probate Court at Adrian to appoint James C. Wainwright guardian of her two minor children, Ezra Allen and Joseph, in order to sell their property in Clinton. On September 5, Wainwright was appointed guardian, and on October 11 he made the following petition to Judge Fernando C. Beaman:

> The petition of James C. Wainwright guardian of said minors shows that said minors are seized of all those tracts a parcel of land situated in the Township of Tecumseh in the County of Lenawee . . . that said

Union School in Clinton, Michigan, built in 1858, which the younger Miner children attended during 1859. The school has since been torn down. Photo furnished to authors by Mrs. Ruth Hoover of Clinton, Michigan.

lots are adjacent and constitute one parcel; that it is necessary to sell said land for the support of said minors.

On December 31 the property was sold to Thomas Adams for five hundred dollars.[12]

In 1860, using the money from the land sale, Harriet Miner and her three youngest children migrated to California, where they settled in the gold-mining town of Yankee Jims, located in Township 5 of Placer County, eighteen miles northeast of the county seat of Auburn. That year, the census taker failed to include Bill and his mother in the Placer County Census, listing only (Mary) Jane Miner, seamstress (her age incorrectly listed as twenty-three), and seven-year-old Joseph Miner on the rolls.[13]

How the Miner family traveled overland or what prompted them to go to California is unknown. They probably joined other families on their trek west and likely had friends or relatives who had previ-

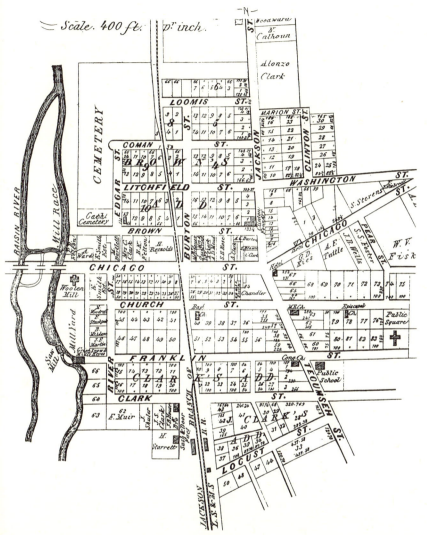

The land holdings of Joseph Miner in Clinton, Michigan, are located on Brown Street, lots 9 and 12 in Plat 10 of Brown's Addition. This map is from the 1874 atlas of Lenawee County, Michigan.

ously settled in the vicinity of Yankee Jims. More important, the impact of this move west would drastically change the course of young Bill Miner's life.

The first settlers arrived at Yankee Jims in the fall of 1850. The following March, the richest surface diggings ever found in California were discovered near Yankee Jims by a party that came west from Georgia. The men named the area Georgia Hill and, after loading their pack mules with clean gold dust, returned to Georgia. Shortly before the Miner family arrived from Michigan, Yankee Jims was the largest town in Placer County and was important enough that the 1857 Placer County Democratic Convention was held there. After Yankee Jims's heyday in the late 1850s, its population and importance began to decline. By 1880 the camp was all but deserted, with only 150 residents left.[14]

When he was an old man, Bill Miner told prison officials at the Georgia prison farm that his mother was a schoolteacher. This may well have been true, as illustrated by the literacy of letters he wrote in an effort to procure a pardon while in San Quentin Prison. However, there is no record of Harriet Miner's having taught school in Placer County. She apparently used her teaching skills to educate her two sons at home.[15]

Bill Miner's brother Henry remained in Michigan, and in 1861 he went to work in Alonzo Clark's dry-goods store in Clinton. He regularly sent money to his mother in California until February 1864. On February 26, with his cousin Frank Miner, Henry enlisted as a private in Company I, Twelfth Michigan Infantry, at Jackson, Michigan, for a period of three years. He was stationed at Niles, Michigan, until March 20, when the company departed for Arkansas. On March 21, Frank Miner deserted.

After the company arrived in Arkansas, it set up headquarters at De Valls Bluff. On May 7, Henry was admitted to the regimental hospital at De Valls Bluff for chronic dysentery, and was returned to duty on May 29. By late July or early August, he was readmitted to the hospital, but his condition continued to decline. On August 5, 1864, Henry Miner died of chronic dysentery and was buried in the national cemetery at Little Rock. Since Henry died in service, his mother later applied for and was granted a federal pension.[16]

The only reference to Bill Miner's early life in California is contained in a letter to Mrs. Miner from her son Henry, dated March 9, 1864, shortly after his enlistment in the Union army. Henry wrote

Yankee Jims, California, in 1857, just before the Miners were living there. Courtesy of the California State Library, Sacramento.

that Allen (Bill) had written from California that he was planning to visit their mother and was thinking of returning east by crossing the plains in the spring. Evidently, at that time seventeen-year-old Bill Miner was not living with his mother, nor did he cross the plains that spring as he had written to his brother.[17]

From April of 1864, Bill Miner's history can be documented with reasonable accuracy. On April 26, 1864, he was recruited into the Union army in Sacramento by Capt. Robert Robinson as a private in Company L of the Second Regiment of California Cavalry Volunteers. Although this is the first documented record showing he changed his name from Ezra Allen Miner to William Allen Miner, it is probable that he had adopted William as his first name a year or so before his enlistment. As recruit No. 23, Miner gave his name as William A. Miner; nativity, Clinton, Michigan; age, eighteen years, four months; occupation, laborer; eyes, hazel; hair, light brown; complexion, light; height, five feet, eight and one-half inches.

Miner was assigned to Camp Union at Sacramento, although most of Company L was at Camp Relief, Utah Territory, and remained in Utah and Wyoming territories until July 1866, when the entire company was mustered out at Camp Douglass near Salt Lake City. Miner arrived at Camp Union on May 7, but apparently military life did not agree with him and his resentment for authority came to light when he deserted on July 22, 1864. On December 5, 1865, regimental headquarters at Sacramento made an inquiry to the commanding officer at Camp Union requesting information on William Miner. The next day, Captain Roper replied that the name William Miner did not appear in the post records and no further action was taken.[18]

On the muster roll, Bill Miner listed his occupation as laborer, and in later life he demonstrated extensive knowledge of the mining profession. Since he was raised in the mining camp of Yankee Jims, it is logical that he had worked in the mines before being recruited. After his desertion, Miner returned to Placer County and continued working, presumably as a mining laborer. It was from these drab beginnings that young Bill Miner took his first step into a lifelong career of crime.

CHAPTER 2

"I'm on the Rob"

DURING his early years at Yankee Jims, Bill Miner had an unblemished record until he was eighteen years old. According to Placer County Deputy District Attorney C. A. Tweed of Auburn, who was a family friend of the Miners, a woman of bad character caused him to turn to crime. In a letter written to California Gov. Fredrick Low regarding a pardon for Miner, Tweed wrote on September 29, 1867:

> She [Harriet Miner] says her son now in prison was a good and upright young man and a *good son* to her until his career of crime was commenced—and I learn that the young man bore an exemplary character at Yankee Jims—Mrs. Miner will tell you of his history after he left that place—She thinks and so does our Sheriff Mr. Poole that the young man had been guilty of no crime until he made the aquantance [sic] of a woman of bad character then living some where below here, perhaps in Sac [Sacramento] County—Poole says that he knows that about the time Miners career of crime was commenced he had fallen under the influence of this woman—He certainly made a very bad record in a few months—but I believe that before that he had been unused to crime—[1]

Other reasons could account for Miner's turning to a life of crime. The prevalent atmosphere in the gold camps of "easy come, easy go" no doubt had its effect. The loss of his father placed the heavy burden of man of the house on the shoulders of Bill Miner, especially after their move to California when he was only thirteen. Without paternal guidance, young Miner was vulnerable to the suggestions and actions of other older males, and stability was not a virtue usually found in the early gold camps in California. The death of his older brother, Henry, who had been the stable force and main provider for the Miner family, put more responsibility on young Bill Miner and likely created more resentment for authority, especially if he considered negligent medical care by the U.S. government as the cause of Henry's death.

But most important were the vast differences between the social and economic status of the mine owners and the working miner. At the beginning of the gold rush, miners, alone or in small groups, had worked the streams with washpans and later with rockers, Long Toms, and sluice boxes. When the easy surface gold was gone, new techniques replaced them, mainly hydraulic mining, in which high-pressure water hoses washed away entire mountains, and tunneling, in which hard rock miners dug deep into quartz veins. By the time the Miner family reached Yankee Jims, tunneling and hydraulicking were used almost exclusively. Gone were the days of the lone prospector, for now large mining companies had been formed to extract the gold. By 1868, hydraulicking alone produced five million dollars from the mines at Yankee Jims and Georgia Hill.[2]

This industrialization of mining created a large social and economic gap between mine owners and laborers. Historian Ralph Mann, in a study of the nearby mining towns of Grass Valley and Nevada City, has traced the disparity which grew between these two groups. He characterizes the period from 1863 to 1870 as "a boom time in industrial mining when clashes of interest between miners and owners . . . were the major civic issues." Mann found that miners' wages were low by national standards and that Grass Valley and Nevada City were poor communities when compared to the national norm. Since these towns were larger and richer than Yankee Jims, it can be inferred that these same conditions existed there also.

Mann's study shows that working miners and residents of the mining towns had another reason to resent the mine owners: "As the mines became heavily capitalized corporate entities, ownership shifted to San Francisco, New York, even Paris. Locals enriched by quartz often left town, and townsmen, with notable exceptions, no longer had investments in the mines." And Mann's analysis throws light on Bill Miner's quickly developing hatred of large corporations: "Nonresident owners would not consider diverting some of the massive capital tied up in mine development to improve the towns themselves. No mine worked uninterruptedly all year; the seasonally underemployed miners lived in the towns while the wealth generated by the mines was spent elsewhere."[3]

The lot of the mine laborer seems to have made a profound impact on young Miner. Throughout his life he would side with and support the workingman. This became so ingrained in him that he later justified his crimes by claiming, "It was no harm to rob an express car that was robbing the people," and cursing corporations, stating, "All of them should be put out of business."[4]

Miner's purported initial criminal act, like the rest of his early life, has been clouded by legend largely created by himself. The following story has been erroneously accepted as fact and has been reported in almost all accounts of his life to date as Miner's first reported crime. Bill claimed that he had organized a band of stage robbers, held up the Sonora stage, and looted it of seventy-five thousand dollars. According to Miner, he gave most of the proceeds of the robbery to his gang members. For this crime he claimed he was sent to San Quentin for three years in 1866.[5]

Bill Miner's career of crime, however, may well have commenced in Los Angeles County one year prior to his enlistment and desertion from the U.S. Army. On June 25, 1863, James Keller and one William Miner stole "five mares of the value of twenty dollars each, five mares of the value of twenty-five dollars each, ten colts of the value of ten dollars each, one mule of the value of forty dollars and one horse of the value of forty dollars" from a prosperous Los Angeles County ranchero, Ricardo Vejar.

Deputy Constable Robert Hester, after several days of pursuit, captured the thieves and fifty or sixty head of stolen horses on July 31 on the Santa Clara River and brought them back to Los Angeles, where they were jailed on charges of grand larceny. On September 18 the Los Angeles Court of Sessions issued warrants and Keller and Miner were indicted on charges of grand larceny for the Vejar theft. William Miner was released on one thousand dollars' bail the same day. On December 5, a nolle prosequi was entered in Keller's case for the reason that the major witness, Lucio Alvitre, was also under indictment for stealing horses from Vejar and his testimony was therefore inadmissible. Although there is no record of the disposition of Miner's case, it is probable that a nolle prosequi was entered for the same reasons.[6]

The first proven crimes that Bill Miner committed were considerably less glorious than he intended for all to believe. In fact, they were amateurish and stupid, lacking any planning or forethought. Early in December 1865 the eighteen-year-old Miner, who was probably working for one of the mining corporations near his Placer County home, robbed his employer of three hundred dollars. A possible motive was that young Bill needed money to carry on his affair with the woman in Sacramento County. Regardless, Miner was

Bill Miner at age seventeen in 1864. Photo probably taken in Sacramento. Courtesy of San Jose Historical Museum, San Jose, California.

lucky, for his employer refused to prosecute because of Bill's youth and he was "let off."[7]

Bill Miner celebrated his nineteenth birthday a day late by committing his first and only single-handed crimes. On December 28, 1865, he boarded a train to Colfax, eight miles from Yankee Jims, and rode to Newcastle. Departing from the train that afternoon, he went to the livery stable of A. H. Smith and hired a horse to ride to Auburn. Promising to return the horse in a short time, Miner rode off on a one-eyed brown mare.

Arriving at Auburn around 8:30 P.M., Bill Miner dismounted and entered Houser's Clothing Store, where he selected a very expensive suit worth ninety dollars. Taking the package under his arm, Miner asked the clerk to accompany him to the house of Mr. Dickerson, the Placer County treasurer, claiming he had left his money there. The unsuspecting clerk accompanied Miner until they reached the secluded alley leading to the treasurer's house. Miner then drew a pistol and demanded the clerk's money, telling him, "I'm on the rob."

When the clerk told him that he had no money, Miner said, "That's a fine watch you have. Hand it over." Under the threat of death, the frightened clerk was ordered by the young bandit to remain there for twenty minutes and count his fingers. According to the *Auburn Stars and Stripes:*

> [The] Clerk was so overpowered by the robber's chivalrous bearing, that he obeyed his parting command, timing himself as well as he could without a watch—stood there shivering, not with cold alone though it was a cold night, until the twenty minutes had expired, and then returned to the store to tell the thrilling story to his astonished and injured employer.

Bill Miner made off with the suit, the clerk's gold watch valued at fifty dollars, and the livery horse, which he did not bother to return. By that evening the livery man in Newcastle had become uneasy and went to Auburn looking for Miner and the horse. He found to his dismay that the young bandit had left just minutes before his arrival. Although local officers were soon scouting the countryside for him, Bill made it safely back to Yankee Jims.[8]

Within a week, young Miner was at it again. On January 4, 1866, he went to a livery stable in Forest Hill, two miles from Yankee Jims, where he hired a bay horse, worth seventy-five dollars, belonging to John Elston. He then headed for the bright lights and wanton pleasures of San Francisco, where he disposed of the two stolen horses. On the way to the city, Bill Miner also picked up an accomplice.

Almost from the beginning of his criminal career, Bill Miner established two practices that he would continue to use in every robbery he committed: he never worked alone, and he tended to choose partners who were weak and gullible men or inexperienced youths whom he could easily influence and control. This became especially true in his later years.

On his way to San Francisco, Bill teamed up with John Sinclair, a seventeen-year-old youth from Petaluma. Before joining Miner, Sinclair had been a waiter at the Weber House in Stockton, where Miner probably met him. Whether Bill had to use persuasion is unknown, but Sinclair became a more than willing partner.

After spending nearly two weeks enjoying the riotous pleasures in the bordellos, gambling halls, and saloons of the Barbary Coast,

Miner and Sinclair took a ferry from San Francisco to Oakland on January 19. That night they hired two horses with saddles and bridles from a livery stable. Instead of returning the horses, the two headed northeast, where Miner traded them to a constable near Georgetown. The pair then drifted down to San Joaquin County.[9]

On January 22 the two stopped a wagon driven by a ranch hand named Porter on the west side of the San Joaquin River near Johnson's ferry, twenty miles south of Stockton. When they first told Porter to hand over his money, he thought the youths were joking and ignored the command. Sinclair drew a revolver, but Porter told him he had no money. Sinclair called him "a damned liar" and told him to "shell out." Porter immediately handed over eighty dollars. When Porter told them that he needed enough money to buy a pair of boots, one of the robbers handed him a five-dollar gold piece that dropped in the mud. As Porter picked up the coin, the robber told him to give it back and he would give him a ten-dollar gold piece. After this transaction, they told Porter that if he reported the robbery, they would kill him, even if it took ten years.

Quickly leaving the area, Miner and Sinclair rode to French Camp. Spotting three law officers they thought were looking for them, they raced on to Stockton, arriving at 3 P.M. Apprehensively, the two headed for Woodbridge, about fifteen miles north of Stockton. Having only one revolver between them, they purchased another in Woodbridge for fifteen dollars and checked into Keith's Hotel for the night.

The two sleeping robbers were unaware that the law was fast closing in on them. Porter had arrived in Stockton that evening and reported the robbery. At ten the same evening, Officer Jerome Myers in Stockton received a telegram from Oakland regarding the theft of the livery horses, giving the same description of the thieves that Porter had provided. Learning that two men answering the description of the fugitives had been seen on the road to Woodbridge, Officer Myers and Deputy Sheriff Joseph Long started in pursuit of them at 11 P.M. Owing to the bad condition of the roads, the two lawmen did not reach Woodbridge until the early morning hours.

At five o'clock on the morning of January 23, Meyers and Long succeeded in catching both of the bandits asleep in their hotel room and had no trouble arresting them. The officers confiscated thirty dollars, two loaded revolvers and two Bowie knives. Awaking, Bill Miner exclaimed, "You fellows think you have done a smart thing arresting us when we were asleep. If you had met us on the road and attempted to arrest us, you wouldn't have found yourself quite so smart."

At noon, Miner and Sinclair were brought to Stockton by the two officers and locked up in jail. On the way to Stockton, Sinclair told the officers they would not have been caught had Miner followed his advice and taken the livery horses back to Oakland and returned them to the stable. That evening, Porter came to the jail and identified the two youths as the robbers.[10]

The preliminary examination of Miner and Sinclair began on January 24, with Justice Baldwin presiding. Under oath, Porter again identified them as the persons who robbed him. At the request of the two prisoners, further examination of the case was postponed. On January 31, Sinclair and Miner were again brought before Justice Baldwin who ordered them committed to jail to await trial at the next term in court. Bail was set at one thousand dollars for each prisoner.[11]

Neither of the young bandits had any intention of remaining in jail and immediately began planning an escape. On February 20, using two bolts taken from the window casings, the two prisoners began to tunnel a hole in the jail wall, hiding the brick dust and mortar in their beds and toilet buckets. They recruited the aid of a Mexican trusty who agreed to empty the buckets on the promise that they would help him escape. Miner and Sinclair told the trusty that they could easily handle the jailer, claiming that they would knock him unconscious. Unknown to the two young prisoners, Jailer Conklin had been closely watching the Mexican and pressured him into revealing the escape plans.

By five o'clock the next afternoon, after digging a hole large enough for a man's body, the youthful pair struck sheet iron, which halted their efforts. Frustrated by their failure, they devised another plan. That evening, with the intention of overpowering the jailer and escaping, they kicked over a water bucket and hollered for Conklin to help them clean up the mess. Aware of their escape plans, Conklin refused to enter the cell or to furnish them with anything to clean up the spilled contents.

The next morning, Conklin called in Sheriff Hook and Deputy Sheriff Long and told them he expected trouble from Miner and Sinclair. With the two officers standing by, Conklin placed the two prisoners in separate cells and investigated the vacated cell. Conklin found brick dust and mortar in the bucket and discovered the escape hole, which was hidden by a box. A slungshot, made from a piece of brick wrapped in the end of a torn towel, was also found in the cell. Confronted with this evidence, Bill Miner ruefully admitted that he nearly broke his teeth off trying to pull out one of the bolts in the window casing. Placing Miner and Sinclair under constant surveillance in separate cells halted further escape plans the two might have harbored.[12]

On March 10, Miner and Sinclair were indicted by the grand jury in Stockton, San Joaquin County, on a charge of robbery. On March 7 and 8, Bill Miner was indicted in Placer County on two counts of grand larceny for the theft of the horses at Newcastle and Forest Hill. Officer Thomas Lewis of El Dorado County, who had been deputized by Sheriff Alonzo W. Poole of Placer County, arrived at Stockton on March 11 with a bench warrant for Bill Miner's arrest. However, the Placer County authorities would have to wait until the San Joaquin County trial was over.

On March 12, both Miner and Sinclair were arraigned, each pleading not guilty. Separate trials were ordered for each youth before Judge H. B. Underhill, with Miner's to begin on the twenty-first and Sinclair's on the twenty-second. District Attorney J. C. Byers prosecuted the cases and James H. Budd represented the defendants. Sinclair was convicted on March 24, and on April 2 he received a sentence of three years at San Quentin.[13]

On the twenty-first, Bill Miner's case was continued and on the twenty-fourth, his trial was set for Friday, March 30. On the morning of April 3, Miner was convicted of the Porter robbery and sentenced to three years at San Quentin. Bill Miner received a stern admonishment and some sound advice for his future from Judge Underhill, and his reaction was recorded in the *Stockton Daily Independent:*

> The prisoner, throughout the Judge's remarks, manifested the utmost indifference, and upon taking his seat after sentence was pronounced, told the officer that he was glad he had not got sentenced for five years instead of three. He left the court as buoyantly and with as much apparent cheerfulness as if it had been some degree of honor conferred upon him as a mark of meritorious distinction, instead of a sentence pronounced consigning him to a penitentiary for crime.[14]

Just before the prisoners left for San Quentin, defense attorney Budd told young Miner that if the opportunity ever arose, he would do anything within his power to help him. Bill Miner would never for-

Jail in Stockton, California, built in 1854 and used until 1869. Bill Miner and John Sinclair attempted to escape from this jail in February 1866. Courtesy of R. Tod Ruse, historian, Stockton Police Department.

get these words, and thirty years later, as governor of California, Budd would regret uttering them.[15]

On the day of Miner's conviction, without wasting any time, Deputy Sheriff Long took Miner and Sinclair aboard the steamer *Julia* and conveyed them to San Quentin. The two prisoners, although chained together, acted as if it were a bon-voyage party. Joyous and completely unconcerned, they stood on the upper deck throwing apples to the crowd on the wharf and waving their handkerchiefs as the ship pulled away. Their actions earned this rebuff in the *Stockton Daily Independent:* "A more thorough evidence of perverted nature we never saw."

Miner and Sinclair entered San Quentin on April 5. Except for using William as his first name, Miner gave the prison officials truthful information about his background. His habit of distorting the truth about his birthplace and of inventing aliases would come later. The following information was entered into the San Quentin Prison Register:

William A. Miner, Convict number 3248; nativity—Michigan; age—19 years old; occupation—laborer; height—5' 8 1/2"; complexion—light; eyes—hazel; hair—brown. Identifying marks—a number of small scars on forehead, pock marks on face, small scar on left forearm, VA in ink on back of left hand; five pointed star in ink on right forearm; brown mole on throat.[16]

Miner's partner, John Sinclair, was registered as convict No. 3249, and after serving two and a half years of his sentence, was released on October 28, 1868. Like Miner, Sinclair would continue to follow a criminal career.[17]

San Quentin would be home to Bill Miner much of his adult life. Its predecessor, the first state prison used in California, was a brig anchored in San Francisco Bay in 1851. Then a two-story stone cellblock was erected in 1854 about ten miles due north of San Francisco at Point San Quentin in Marin County. It was called "the Stones" by the convicts and guards. Two three-story brick buildings were added to the site in 1864, and finally a brick third story was added to the old stone cellblock.[18]

By the time Bill Miner entered San Quentin, conditions had improved slightly from those of the 1850s, when one visitor described convicts "in such tattered, torn, forbidding, filthy condition that the commonest street beggers, sleeping by the wayside and begging their daily bread, would by comparison have the appearance of newly Parisian clad gentlemen."[19]

San Quentin in the 1860s was certainly not noted for social reforms or mollycoddling prisoners. It was a tough place utilizing tough measures in handling the imprisoned men. Some of the methods employed against a prisoner who broke the rules included beating with rubber truncheons; being forced to stand for hours inside a small circle painted on the floor; "showering," or placing a pressure hose in the mouth which forced water into the throat and nose to the point of suffocation; and a discipline measure known as "the hooks." In this brutal torture the prisoner's hands were tied behind his back and attached to a hooklike device that stretched his arms upward until he was forced to stand on tiptoe. The unfortunate convict was kept in this condition until he passed out.[20]

In 1866 the prison held about seven hundred convicts, with the six-acre grounds surrounded by an eighteen-foot-high wall. The tiny cells measured four by nine feet and held two men each; they were sparsely furnished with a pair of bunks, straw ticks, threadbare blankets, and a bucket. To shield themselves from the winter cold, many convicts sewed newspapers between their blankets for insulation. They were issued uniforms of brown and black striped woolen shirts and pants.

San Quentin was heavily guarded, with several guard towers armed with grapeshot-loaded cannon, which later were replaced with Gatling guns. Sentinels patrolled the walls, and horse guards watched the grounds. Those guards (called "freemen") who worked inside the yard were not armed but did carry heavy canes for protection.

Most convicts were employed in the brickyards outside the wall. Another two hundred worked under contract for the state, making harness, saddles, whips, shoes, and barrels. A handful of others were employed in the blacksmith shop. Others worked on their own, making wood carvings or other handicrafts and selling them to infrequent visitors. Later a large jute mill was constructed, where convicts made burlaplike sacks. Many prisoners did not work at all but spent their time in idleness.

Prison life was a monotonous one for Bill Miner and his fellow convicts. The prison bell awakened them between 5 and 7 A.M., depending on the season, and each man had ten minutes to dress in his woolen stripes before the cells were opened by the turnkey. The convicts were permitted to stretch and walk about in the yard for half an hour, then breakfast was served, with only fifteen minutes allowed for them to wolf it down before they began work. The noonday meal was served at eleven-thirty. For safety, no knives or forks were allowed, only spoons, and absolute silence was enforced. The supper call was at four-thirty, after which all convicts were locked in their cells, where they could read or play cards until "lights out" at nine o'clock.[21]

A major problem that plagued the prison officials at San Quentin was that of sexual abuse, especially of the younger prisoners. According to author Kenneth Lamott, chronicler of San Quentin's history:

> Administratively, boys are always a major nuisance in prison for two reasons. First, they are wild, unpredictable and violent in their actions, and second, they are prime bait for the aggressive homosexuals, the wolves and the jockers. So far as his capacity for stimulating bloodshed goes, a fresh, attractive boy might as well be a shameless wench of sixteen. Beyond this the presence of young boys in prison had acted as a burden on the public conscience and stimulated professional reformers to bedevil wardens and legislatures.

Not until 1877, upon the arrival of Dr. J. E. Pelham, was a crusade launched against homosexual practices at San Quentin. Pelham advised solitary confinement as curative therapy but admitted that he was faced with a herculean task. An administrative solution was to separate the boys from the men. The boys were placed under the direction of the moral instructor and kept under guard except when in quarters.

When Bill Miner arrived in 1866, homosexuality was still unchecked. In later years a favorite trysting place was the jute mill, where the dark corners and the piles of material afforded the convicts relative safety from observation. Nineteen-year-old fresh-faced Bill Miner, who had a slender, girlish figure, no doubt was a target for sex-starved older and stronger convicts. Miner himself had a strong libido, and it must have been a bitter pill to swallow for him to be segregated from women for four long years during a period in his life when most men are at their sexual peak.[22] Sociologist Gresham M. Sykes has noted: "It is clear that the lack of heterosexual intercourse is a frustrating experience for the imprisoned criminal and that it is a frustration which weighs heavily and painfully on his mind during his prolonged confinement." The result, in many cases, is "prisoners who have turned to homosexuality as a temporary means of relieving their frustration."[23]

Like many other convicts, Bill Miner seems to have adapted to prison life by seeking alternative outlets for sex. Yet the absence of females may not have been the only reason for his homosexual behavior in San Quentin. One study of prison homosexuality sheds additional light on Miner's character:

> The male whose primary source of masculine validation in the outside community has been his sexual success (rather than work, family, etc.) and who has conceived of himself as aggressive and controlling in his responses to his world finds himself in prison deprived of these central supports for his own masculinity. In reaction to this he enters into homosexual relationships in which he can be conceived as the masculine, controlling partner and which for him and for the other males validate continued claims to masculine status. A complicating factor here is that some men suffer a profound psychological crisis when the supports for their masculine identity are removed. In these cases both severe homosexual panics or falling into "passive" homosexual roles are likely to result.[24]

Apparently, Bill Miner's introduction to homosexual behavior in San Quentin would become part of his character during his many years of confinement, a habit which would stay with him the rest of his life. Homosexuality, of course, was not an openly discussed topic during that era, and Miner's homosexual tendencies would not come to light until 1903, when they were revealed by the Pinkerton Detective Agency.[25]

Even though Bill Miner was in prison, Placer County authorities did not drop their charges against him. Pursuant to a court order dated June 7, 1866, Bill was discharged from San Quentin on June 9 and returned to Auburn to face charges of grand larceny for the theft of the horses at Newcastle and Forest Hill. For some reason he was not charged with the Houser store robbery. On June 16, Miner pleaded not guilty to both indictments before Judge H. Fellows and trial was set for June 25. On the trial date, Miner withdrew his plea in both cases and pleaded guilty. On June 29, the young bandit was sentenced to serve one year at San Quentin for each case. The new sentences were to commence at the expiration of his current three-year term. On July 3, Miner was returned to San Quentin as convict No. 3313.[26]

In the autumn of 1867, Miner's mother, Harriet, made a personal plea to Governor Low to pardon her son, carrying with her a letter of recommendation from her friend, attorney C. A. Tweed of Auburn, who had prosecuted Miner's case in Placer County. It was a vain appeal. Nonetheless, Bill was released from prison almost a year early on "coppers" (time credits granted for good behavior). On July 12, 1870, twenty-three-year-old Bill Miner, somewhat tarnished but certainly prisonwise, walked out of San Quentin a free man.[27]

CHAPTER 3

"Hello, Stranger, Stop a Minute"

THE brutal treatment and the hardships at San Quentin should have been enough to make an intelligent young man think twice before committing further crimes that could return him to that inhumane environment. Bill Miner was an exception. Six months after his release, he was in trouble again. This time, however, Miner had graduated to a higher class of crime: stagecoach robbery.

The young outlaw fell in with James ("Alkali Jim") Harrington, a Tennessean who presumably had been a San Quentin chum. Of all Bill Miner's criminal associates throughout the years, Alkali Jim was probably the most dedicated and hardened. Through Harrington, Miner was introduced to the loftier crimes of burglary and stage robbery. He also learned to conceal and use escape tools and, sadly, to betray an associate. Neither Miner nor Alkali Jim was a gunman, or "shooter," but Miner got his first taste of gunfire through their association. The two became so notorious that they were chained in irons throughout the entire proceedings of a subsequent trial.

When Harrington met Miner, he was serving his third prison term in San Quentin. His first conviction, under the alias William Waverly, was in El Dorado County in 1864 for grand larceny. Released in 1865, he was again convicted of grand larceny a year later in San Francisco County under the alias James W. Clark. After his release in 1867, Harrington stayed out of trouble until May 1869, when he was sentenced to one year and three months for burglary in San Francisco County under the name of William Harrington. He was released on June 3, 1870, one month before Miner's term expired. He and Miner apparently made plans to reunite after Bill's release. The twenty-six-year-old Harrington was also known to use the aliases of Walter Scroggins, Clifton, and "the Emigrant Boy," but was best known as Alkali Jim.[1]

Exactly when Bill Miner and Alkali Jim joined forces is unknown, but around the first part of January 1871 they were suspected of burglarizing several homes, including the house of J. Levy, in Alkali Jim's old stomping grounds of San Jose. Entering Levy's house at night, the thieves stole an expensive gold watch and other valuables. Learning that Alkali Jim and Miner were in the area, Officer Mitch Bellew searched unsuccessfully for them. He would find them later, much to his chagrin.[2]

Although proof is lacking and charges were never brought against them, Miner and Alkali Jim may have been the two bandits who robbed the Murphys-to-Stockton stage on January 17. About three miles west of Angels Camp, two men stopped the stage and took two thousand dollars in treasure. Sheriff Ben Thorn of Calaveras County scouted the area for the bandits but never caught them. A reward of five hundred dollars for each bandit was offered, plus one quarter of the loot if recovered.[3]

On the day of the stage holdup, Miner and Alkali Jim allied themselves with one Charles Cooper. The twenty-four-year old Cooper claimed he had come to California from the East with two thousand dollars in his pocket. His plan, supposedly against the wishes of his well-to-do parents, was to see California and return east when his money ran out. When this occurred, however, he decided to remain in California, taking a job with the Stockton-Copperopolis Railroad setting rails.[4]

In reality, Charlie Cooper was an alias for George Robertson, a Philadelphia native who also used the alias Charles Williamson. In 1869, Cooper committed a robbery in Sacramento for which he was convicted and sentenced to one year's imprisonment. Cooper entered San Quentin on December 14, 1869, as convict No. 4301, where he met Miner and Alkali Jim. He was released on October 20, 1870, and soon obtained his job with the railroad.[5]

On January 17, 1871, Alkali Jim and Bill Miner approached Cooper at his job site. According to statements made later by Cooper, they flourished their revolvers and said they wanted him to go with them. Cooper claimed that he did not want to leave his job and that they forced him to go with them. Using the age-old excuse that he did not know why they wanted him to join them, Cooper obtained his wages from the foreman of the job, bought provisions, and met Miner and Alkali Jim about twelve miles above Mormon Slough. He claimed he found the two outlaws armed with two shotguns, two six-shooters, one seven-shooter, and two derringers. Cooper subsequently recanted the story, admitting they later burglarized a store for some of the weapons.

Starting off that night on foot, the three made their way to Mokelumne Hill the next day. Here they remained all night and then headed for San Andreas, reaching there the following evening. Miner and Alkali Jim remained on the outskirts while Cooper went into town and bought crackers. The trio found an unoccupied house in the western portion of town, where they remained until the next morning, Saturday, January 21.

At daybreak they had started toward Stockton when Miner spotted a turkey, which he tried to catch. Cooper was quicker and seized the turkey, wringing its neck. They soon found another unoccupied cabin and moved in. To prevent detection, the trio placed gunnysacks over the windows, then started a fire and enjoyed a turkey dinner. During the day, Alkali Jim went to Hickman's Store in Stockton, apparently to familiarize himself with the interior and merchandise. Shortly thereafter, all three robbers broke into the store and stole two shotguns and other weapons.

In the early hours of Monday, January 23, they headed for their destination on the San Andreas–Murphys stage route. Cooper later claimed dubiously that it was only then that he realized they were going to rob a stagecoach.[6]

Before daybreak the trio reached a spot one and a half miles west of San Andreas on Murrays Creek and anxiously waited for the Sisson & Company stagecoach from San Andreas to Stockton, which was to arrive at 5 A.M. As the stage reached Murrays Creek, it was stopped by Bill Miner, who stepped forward and called out, "Hello, stranger, stop a minute."

"Do you want a ride?" asked the the driver, William Cuttler.

"Yes," was Miner's response.

"Just unbuckle those straps and jump in," Cuttler replied.

As Miner took considerable time in unbuckling the straps, Cuttler impatiently called out, "Are you ready?"

"No, not quite yet," Bill answered. "You had better not go any further. You had better stop here a little longer."

Cuttler, now noticing Alkali Jim and Cooper standing in front of his lead horses and pointing shotguns at him, exclaimed, "Now, gentlemen, you've got me, you had better drop those guns as there is no passengers."

Left: Alkali Jim Harrington in 1866 when he was using the alias James Clark. Courtesy of Wells, Fargo Bank History Room, San Francisco, California. *Right:* Charlie Cooper circa 1869. From John Boessenecker's collection.

Miner, with a pistol and hatchet, demanded Wells Fargo's money chest. Cuttler amiably answered, "Certainly," and threw down the chest and started to release his brake.

"Hold on, we'll let you carry the box with you," Bill called out and started to open it with the hatchet. Finding the chest difficult to open, Miner remarked, "You've got this fixed up pretty tight. I guess we will have to keep the box."

"Yes," agreed Cuttler, "We've fixed it up pretty tight because we've just been robbed the other day."

Miner then asked, "Have you any more baggage in there?" to which Cuttler replied, "No."

Spotting the mail pouch, Bill asked him, "What is that in the coach there?"

"That is the letter bag," Cuttler replied.

"I guess we will have to have that, too," said Bill.

To this Cuttler remarked, "Gentlemen, I don't see what you want with that bag, there is none but letters in there."

Miner answered, "Well, we better let that go," and then spotting a bag under the driver's seat asked what was in it. Cuttler stated that it held nothing but straps and ropes to fix harnesses. Miner then asked if there were any boots aboard, to which Cuttler told him there were none except what he had on.

"Haul them off then," demanded Miner. "One of my boys out here wants a pair of boots."

Cuttler indignantly replied, "Look here, gentlemen, this is pretty rough, making a fellow take off his boots and drive all the way barefooted."

"Can't help it," countered Miner. "Haul them off."

Cuttler did as he was told and was given Alkali Jim's old boots, which were cut up and dirty. Bill handed the the driver's boots to Alkali Jim.

Complained the driver, "I don't want to put on these; I'd rather go without them. They'll dirty my stockings."

Miner forced him to put them on but when Alkali Jim exclaimed, "I can't get on these boots," driver and robber again swapped boots.

Still not satisfied with their haul, Miner asked, "Have you got any money?"

In resignation, the driver replied, "I've got three and a half or five and a half [dollars], I don't know which."

Bill ordered him to "shell out."

"This is pretty rough," lamented Cuttler, "I haven't any change to go on."

"I can't help that, come out," the callous bandit replied, and the driver gave him five and a half dollars.

"Have you got a watch?" Bill asked. And Cuttler said that he did.

"Come out," said Miner.

"You'd better leave me something to keep time with," rejoined the driver.

Miner again told him to "come out," to which Cuttler pleaded, "Look here boys, take my coat, take anything, but I don't want you to take my watch. It was a present to me."

Cooper asked him who gave it to him and Cuttler told him, "It is a keepsake from my mother, who is dead."

Cooper replied, "Well, you are a pretty good fellow, and out of respect to your mother you may keep the watch."

Relieved, Cuttler replied, "I wish I had a bottle of cocktails, I'd like to treat you fellows."

To this, the robbers answered in unison, "I wish you had too."
After this exchange, Cuttler was allowed to drive off.[7]

According to a legend fostered by William Pinkerton, head of the Pinkerton Detective Agency, Bill Miner originated the term "Hands up!" The foregoing account of Miner's first stage robbery is based upon the detailed statements of Cuttler and Cooper, but nowhere in the reported conversation can be found this cliché. The phrase Miner did use, "Come out," was commonly used by robbers from the 1850s through the 1870s. This is just another example of the many legends surrounding the life of Bill Miner.[8]

Leaving the robbery site, Miner and Alkali Jim picked up the treasure box and carried it some distance from the road, where Alkali Jim opened it with their hatchet. Cooper removed the contents of the chest: two hundred dollars in gold coins and twenty-four hundred dollars' worth of gold dust. In his haste, Cooper almost left one thousand dollars behind but caught his error after going a short distance. Retrieving the money, the three walked north along the Mokelumne Road, covering eight miles in two hours.

Bill Miner, who had obtained directions from a German in San Andreas, led them over the mountains toward Jackson. Three miles outside Jackson they spotted two lawmen who turned off the road without seeing the bandits. Stopping at an old man's cabin about a mile below Jackson, Alkali Jim went inside and changed his old boots for a new pair, leaving the old ones at the cabin. A short distance from the cabin, Alkali Jim tossed their two shotguns into a creek. The trio then headed for Sacramento by way of Ione Valley. Reaching Ione after dark, they took lodging at a hotel after hiding the loot under a shed.

The next morning they retrieved the money and walked to Brighton, arriving after dark. Here they intended to hop a freight train, but they were half a mile away when it passed and were forced to remain in Brighton overnight. The next morning they caught the train to Stockton.

Fourteen miles outside Stockton, the brigands disembarked and walked the rest of the way, reaching the town at dusk. Miner and Alkali Jim remained outside town and sent Cooper in for food. When Cooper returned, he and Alkali Jim went to the railroad depot. Bill Miner, satisfying his penchant for fashionable clothing, went into town and bought a new suit for twenty-three dollars, equivalent to a month's wages for a laborer.

Leaving Cooper at the depot, Alkali Jim hid the loot under a sidewalk. When he returned he told Cooper he had successfully dodged two San Francisco policemen and therefore had been unable to buy a shirt. Giving Cooper two dollars, Alkali Jim asked him to go into town and purchase one. When Cooper returned, much to his dismay, he found that Alkali Jim, Miner and the loot were gone, leaving him with only eighty dollars in gold coin and Alkali Jim's new shirt.

Unsuccessful in finding his vanished partners in Stockton, Cooper caught a train for San Francisco. Unable to locate them there, he headed for San Jose to search for Alkali Jim but again was unsuccessful. Returning to San Francisco around January 29, Cooper was arrested by Detectives Sellinger and Appleton W. Stone. Because of the double-dealing by Miner and Alkali Jim, Cooper "peached" on them and readily confessed to the stage robbery.

While Cooper was searching for them, Bill and Alkali Jim had gone to San Francisco. On January 26, one of the two, probably Miner, went to a garment store on Main Street across from City Hall and tried to buy clothing with the gold dust. The clerk asked that the dust be weighed by Wells, Fargo & Company. Because the gold had been stolen from a Wells, Fargo express box, the bandit made some excuse and hurriedly left the store. Fearing this could cause them trouble, Miner and Alkali Jim immediately departed for San Jose.[9]

At 6 A.M., on January 27, San Jose police officer Mitch Bellew was informed that the "two State Prison birds" had been seen prowling about the streets. Bellew immediately set out to find them. At seven o'clock he spotted Bill Miner and Alkali Jim at a box factory near the San Pedro depot. When the officer commanded the two suspects to halt, Alkali Jim drew a derringer and Miner pulled out a Navy revolver. Bellew's belted pistol had slipped around behind his back and when he finally managed to draw it, Alkali Jim pulled the trigger of his derringer but only the percussion cap exploded. Bellew quickly fired two rounds at Alkali Jim, who took to his heels and disappeared into the fog.

During the exchange between Bellew and Alkali Jim, Bill Miner frantically tried to fire his revolver, but the cap was defective and he dodged for cover behind a telegraph pole. Bellew turned his attention to Miner, fired a shot at his shoulder, and "the fur flew" from Bill's coat. Without further inducement, Bill prudently hightailed it in the direction opposite that taken by Alkali Jim and also escaped into the dense fog. Bellew immediately went to San Francisco and related the details of the confrontation to Police Chief Patrick Crowley and requested that Alkali Jim be arrested on a charge of assault to murder.¹⁰

Deciding that San Jose was too hot for them, Miner and Alkali Jim returned to San Francisco and rented a room in the western portion of town. Obtaining a set of grocer's scales, the two weighed out a total of three and a half pounds of gold dust into three bags. Within a few days, Bill Miner traded the gold dust to a broker for twenty-dollar gold pieces and split the loot with Alkali Jim. The fugitives then hired a team of horses at the Fashion stable on January 31 and left San Francisco for Mayfield (now part of Palo Alto), arriving that night. Leaving the team at McComb's Stable, Alkali Jim split up with Miner and went to the house of a Mexican girlfriend.

Cooper had told the San Francisco officers that Alkali Jim was in the habit of staying with a Mexican woman in Mayfield and that he intended to depart with her for Mexico after the robbery. With the information from Cooper and Bellew, Police Chief Crowley sent a dispatch to San Mateo County Sheriff Tom Lathrop that Alkali Jim was probably in Mayfield and to arrest him.

Late the same night Alkali Jim arrived in Mayfield, San Mateo County officers, led by Deputy Sheriff Freeman, surrounded the Mexican woman's house. When the woman refused to open the door, Deputies Freeman and Whitlock and Constable Walker of San Mateo broke it down and rushed upstairs, where they found Alkali Jim in bed. Outnumbered, the outlaw surrendered without resistance.

Searching their prisoner and the room, the officers found ninety-seven dollars, several new derringers and boxes of cartridges, and an "Arkansas tooth-pick"—a knife with a razor-sharp fourteen-inch blade. The officers took Alkali Jim to Redwood City and jailed him on the warrant from San Jose. The next morning, Sheriff Lathrop notified Chief Crowley of Alkali Jim's arrest, and Detectives Stone and Sellinger immediately left for Redwood City to pick up the prisoner and return him to San Francisco.¹¹

For two days following Alkali Jim's arrest, Sheriff Lathrop and San Francisco Detectives Stone and Sellinger futilely searched the Mayfield area for Bill Miner. According to records of San Francisco police detective Edward Byram, "Feb. 5th/71 Miner was arrested on 3rd St. near Market by [Captain Henry] Ellis and [Detective Billy] Jones who went out in a hack, drove right on top of him and bounced him into the hack before he knew where he was. He was armed, but he had no chance to use his weapons." The *San Francisco Call*, reporting that Detectives Ginton and Sellinger were also in on the arrest, stated: "When arrested, Miner made an attempt to draw a weapon and use it on the officers, but he was prevented, and marched to the calaboose."[12]

On Saturday, February 4, Alkali Jim's lawyer, G. W. Tyler, berated the police clerk after being refused admittance to see his client. Tyler sued for a writ of habeas corpus, which was served on Chief Crowley. On the morning of the sixth, Chief Crowley, along with Alkali Jim and his counsel, appeared before Judge Stanley in county court to show why the prisoner was being held in the county. Tyler argued that Alkali Jim was illegally detained and asked that he be released. When Tyler could show no statute to back his allegation, the court remanded Alkali Jim into Chief Crowley's custody.[13]

On the afternoon of February 6, Chief Crowley and Detective Stone of San Francisco, Lee Matthews of Wells, Fargo & Company, and Deputy Sheriff Abbot G. Thorn of Calaveras County brought Bill Miner, Alkali Jim, and Charlie Cooper to Stockton on the first leg of trip through the area to establish positive identification. The three prisoners were placed in the county jail and later taken to Hickman's Store, where the proprietor identified Alkali Jim as the man who had been in the store on the day of the burglary.

Jerome Myers and Joseph Long, who had arrested Bill Miner in 1866 at Woodbridge, came to the jail and conversed with him, reminiscing about "the good old days." Miner jocularly recalled his long ride from Woodbridge to Stockton but later remarked with a little less humor that he was indebted to Myers for his prolonged residence at San Quentin and did not thank him for that.

On the seventh, the three bandits were taken aboard the noon train for Galt and then proceeded to Ione, where all three were positively identified. From there they continued to Jackson, in Amador County, where the old man recognized Alkali Jim Harrington as the man who changed boots in his cabin. Cooper took Chief Crowley and Officer Stone to the creek, where they recovered the badly corroded shotguns. Every detail of Cooper's confession was verified, and through him, Wells, Fargo agents Matthews and S. D. Brastow recovered some eight hundred dollars of the stolen booty.

From Jackson the officers and their prisoners headed for Mokelumne Hill, and on the way they stopped to eat. During the meal, Miner stole a steel table knife and slipped it in his coat sleeve. Not taking any chances with their prisoners, the alert officers searched Miner and found the knife. The three prisoners then were taken to Mokelumne Hill on February 10 and brought before Judge Tibbits for examination. Waiving preliminary examination, the prisoners were committed to jail on default of five thousand dollars' bail each to await action by the grand jury. Upon their delivery to the jail at San Andreas, Sheriff Ben Thorn had Miner and Alkali Jim manacled and ironed to the floor with chains weighing forty-five pounds each.[14]

During the week of February 21, Alkali Jim agreed to return part of the stolen loot. Taken to Santa Clara County, he showed the officers where he had hidden six hundred dollars. According to the *Calaveras Chronicle,* two thousand dollars of the stolen plunder had been recovered by late February.[15]

On March 5, Miner and Alkali Jim were caught making a desperate attempt to escape. Jailer G. W. Smith heard unusual noises coming from the jail and thought it was a diversion to cover an escape. He soundlessly made his way to the jailer's room, adjacent to Alkali Jim's cell, where he heard the sound of filing. He discovered that the bandit had filed his irons off with a case knife and was furiously trying to file through the bolt attached to Miner's chain, who was in the next cell. Alkali Jim admitted that they were planning to escape that night and rob a stage the next morning. Alkali Jim was furnished with a new forty-pound chain, which he later nearly managed to cut through with a bail from a water bucket. Referring to Harrington as "the alkalescent James," the editor of the *Calaveras Chronicle* quipped, "A forty pound steel chain ought to form an alkalimeter of sufficient capacity to test the strength of any alkali."[16]

During the March, 1871 term of court in Calaveras County, robbery indictments were drawn up but then quashed, likely because of Cooper's willingness to turn state's evidence. Miner and Alkali Jim were remanded to jail to await the June term of Calaveras County Court.[17]

Cooper's cooperation and testimony against Miner and Harrington brought about his discharge, and he was never tried for his part in the stagecoach robbery.[18] Nevertheless, his criminal career in California continued for the next thirteen years.[19]

On June 6, 1871, Bill Miner and Alkali Jim again were indicted for robbery. At 5 P.M. on June 22 their trial began, with Judge James Barclay presiding and District Attorney Wesley K. Boucher handling the prosecution. Sheriff Ben Thorn brought the prisoners to the courtroom in manacles and chains, prompting an objection from their counsel, G. W. Tyler. The court overruled the objection and ordered the prisoners to remain chained for security reasons. At nine-thirty that night, the jury quickly returned a verdict of guilty. The next morning, Bill Miner and Alkali Jim were sentenced to ten years each in San Quentin.[20]

CHAPTER 4

The Old Con

BILL Miner and Alkali Jim Harrington were transported to San Quentin on June 28, 1871, and given consecutive convict numbers: Bill Miner was 4902, Alkali Jim Harrington 4903. The two old cons knew the procedure, adapting themselves quickly to the routines of prison life.[1]

Interestingly enough, Miner and Alkali Jim were officially discharged from San Quentin on February 9, 1872, by a court order from Calaveras County and returned to the San Andreas jail. Their defense attorney, G. W. Tyler, had appealed to the California Supreme Court for a new trial on grounds that the defendents had been tried in court while shackled, thus prejudicing the jury against them. On these grounds, the judgment was reversed in November 1871 and Miner and Harrington were granted a new trial.[2]

Sheriff Ben Thorn was an astute officer and, knowing the character of Bill Miner and Alkali Jim, searched them thoroughly on their arrival at his jail on February 11. In the band of Alkali Jim's pants, Thorn found a four-inch saw blade. With this discovery, Thorn then searched Miner and found another saw concealed in the sole of one of his boots. With a grave expression on his face, Alkali Jim remarked with great innocence, "By God! Them chaps in San Quentin would play anything on a feller."[3]

On March 18, both Miner and Alkali Jim were brought to trial before Judge W. B. Norman in San Andreas, with Wesley K. Boucher again serving as prosecutor. If Miner and Alkali Jim had known the outcome of this trial, they certainly would have rejected the appeal and accepted their original sentences.

The fact that no new evidence was presented at their second trial did not please Judge Norman. On March 21, using this case to discourage other appeals of this nature, he sentenced Bill Miner and Alkali Jim to thirteen years' imprisonment. Their previous time in prison was not counted against this sentence, so both Miner and

Alkali Jim could look forward to a total of almost fourteen years in San Quentin. Such a penalty for making an appeal is not allowed under modern law.[4] On March 30, the two disgruntled bandits were returned to San Quentin. They both received a new convict number, Miner as 5206 and Alkali Jim as 5207.[5]

On July 17, 1875, Alkali Jim escaped from San Quentin but was quickly apprehended and returned to prison. After serving nine years and five months of his sentence, he was released on January 28, 1881. Alkali Jim was never to join forces with Bill Miner again. Following his discharge, he drifted through Arizona, New Mexico, and back to California, where he died at Colusa in the county hospital on April 21, 1884.[6]

By now, Bill Miner was considered an old con by the guards at San Quentin. The term means the same today as it did a century ago. Sociologists classify the "old con" as one of the principal types in any prison:

> The old con tends to carve out a narrow but orderly existence in prison. He has learned to secure many luxuries and learned to be satisfied with the prison forms of pleasure—e.g., homosexual activities, cards, dominoes, hobbies, and reading. He usually obtains jobs which afford him considerable privileges and leisure time. He often knows many of the prison administrators—the warden, the associate warden, the captain, and the lieutenants, whom he has known since they were officers and lesser officials.[7]

The results of Bill Miner's second trial made him a desperate man, one who would employ any means to get out of prison. On May 7, 1874, he made a futile attempt to escape by staging a fight with a fellow prisoner named John Wheelan. Both prisoners were caught and, as the instigator, Miner's punishment was nine days in the dungeon and twenty lashes plus the loss of all time credits, or coppers earned for good behavior. Wheelan got two days in the dungeon.[8]

Less than a year later Miner was in trouble again, but this time he was the innocent victim. In March 1875 a convict named Charles Marshal reported to Warden William Irwin that Bill Miner was plotting to escape from prison again. As a result, Miner was punished by confinement in the dungeon and a loss of his four months' credit time. Marshal had concocted the escape plot to ingratiate himself with the prison officials in hopes of receiving executive clemency for his help. His scheme succeeded, and Marshal was pardoned for exposing Miner's supposed escape plan. After an investigation by A. C.

McAllister, captain of the yard at San Quentin, and Lt. Gov. James A. Johnson, Marshal's charge was found to be entirely false. They reported their findings to Gov. George Perkins on January 17, 1880.[9]

Bill Miner's failed escape attempt, his loss of coppers, plus the increased prison sentence he received in his second trial spurred him to pursue a different avenue to get out of San Quentin. He turned to the legal system. Between August 4, 1876, and February 16, 1880, Miner wrote eleven letters requesting commutation of his sentence. He made his plea to Wesley K. Boucher, the prosecutor during his trials in San Andreas; to his defense attorney G. W. Tyler; and to two governors of California, William Irwin and George Perkins. In his letters, Miner based his appeal on three factors: the unfairness of his second sentence (thirteen years), which did not consider the previous eight months he had spent in prison; his loss of credit time because of false allegations regarding the escape plan; and his meritorious conduct during the construction of building improvements in the summer of 1877, for which a six-month reduction of his sentence was granted by legislative act. He also brought out his concern for his mother's deteriorating health. His letter to Governor Irwin dated December 6, 1878, reads:

> A few days since I addressed to Your Excellency a letter of entreaty praying that Your Excellency would pardon me on condition that I leave the State. I was induced to do this from the fact that I had understood, as I stated in the letter referred to, that the prosecution in the case would oppose my being pardoned unconditionally and I felt that perhaps they were entitled to be heard in the matter. I also stated in my letter to Your Excellency that I had written to the representative of the prosecution in such matters and had received an indefinite reply with the intimation that the matter would be considered. I have now received a definite reply verbally through Dr. Pelham Resident Physician here from Mr. Brastow, the representative referred to, to the effect that no opposition had or would be made that he knew of and that if any had been made it would be withdrawn and that personally he hoped that my prayer would be granted. I have now served a term equal to the sentence on which I am held with credits. But nearly one year of the time I have served on this charge was served on the original sentence which was for only ten years and would long since have expired. I was only a youth at the time of my conviction and had recklessly formed bad associations which my record for the last four or five years will I think show that I have freed myself from. As I have before stated to Your Excellency my anxiety for an early release is on account of the condition of my mother, which I hope will plead an excuse for my importunity.

San Quentin Cal.
6th Dec. 1878

Sir:

A few days since I addressed to Your Excellency a letter of entreaty praying that Your Excellency would pardon me on condition that I leave the State. I was induced to do this from the fact that I had understood, as I stated in the letter referred to, that the prosecution in the case would oppose my being pardoned unconditionally and I felt that perhaps they were entitled to be heard in the matter. I also stated in my letter to Your Excellency that I had written to the representative of the prosecution in such matters and had received an indefinite reply with the intimation that the matter

One of eleven letters written by Bill Miner requesting early release from San Quentin during his second term, 1871–80.

would be considered, I have now received a definite reply verbally through Dr. Pelham Resident Physician here from Mr. Brastow, the representative referred to, to the effect that no opposition had or would be made that he knew of and that if any had been made it would be withdrawn and that personally he hoped that my prayer would be granted. I have now served a term equal to the sentence on which I am held with credits. But nearly one year of the time I have served on this charge was served on the original sentence which was for only ten years and would long since have expired. I was only a youth at the time of my conviction and had recklessly formed bad associations which my record for the last four or five years will I think show that I have freed myself from. As I have before stated to Your Excellency my anxiety for an early release is on account of the condition of my Mother, which I hope will plead an excuse for my importunity. Most respectfully

William A. Miner

To His Excellency William Irwin
Governor of the State of California

In another 1878 letter, Miner stated that if his sentence was commuted, he would leave California, go to Colorado where his sister was living, and work as a shoemaker, a trade he learned in prison. He wrote convincingly that he saw the error and folly of his earlier life and that reformation was inevitable. These letters, though repetitious in content, showed Bill Miner to be well educated and literate.

Even though Miner had spent two terms in prison, he remained a likable, soft-spoken man whose sincerity impressed others. This fact is borne out by favorable letters written by District Attorney Boucher, California Lieutenant Governor Johnson, and Captain McAllister. These letters were written to the governor in support of Miner's plea for commutation.[10] Miner's sister Mary Jane also made an appeal for his release. Having married a mining man named Louis Wellman, Mary Jane followed her husband from California to Colorado in 1871. They established a winter home in Colorado Springs and spent the remaining nine months of each year developing their mining interests around Leadville.[11]

On October 30, 1878, Mary Jane Wellman wrote to Governor Irwin expressing her faith in her brother, stating that she would be willing to give him a home and that her husband would provide a job for him in one of the mines near Leadville in which he had interest. She also appealed to the governor on the grounds that her mother was in poor health and that Bill Miner was her only son. Both statements were true. Harriet Miner suffered severely from rheumatism, and her youngest son, Benjamin, had died tragically six years before.[12]

The life of nineteen-year-old Ben Miner was as lamentable as his older brother's was notorious. During the Civil War, young Ben was made drummer boy in Capt. John Keiser's Yankee Jim Rifle Company. Ben was considered an unusually intelligent youth despite his lack of education, and friends of the Miners secured employment for him in March 1869 as a telegraph operator for the Central Pacific Railroad Company at Truckee, California. According to the *Truckee Republican:*

> For a while he was steady, earned good wages, and aided his widowed mother, who was in somewhat straightened circumstances. But he soon became what is termed a "fast young man," failed to properly remember his mother, squandered his earnings, and neglected his duties. His shortcomings were overlooked for some time by the railroad company, and efforts were made by his friends to give him good

counsel and induce him to reform, but to no purpose. He was discovered to be guilty of sleeping at his post, and the company found it necessary to discharge him in August 1871. Soon after his discharge he forged a pass over the railroad to Salt Lake, and went to the Atlantic States. On account of his youth, and influence of friends in his behalf, he was not prosecuted by the company.

Ben Miner returned to Truckee around June 5, 1872, and began loitering about gambling houses, playing faro and other games of chance, although he did not have much money. A few days later, Ben informed his friends that he was broke and asked if they knew how he could make a "raise." Local wags advised him to lecture on the resources of the frontier areas he had visited. Taking their facetious advice seriously, he ordered handbills from the newspaper advertising himself as "Professor Miner" who would lecture at the Good Templars Hall on the night of June 15.

A very sensitive and high-spirited young man, Ben Miner was subject to periods of despondency. In April 1871, while living with John Keisler's family in Truckee, a package of poison was found in his bed which Miner confessed he planned to use to commit suicide. During his trip across the country, Ben tried to kill himself in Salt Lake City during a spell of sickness but was prevented from committing the act by his host.

On June 10, Ben went to a store owned by Frank Stevens, pulled out a pistol, put it to his head, and told Stevens he had a notion to pull the trigger. Stevens took the pistol away and Miner declared that he had come three thousand miles to die in Truckee. On the fourteenth, Ben returned to Stevens's store with a package of poison, which he threatened to take. Stevens managed to throw the poison into his stove and then took the despondent youth to the back of his store, where, for the next two hours, he tried to reason with him. It did little good, and as Ben Miner left the store, he insisted that he no longer wished to live.

At 1 P.M. on June 15, the morose youth went to the Eureka Saloon, where he encountered a patron, Gus Heyman. During their conversation, Miner suddenly pulled out a derringer, pointed it at his head, and threatened to fire it. Heyman calmly talked the youth into giving him the derringer, but he later made the mistake of returning it. Heyman and Miner left together and headed for a pile of lumber on the west side of the saloon, where they sat down. Ben then told him that he might be dead in three hours.

Ben Miner went back to Stevens's store at 2 P.M. and Stevens asked him if he was ready for his lecture that night. Stevens recalled that the youth was extremely distraught and despondent over the considerable amount of ribbing he had taken over his upcoming lecture as Professor Miner. Ben told Stevens he did not know whether he would lecture or not as he thought he would kill himself first.

At eight o'clock that night in Room 32 of the Truckee Hotel, Ben Miner pulled out the derringer for the last time, placed it above his right ear, and pulled the trigger. His body was discovered a short time later with a note that read:

>TRUCKEE, June 15th.
>
>Enclosed please find key to my valise in room 32. Make such disposal as you think best. I am lost.
>
>B. F. [sic] Miner

Ben Miner's former employer, the Central Pacific Railroad Company, with uncharacteristic compassion, had his body shipped, expense free, to his mother in Sacramento for burial.[13]

The funeral was held in Sacramento at the residence of his mother's landlord, A. T. Smith, on Twelfth Street between G and H, where she had resided since 1870. The *Sacramento Bee* reported, "Funeral at 5 o'clock this afternoon [June 17]. . . . Friends invited to attend."[14]

It was sad blow to add to the lonely existence of Harriet Miner, with her remaining son in the penitentiary and her daughter now living in faraway Colorado. But the family bond remained strong, as her deep feelings for her wayward son were expressed when she concluded an 1878 letter to him at San Quentin with "God bless and keep you in the constant prayers of your ever loving Mother."[15]

Although Bill Miner never made another attempt to escape during this prison term, he did run afoul of the San Quentin rules. A prison feud had developed between convicted stage robber Austin Smith and Peter ("Scotty") Gibson, a prison chum of Miner serving a six year sentence for burglary. Miner and Gibson went to Smith's cell on August 10, 1879, and beat him brutally. On August 13, the State Board of Prison Directors sentenced both Miner and Gibson to be flogged. Miner received twelve lashes, but this did not put an end to the feud. A month later, on the morning of September 17, Gibson stabbed Smith to death while returning from the prison dining room.[16]

The barrage of requests for Bill Miner's release had no effect; however, his credits were restored, and, after serving a little over nine years in San Quentin, he was discharged on July 14, 1880.[17] Now thirty-three years of age, Miner had spent thirteen years of his life behind bars. After his discharge from San Quentin, Bill Miner did leave California, as promised in his petitions, and he did head for Colorado. But he had no plans for honest work as a shoemaker or miner.

CHAPTER 5

Old Tricks—New Turf

BILL Miner arrived in Colorado soon after his release from San Quentin. It seems probable that he spent some time in Colorado Springs at the home of his sister and brother-in-law, Mary Jane and Louis Wellman, or at their mines in Leadville. By mid-September of 1880, Miner was in Denver and no doubt learned that a considerable amount of bullion from the mines in southern Colorado was being transported by the Barlow-Sanderson Stage Line. Boarding a southbound train at Denver, Bill was soon engaged in conversation with a twenty-three-year-old passenger, a small-town Iowan named Arthur Pond, who was en route to Silver Cliff to work for the railroad.[1]

The impetuous and headstrong Pond was attracted to the older man's soft speech and gentlemanly manner, while Bill Miner was drawn to Pond's immaturity and youthful enthusiasm. Another factor that appealed to Miner was Pond's familiarity with southern Colorado, Pond having worked and traveled there the previous summer. Calling himself California Bill and no doubt exaggerating his criminal experiences, Miner convinced Pond that there were quicker ways to obtain money with much less effort than working for the railroad. Pond fell in with Miner's scheme and the two got off the train at Canon City, Colorado.[2]

If Bill Miner had the impression that Arthur Pond would prove to be a docile, gullible, and obedient follower, he was badly mistaken. Pond, who is known to this day in Colorado by his alias of Billy LeRoy, developed into a dangerous, callous, and desperate character. It was a strange partnership, as these two men were opposites in every conceivable way.[3]

Miner and Billy LeRoy first earned a few dollars as common laborers in Canon City. With this small stake and both now armed with six-shooters, they headed west. Crossing the South Arkansas River, they traveled over Marshalls Pass to Parlin's Ranch (now Parlin) at the junction of Tomichi and Quartz creeks. During the previous summer, LeRoy had worked for a sawmill belonging to Warren Patten in Pitkin and knew that the Barlow-Sanderson stage line, running between Alpine and Gunnison, transported ore and bullion from the mining areas. Miner and LeRoy decided to rob the stagecoach running from Alpine.

Heading up Quartz Creek, the two stopped and made camp one-half mile north of Ohio City and six miles southeast of Pitkin. Leaving Miner hidden in the brush, Billy LeRoy went into Pitkin and, with their last twenty-five cents, purchased two loaves of bread. LeRoy made his way back to camp around 9:30 that evening by furtively avoiding the main road. For the next half hour, the two anxiously awaited the arrival of the stage.[4]

To the bandits' disappointment, it was not a stage that drove up at 10 P.M. on September 23, but the Barlow-Sanderson buckboard from Pitkin that connected with the stage to Buena Vista. Nevertheless, Miner and LeRoy made the best of a bad situation and carried out the robbery anyway, thus setting the dubious record of committing the first such robbery in Gunnison County.

Stepping from the side of the road, Miner and LeRoy commanded the driver, Jack Hausbrough, to stop the ill-fated buckboard, which contained one passenger, Union Pacific agent Harry White of Leadville. Ignoring the passenger, Bill Miner pointed his revolver at the driver and demanded the treasure box while LeRoy held the team of horses. When the driver informed Miner that the buckboard did not carry a treasure box, the bandit asked for the express box. Again receiving a negative reply, Miner, now frustrated, demanded the two mailbags, which the driver reluctantly handed over. Bill then allowed the driver to depart. In their haste to procure the money, the robbers quickly rifled one of the sacks by the road. Realizing they were in the open and might be seen, they took the other sack and headed up the mountain for cover. Upon opening the sack, the disgruntled bandits found that their efforts had netted them a paltry fifty dollars.[5]

The *Colorado Chieftain* reported these observations from passenger Harry White, who claimed he had watched Miner closely during the entire operation:

> Mr. White describes the man who seized the pouches as of about five feet ten or eleven inches high, with a beard and moustache, and about forty years old. From the coolness and method with which the whole

Arthur Pond, alias Billy LeRoy, from a photograph probably taken in Denver in 1881. From Mark Dugan's collection.

affair was managed and from the expressions used, Mr. White would judge that these men were old hands at the business, and had probably attempted the same thing in the Black Hills.[6]

Although White professed to have keenly observed Miner, his description was not accurate, especially his assessment of Miner's age. This illustrates how difficult it is for a victim to give a precise identification of a robber under threatening conditions.

Deciding to head back to Parlin's Ranch, Miner and LeRoy somehow lost their way, although the distance was only about eight miles. Late the following evening they finally reached Parlin's Ranch. Having run out of provisions, they were only able to obtain some bread before heading south. By keeping out of sight during the day and traveling by night, they reached Lake City, where, in a few days, they squandered the fifty dollars. Finding themselves flat broke, the two decided to rob another stage.[7]

On October 7 the stagecoach to Lake City was halted by Bill Miner and LeRoy at Slumgullion Pass, five miles northeast of Lake City. LeRoy, armed with a rifle, held up the driver, James Davidson. Miner hauled out four mail sacks, but in his haste to complete the robbery, he failed to notice the registered mail pouch, which usually carried cash or valuables. Wilson Hunter of Del Norte, the only passenger aboard, was not molested. The contents of the mail sacks tallied a meager one hundred dollars and five thousand dollars in drafts and nonnegotiable money orders. This trivial haul spurred the bandits into executing a third strike on the Barlow-Sanderson stage line.[8]

Deciding to head for the San Luis Valley, Miner and his partner set out southward into the Cebolla country. By skirting the roads and using the timber as cover, they soon became lost in unfamiliar terrain. Traveling in circles for two days, they went without food or rest until they became weak from fatigue and hunger. Several times they were forced to lie down and rest until they regained their strength. With great effort, they mustered enough energy to rise and continue their laborious journey. Finally, by a stroke of luck, the exhausted and famished bandits stumbled upon the small community of Wagon Wheel Gap on Sunday, October 10, after three days of torturous wandering. Fortunately for the pair, they escaped being caught in a blizzard which began on the day of their arrival.

Billy LeRoy immediately went to the hotel and purchased some bread and meat, leaving Miner hidden in the timber. Finding some shelter from the storm, they first ate their provisions and then slept from nightfall until the next evening. Their strength regained, the outlaws made their way eastward on foot through the timber toward Del Norte. Running out of provisions again, they stopped about fifteen miles west of town and obtained more food. At midnight they reached Del Norte and walked cautiously through town, unnoticed. They continued eastward and on the night of October 13 reached a point ten and one-half miles west of Alamosa and three-quarters of a mile east of Banshee Station, the first stage stop on the Barlow-Sanderson route. Preparing a crude camp, Miner and LeRoy rested and waited for the morning stage from Alamosa to Del Norte.[9]

At 3 A.M. on October 14, the two highwaymen stopped the westbound stage. For the first and only time in his career, Miner faced a unique dilemma during a robbery: the inability to control one of his men. To Miner's chagrin, LeRoy took charge of the operation and went through the empty coach while Bill was left with the secondary role of guarding the stage driver, Joseph Benedrum, with his rifle. After the four mail sacks and the registered-mail pouch were hauled out to the roadside, the robbers allowed the coach to proceed.

The two bandits cut open the registered-mail pouch and saw they had finally struck it rich. The pouch held four thousand dollars, a small fortune in those days. Quickly dividing the spoils, Miner and LeRoy returned to their camp and alternately stood guard throughout the night.[10]

The two satisfied bandits decamped for Fort Garland the next morning. From there they took a train to Pueblo, where they separated. The fact that their only profitable robbery was the one that LeRoy engineered was likely discomforting to Miner. No doubt with feelings of relief at ending their association, Bill Miner headed north, LeRoy east.

Billy LeRoy later returned to Colorado with his brother Silas Pond, alias Sam Potter. The two brothers and a third man robbed a stagecoach near Del Norte in May 1881. In 1882, U.S. Postal Inspector L. Cass Carpenter, in an interview with the *Denver Republican* regarding Bill Miner, erroneously reported that Miner had rejoined LeRoy as the third member of his new gang. The third man, in reality a badman named Frank Clark, eluded capture, but LeRoy and his brother were caught and jailed by local officers. The citizens of Del Norte had had enough of stage robbery, so they stormed the jail, seized the two men, and lynched them on May 23. These events made LeRoy one of the most noted of the Rocky Mountain bandits.[11]

Never before in his career had Bill Miner committed a profitable stage robbery without getting caught. Now that he was flush, he made new plans. From Pueblo, he entrained for Chicago, where he bought several new suits in the latest fashion. Now attired in the height of style, and with two Saratoga trunks loaded with fashionable clothing, Bill Miner headed for his hometown of Onondaga, Michigan, with a new scheme in mind.[12]

CHAPTER 6

"Oh, But It Was Great Fun"

LIKE many other small Michigan towns, Onondaga was settled in the 1830s. Laid out along the banks of the Grand River some eighty miles west of Detroit, the village was situated on the stage route from Jackson to Lansing. The first documents of land ownership in Onondaga were recorded in 1834 and the township was organized two years later. The railroad arrived in 1864 and by the time Bill Miner got there in 1880 the town boasted a population of eight hundred, as well as three sawmills, three churches, three general stores, two hotels, one flour mill, and several mechanical and blacksmith shops.[1]

Bill Miner had left Vevay Township as a boy of five, so when he arrived at his birthplace at age thirty-three, no one recognized him. Bill no doubt thought it a great joke to deceive and dazzle the citizens who had known him as a child. Posing as William A. Morgan, a cultured and prosperous California mining man, Miner claimed that he had come east to settle an estate of which he was the lone surviving heir. One cannot help wonder whether his ironic sense of humor prompted him to adopt the surname of rising financier John Pierpont Morgan.

Bill Miner's charade worked. Taking lodging in the town's best hotel, the Sherman House, he liberally spread his money around and quickly made many friends. His soft-spoken ways, witty charm, and courteous manners soon allowed Miner to ingratiate himself with Onondaga's leading citizens. Six years later a reporter for the San Francisco *Alta California* interviewed the outlaw in prison and heard the story firsthand. "Miner told all manner of Munchausen tales of his fabulous wealth in California, of great blocks of houses in Sacramento and San Francisco, and rich gold mines without number."

Bill's elegant clothing, his gentlemanly demeanor, and his extravagant spending made his stories plausible. Soon he was high on the list of the town's eligible bachelors, and it was not long before he

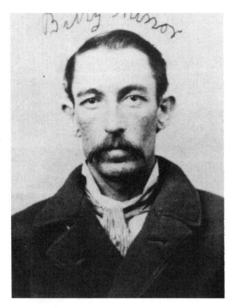

Bill Miner in 1881, a year after his affair with Jennie Willis. Photo made following his arrest for the Sonora stage robbery. Courtesy of Wells, Fargo Bank History Room, San Francisco, California.

became engaged to marry a daughter of one of the leading families. Outside prison, the outlaw seems to have reverted to his interest in the opposite sex in lieu of the homosexual outlets available behind bars.[2]

The object of Miner's romantic interest was twenty-year-old Jennie Louise Willis, daughter of Henry S. Willis, a well-to-do Onondaga businessman. The Willis family was highly respected. Henry and his wife, Jane Goodfellow Willis, had migrated to Onondaga from New York in March 1856. Enterprising and energetic, Willis first found work as a carpenter until January of the following year, when he purchased and enlarged the Onondaga Hotel. Four years later he sold out and began dealing livestock, grain, and produce. When a chapter of the Odd Fellows Lodge was founded in 1871, Henry Willis was installed as noble grand. He also served as a township officer and in 1880 was secretary of Onondaga's Masonic Lodge. Willis and his wife raised seven children; their youngest daughter, Jennie Louise, was born in Onondaga on January 10, 1860.[3]

It was probably through Henry Willis that Bill Miner met his youngest daughter, who was approaching the ripe old age of twenty-one, almost an old maid in those days. Willis no doubt saw Miner as a splendid prospect for a son-in-law. According to descendants of Jennie Willis, as well as local historians, Henry Willis encouraged the courtship and Bill literally swept Jennie off her feet, hiring the fanciest horse and buggy in Onondaga and wining and dining her in the area's best restaurants. To Jennie, Bill was a dashing, elegant, and wealthy older man, and soon she fell headlong in love with him. It was not long before the couple were engaged to be married.[4]

However, Bill Miner's facade of riches and respectability was quickly wearing thin. After three months of lavish spending, he found himself nearly broke. Miner quickly solved his dilemma by telling his new friends that he was desperately needed back in California. His aged mother's health was rapidly declining and it was necessary for him to leave immediately and take her on an ocean voyage to restore her health. Bill's alleged devotion to his mother must surely have impressed both his fiancée and his friends.

The people of Onondaga were not happy to see Miner leave. Wrote the reporter for the *Alta California*, "On the eve of his departure the prominent citizens of the town gave him a banquet, at which the mayor, with becoming dignity, presided, and Bill was the hero of the hour." A correspondent for the *New York Sun*, who also interviewed Miner in San Quentin, reported the identical story, while other accounts had the mayor acting as toastmaster. The more likely scenario is that Henry Willis organized a dinner party for his daughter's fiancé and invited the most prominent Onondaga citizens. Onondaga has never had a mayor, but instead a township superintendent, a position which in 1880 held by was Pomroy Van Riper. If Van Riper indeed had been duped into toasting one of the West's most noted outlaws, it would surely have been an experience he would prefer to forget.[5]

Bill Miner faithfully promised Jennie that he would return to her immediately after completing the voyage with his mother. After he left, Jennie bought her bridal gown in anticipation of a sumptuous wedding in the very near future, but she never saw Bill again. Eventually Jennie discovered her fiancé's identity, possibly a few years later when the *New York Sun* report, which included a lengthy account of Miner's criminal career, hit the wire services. No doubt she was devastated, first by Bill's failure to return and later by the knowledge that her wealthy lover was a notorious bandit. But Jennie seems to have recovered fully from the experience, for in later years she had no reservations about telling of the affair. She lived a long and full life, remaining in Onondaga and marrying Joseph Edward Boucher, who fathered her six children. Jennie lived to the grand old age of eighty-five, passing away in Onondaga on September 18, 1945.[6]

For Bill Miner, the three months he spent in Michigan society were the highlight of his checkered career. Although he would be questioned by newspapermen several times over the years about his love affair in Onondaga, he was too much of a gentleman to reveal Jennie's name. While in a Georgia jail in 1911 for train robbery, the now aged Miner admitted that the whole episode was true, but he did not reveal that he was born just outside Onondaga. E. C. Bruffey, a skeptical reporter from the *Atlanta Constitution*, decided to investigate the story. He was able to contact Jennie Willis, who was now married, and received confirmation from her. The newspaperman was likewise too much a gentleman to name Jennie in his report. When Bruffey questioned Miner about the love affair and the yarns he had spun in Onondaga, the old bandit replied ruefully, "Of course it was all hot air. If I had saved that money, I might be right there now, the head of a happy family. Oh, but it was great fun. Why didn't I try a hold-up where I was? you ask. Oh, no, I had too much respect for that girl who had told me she loved me."[7]

When Bill Miner left Onondaga, he had no intention of returning to California to visit his aged mother or to make a much-needed

Jennie Willis Boucher's grave in Onondaga, Michigan. Photographed in 1990 by Isabelle Moyer of Onondaga.

withdrawal from Wells, Fargo. Instead, he headed for Colorado, where he had been so successful the previous fall. Since Bill did not like to work alone, he had befriended an itinerant laborer named Stanton T. Jones, who had been working on a Michigan farm. Little is known about Jones, and most sources state that he was a criminal from Chillicothe, Ohio. But existing Ohio jail and prison records do not substantiate this and he has probably been confused with Jim Crum, a later confederate of Bill Miner, who had family ties in Chillicothe. Stanton T. Jones seems to have been a restless farm hand who met Miner during his stay in Michigan and fell victim to the crafty outlaw's persuasiveness.

The two arrived in Denver sometime in late January 1881, with Miner still using the alias William A. Morgan. Perhaps Bill should have remained in Michigan, for the Onondaga episode attested to the fact that he was a much better con man than a highwayman. Nonetheless, he visited a secondhand shop and sold all his fancy clothes. With the money he received he bought the tools of his trade: a knife, two six-shooters, and a Winchester rifle. Roughly dressed and well armed, Miner was just as at home on the Colorado frontier as he was in Michigan society. With his new partner, Bill Miner was back on the road, headed for Del Norte, 260 miles to the south.[8]

CHAPTER 7

On the Road Again

ALWAYS on the lookout for ready accomplices, Bill Miner fell in with a tall and ungainly youth of nineteen named Charles B. Dingman in the vicinity of Del Norte. What especially appealed to Miner was that Dingman worked for the Barlow-Sanderson stage line as a stock tender at its Venables Station stop, some thirteen miles east of Del Norte. Recruiting Dingman was not difficult for the oily-tongued Miner, and the youngster agreed to join in Bill's plan to rob one of Barlow-Sanderson's stages. Dingman's task was to hold the horses while Miner and Stanton T. Jones robbed the coach. They planned to hold up the stage from Del Norte to Alamosa on the night of February 3.

Whether Miner knew it or not, Charles Dingman was not a novice at crime. He was born in Minnesota in 1861 to William and Abbie Dingman. Moving twice in the next ten years, the Dingman family first went to La Porte City, Iowa, when Charles was three, and then to Louisville, Pottawatomie County, Kansas, seven years later. When Charles was sixteen, he left Kansas, setting out on his own for Colorado.

It was not long before Dingman fell into criminal ways. Arrested in El Paso County for cattle theft, he was convicted of grand larceny on October 23, 1878, and sentenced to serve one year in prison. He entered the Colorado State Penitentiary at Canon City on October 24 as inmate No. 338. He was mistakenly registered as Cyrus B. Dingman. The records show that he was six feet, three-fourths of an inch tall, had light hair and blue eyes, and was sixteen years of age. Dingman was released September 17, 1879, after serving eleven months of his sentence. He soon found work as stock tender for the Barlow-Sanderson stage line where he became known as "the Swede."[1]

There had been no stage robberies on the Barlow-Sanderson stage line for almost four months, so just past midnight on February 4, driver George Stout was startled when two of Bill Miner's band forced him to stop the eastbound coach five miles out of Del Norte. Leaving Dingman to hold the horses, Miner and Jones commanded the four passengers to put up their hands and then took four mail sacks and the treasure pouch from the driver. A resident of Wagon Wheel Gap named Peck had the misfortune of sitting next to the driver and the bandits relieved him of ten dollars. However, they ignored the three passengers inside the coach. The bandits then permitted the coach to continue on to Alamosa.

Quickly rifling the pouches, the bandits, in their haste to obtain loot, carelessly threw out drafts and money orders, only to discover there was nothing of value to show for their efforts. As strangers in that region, the disgruntled robbers realized they would soon be prime suspects. Miner and Jones separated from Dingman and promptly fled the area. After news of the robbery reached Del Norte, two townsmen named Dawley and Windspear went to the robbery site in a buggy, recovered the drafts and money orders, and returned them to Del Norte.[2]

If Dingman remained in the area around Del Norte thinking no one had recognized him during the robbery, he was badly mistaken. Within two weeks' time, he was spotted by one of the stage passengers, a local rancher named H. C. ("Hank") Dorris. Following Dingman to Alamosa, Colorado, Dorris immediately relayed the information to Alamosa City Marshal Cicero Wiedner. On February 16, Wiedner easily captured the surprised bandit on a road just outside town.

Immediately after his incarceration in the Alamosa jail, Dingman made a violent attempt to escape. He seriously injured the jailer by clouting him over the head with a board but was stopped before he could break out of the jail. Realizing his predicament, Dingman broke down and confessed to his part of the robbery. "I did nothing but hold old Eagle," he declared, referring to one of the lead stage horses.

U. S. Postal Inspector Robert Cameron and U.S. Marshal P. P. Wilcox took custody of Dingman and brought him to Denver in the morning of February 20. He was locked up in the Arapahoe County Jail to await his hearing in the U.S. commissioner's court.[3] On February 27 the court set Dingman's bail at three thousand dollars pending examination by a grand jury. Unable to raise bail, Dingman remained in the Arapahoe County Jail until his trial. The grand jury met on May 12 and on the nineteenth indicted Dingman for robbery and bound him over for trial, which was scheduled for the September term of court.

Dingman's trial began on September 12, under presiding Judge Moses Hallett in U.S. District Court at Del Norte. Although Dingman had made a previous confession, he now entered a plea of not guilty. It took the jury only one day to reach a verdict: guilty of robbery but not guilty of carrying firearms. On the fourteenth, the young highwayman was brought back to court. Judge Hallett sentenced him to serve ten years' hard labor in the Wyoming Territorial Penitentiary at Laramie, as there was no federal prison in Colorado.

On September 24, U.S. Marshal Sim Cantril took custody of Dingman and brought him back to Denver. Cantril reported that a mob in Alamosa had threatened to take Dingman from the train; however, the *San Juan Prospector* claimed the charge was false. Without further incident, Cantril left Denver with Dingman and delivered him to the authorities at the Wyoming Territorial Penitentiary on October 8.[4] The Wyoming prison officers recorded the following data on Dingman:

> Convict No. 106; age-nineteen; occupation-stage driver; height-six feet three quarter inches; complexion-light; hair-brown; eyes-blue; education-fair; general remarks-a small scar under right jaw (a razor cut), a stout muscular and well built man.[5]

An appeal to pardon Dingman was initiated by his parents in 1882, and by 1884 they had managed to enlist the aid and support of U.S. Marshal Sim Cantril, U.S. Postal Inspector Robert Cameron, U.S. Attorney for Colorado Edward L. Johnson, and U.S. District Judge Moses Hallett. In a letter dated March 31, 1884, to U.S. Sen. A. B. Plumb, Marshal Cantril expressed his support for the pardon and made reference to Bill Miner's influence on Dingman. Marshal Cantril astutely wrote: "I had charge of Dingman during his trial, and believe that he was led into the act by older persons, he being only 20 at the time." Their efforts were rewarded on March 18, 1885, when President Chester A. Arthur granted Dingman a presidential pardon. Dingman walked out of the penitentiary a free man on March 26, 1885.[6]

Bill Miner and Stanton Jones were never charged or arrested for the stage robbery. Either Dingman did not know their true identities or he refused to name them. It was reported that the missing bandits had escaped to Texas, and this information likely was given to the arresting officers by Dingman.[7]

It is doubtful that Miner and Jones went to Texas, for there is documented proof that the two men were in Colorado in April. As they were flat broke, a reasonable assumption is that they escaped into the mountains and beat their way to the home of Miner's sister and brother-in-law, Mary Jane and Louis Wellman, in Colorado Springs. It was a perfect hideout and they could earn much-needed cash by working in one of Wellman's mines near Leadville.

In the spring, Bill Miner and Jones picked up a third man named James East and returned to the San Luis Valley. East, a pleasant looking twenty-three-year-old farmer, had come to Colorado from Tilden, Illinois. East was an easy mark for Bill Miner and was a new addition to the increasing number of younger men to fall under Miner's persuasion and influence.[8]

Still using the alias William A. Morgan, Bill Miner surfaced in Saguache County in mid-April with Jones and East. Apparently the three were on foot, but on April 18 they stole three horses near the town of Saguache. Two of the horses, valued at $175, belonged to Thomas Wells; the third horse, which was worth $100, was taken from Samuel Ashley.[9] For more than a week no trace of the thieves could be found. During this period, however, a stage was robbed in the area, which probably was more than mere coincidence. Prime suspects were Miner and his two confederates, who were in southern Colorado at the time, although the robbery was not committed in Bill Miner's typical style.

Leaving Ouray on April 23, the stage to Gunnison lumbered through three post office stops between Uncompaghre and Barnum. The stage reached the post office at Barnum on the twenty-fourth where the postmaster discovered that someone had cut open both the mail pouch and the registered pouch and had stolen the contents at one of the three stops. The value of the stolen postal material was undetermined. The *Denver Republican* speculated upon how the robbery was conducted:

> The theory is that it was the work of experienced road-agents, who forsook the more romantic and bolder "hold-up" style for the safer and quieter plan of robbing while in the guise of passengers. It is held that the pouches could easily have been cut and rifled while the drivers took their meals or changed their horses.

Prison photograph and identification card of James East after being received at the Colorado State Penitentiary at Canon City on June 1, 1881. Courtesy of the Colorado Department of Corrections, Colorado Springs.

Following the same opinion, the *Daily News* offered a more comprehensive account:

> Persons who have occupied a seat in the "boot" with the driver over some of our long mail routes, are aware of the fact that most of the mail is carried in the front boot and is thrown off and taken on the various postoffices which are passed on the line. At night when the horses are changed at the several relays an excellent opportunity is afforded the "light-fingered gentry" to cut open a sack of through mail left on the coach, and no one would be the wiser for the deed until the destination of the rifled sack was reached.[10]

If Bill Miner actually engineered this stage robbery it was his shrewdest. It is known that before and after the robbery Miner and his confederates were no more than twenty miles or so from where it was committed. Although the robbery was not characteristic of Miner's style, he was perceptive enough not to pass up such an easy mark, especially with his knowledge of local stage routes and what treasures the coaches carried. Three days after this robbery, Miner and his accomplices reappeared in Saguache County, and their subsequent actions can be accurately accounted for.

On April 27 the trio stopped and purchased oats for their horses at the ranch of Sam Goodaker in Saguache County and took a saddle from him without paying for it. The irate rancher immediately started in pursuit of the thieves and enlisted the aid of a Del Norte resident named Eagen. The two men trailed the outlaws to Hot Springs, five miles north of Del Norte. While Goodaker continued to keep the thieves in sight, Eagen went after Sheriff Lew Armstrong in Del Norte. By the time that Armstrong and a posse reached the area, Miner, Jones and East had escaped by bearing west into the mountains and then turning southwest until they reached the Hunt ranch on the Rio Grande River.

Meanwhile, Sheriff W. A. Bronaugh of Saguache County had joined Goodaker at Wagon Wheel Gap. On the twenty-eighth, after learning that the thieves had passed a toll gate at nine o'clock the previous evening, the two lawmen trailed the thieves upriver. Bronaugh shrewdly predicted the course the robbers would take. Arriving at the Pokins ranch above Wagon Wheel Gap, Sheriff Bronaugh and Goodaker waited for the thieves to arrive. The weary outlaws rode up at sundown and before they could make a move were ordered to drop their weapons. The three outlaws were taken completely by surprise and meekly surrendered. The subsequent actions of both the lawmen and their captives have never been accurately reported. Because of the ambiguity of all previous accounts, the following detailed article is quoted from a firsthand report in the *San Juan Prospector:*

> The men were handcuffed with hay bailing wire and brought to Kinders where, worn out and weary with sleepless nights and hard riding, Goodaker and the Sheriff proposed to remain overnight. They put the three thieves to bed and tied them together after being sure, as they supposed, unarmed. Being worn out, both men fell asleep and during the night the prisoners unfastened the wire and, with a small .32 cal. pistol which had escaped the notice of the officers, they shot Goodaker twice in one arm and once in the other. They then shot the Sheriff in one arm after which two of the prisoners [Miner and Jones] bounded through the window and escaped. The other [East] gave himself up without any resistance and was brought to Del Norte yesterday.
>
> As soon as Goodaker saw the situation, wounded as he was, he grabbed his revolver and sprang through the window after the prisoners. But he was so badly wounded that he could not raise his weapon to fire. The two thieves started west and were tracked as far as the bridge where they turned and came back this way. Dr. Pittman was telegraphed for to go and dress the wounds and a party of men from the vicinity went in search of the prisoners who escaped.

Although the newspaper neglected to state how the outlaws concealed the pistol, the *New York Sun* reported that it had been hidden in one of their boots. This report also claimed that Miner was the one who shot Bronaugh and Goodaker.[11]

East was taken to Saguache around the first week of May and locked up in the Saguache County Jail until he was brought to trial. East confessed and named W. A. Morgan and Stanton T. Jones as his partners in crime. The three men were indicted on two charges of grand larceny, one for the theft of two horses belonging to Thomas Wells and the other for stealing Samuel Ashley's horse.

On May 25, East was brought before Judge Charles D. Bradley in Saguache County District Court. Pleading guilty to both charges, East received a sentence of five years' imprisonment: four years in the first case and one in the second. Judge Bradley ordered Sheriff Bronaugh to deliver East to the Colorado State Penitentiary at Canon City within ten days after the trial date. East entered the prison walls on June 1 as convict No. 575.

On June 7, 1882, East's attorneys appealed for a writ of habeas corpus which was denied immediately by the Saguache County District Court. On July 24, 1884, East was discharged and released from prison, having served just over three years of his sentence. Miner and Jones were never brought to trial on these charges.[12]

Bill Miner's friendship in Colorado with the boyish Charles Dingman and James East gives rise to further speculation about his bisexual nature. His habit of attracting such youths lasted throughout his career, but there is no solid evidence that Miner had a homosexual relationship with either Dingman or East.

Now that his description and alias were known, Bill Miner must have realized that his days of freedom would be short lived if he attempted any more crimes in Colorado. Stealing horses and robbing stages were serious offenses, but shooting a sheriff and his deputy was extremely bad business. Miner knew that he must either find a safe hideout or shake Colorado's dust from his boots as quickly as possible. This period of Miner's life, including his Colorado sojourn, remain the most obscure and confusing of his entire career. Several conflicting accounts of his actions during this time, all of which are unfounded, have given rise to much misinformation.

Wells, Fargo detectives James B. Hume and John Thacker stated that, after his release from San Quentin in July 1880, Bill Miner went to Colorado Springs, where his sister was living. The detectives reported that Miner returned to California by mid-September and single-handedly robbed the Forest Hill and Auburn stage near Grizzly Bear House on September 22, 1880. Shortly after the robbery, Congressman Frank Page arrived at the scene in his buggy and was also relieved of three hundred dollars and his gold watch. The bandit was described as medium-sized and with a light complexion. Hume and Thacker further reported that, after the robbery, Miner went to Colfax, bribed a brakeman to let him ride a boxcar to Reno, Nevada, and then caught a train for Denver, where he pawned Page's watch for sixty-five dollars.[13]

This robber could not have been Bill Miner as Thacker and Hume claimed. It is well established that he and LeRoy robbed the Gunnison stage one day after the Auburn stage robbery occurred. It would have been impossible for him to do both. Further, the California robbery does not fit Miner's pattern: he never committed any robberies alone.

Bill Miner's own story is as far fetched. Years later, Bill claimed that he and a companion left Colorado and set off on a world tour. On reaching San Francisco, they set sail for England and crossed Europe to North Africa, where, as a desert slave trader, Bill abducted

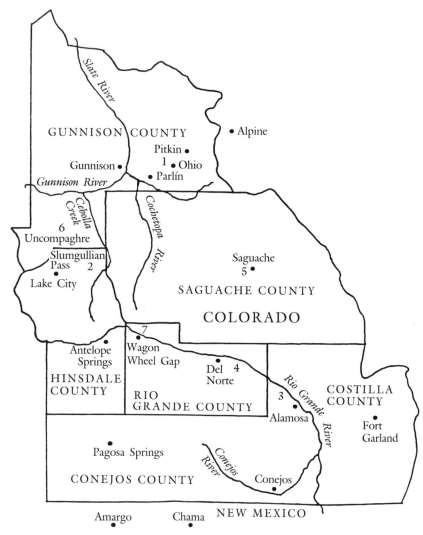

BILL MINER'S CRIMINAL CAREER IN COLORADO, 1880–81
1 Robbery of the Gunnison-Alpine stage, September 23, 1880, Miner and LeRoy.
2 Robbery of the Lake City stage, October 7, 1880, Miner and LeRoy.
3 Robbery of the Alamosa-Del Norte stage, October 14, 1880, Miner and LeRoy.
4 Robbery of the Del Norte-Alamosa stage, February 4, 1881, Miner, Jones, and Dingman.
5 Theft of three horses, April 18, 1881, Miner, Jones, and East.
6 Robbery of the Ouray-Gunnison stage, April 24, 1881, Miner, Jones, and East.
7 Arrest of Miner, Jones, and East for horse theft, April 29, 1881, resulting in the wounding of Sheriff Bronaugh and Goodaker and the escape of Miner and Jones.

women for harems. Deciding to rob diamond trains in South Africa, Miner headed for Capetown. He quickly gave up this plan after observing that the trains were too well guarded. Sailing to "Rio de Janeiro, Argentina," Miner claimed he became a gun runner. He then crossed the Pacific to China before returning to the United States. Miner related this account in 1913 as an aged convict on the Georgia prison farm at Milledgeville.[14]

This story is fabricated from start to finish, the ramblings of a garrulous old man who, incredibly, convinced his listeners that the yarn was true. There is documentary evidence that Miner was in California during the fall of 1881; it would have been impossible for him to complete his world tour in a scant six months' time. Miner's ignorance of geography is also a dead giveaway when he placed Rio de Janeiro in Argentina. Had he been there, he surely would have known that it is in Brazil.

There are other conflicting reports regarding the activities of Bill Miner and Stanton Jones after their confrontation and escape from Sheriff Bronaugh. One account states that they traveled to Arizona, where they supposedly committed several bold stage robberies before fleeing to California. Considering the fact that Arizona was foreign territory to Miner and Jones, it is doubtful that they would have been foolhardy enough to take that chance. Detectives Hume and Thacker stated that Miner and Jones went to New Mexico, where they held up a stagecoach en route from Deming to Silver City. This is also in error, for there is no record of a stage robbery occurring from February to November of 1881 between Silver City and Deming.[15]

U.S. Postal Inspector L. Cass Carpenter of Denver, who had been instrumental in tracking down other Colorado stage robbers in 1881, related an account of Miner's career in Colorado to a reporter for the *Denver Republican* in April 1882. Although Carpenter gave some incorrect information in the article, titled "California Bill," in all likelihood he was close to the facts when he made these statements about Miner's actions after his escape from Bronaugh:

> They made their escape although hunted for days. Nothing has ever been heard from the partner, and "California Bill" was not heard of again until his arrest in California.
> It seems he made his way directly across the country until he reached California.[16]

In all probability, Miner and Jones either returned to Leadville, where they could safely hole up until the situation cooled down and at the same time earn pocket money working for Miner's brother-in-law or, according to local legend in Onondaga, Michigan, Miner returned for one last fling in his courtship with Jennie Willis. Whatever the two did, by late summer or early fall, Miner and Jones had returned to California.[17]

Considering his notoriety and reputation in California, this was a dangerous move for Bill Miner, but not nearly as dangerous as remaining in Colorado. No one was looking for him in California, and Miner, who was now using the alias William Anderson, knew the area well. It was not long before the inveterate highwayman was again plying his trade.

CHAPTER 8

"The Drivers on This Line Are All Damned Fine Fellows"

FOLLOWING their arrival in California, Bill Miner and Stanton T. Jones made their way directly to Yolo County. Here they teamed up with James Crum, a forty-two-year-old former prison mate of Miner who at the time was stealing horses on a large scale along the Pacific Coast. Bill knew that the stages from Sonora usually carried large amounts of cash or gold from the surrounding mining areas and began formulating plans to relieve a stage of this valuable cargo. With Crum's assistance, Miner contacted another former prison chum, William A. Miller, who was then farming in Yolo County.[1]

Miner, Crum, and Miller had all been incarcerated at San Quentin in 1871. Jim Crum, a native of Missouri, was undoubtedly the most notorious horse thief on the Pacific Coast. He was first arrested for stage robbery in Sacramento in December 1866 but soon was released owing to lack of evidence. In December 1871, Crum was convicted and sentenced to ten years on charges of grand larceny for stealing a herd of horses in Sacramento County. As convict No. 5061, he entered San Quentin on December 16, 1871, and was released on June 8, 1878.

Crum immediately resumed his career as a horse thief with forty-six-year-old Ben Frazee, who was then living near Rough and Ready in Nevada County. Frazee was another San Quentin ex-convict who had been released in February 1874 after serving four years for grand larceny in Sutter County.

In November, Crum and Frazee were joined by ex-convict Charles Dorsey, alias Charley Thorn, and the trio spent the winter stealing horses and playing cards. In June 1879, yet another ex-convict, John C. Collins, alias Patterson, joined the trio at Frazee's house. Dorsey and Collins soon began planning a stage robbery and asked Crum to join them. Knowing the two outlaws were extremely dangerous men, Crum declined their offer, but he did lend them his shotgun. On

September 1, Dorsey and Collins robbed a stage at Moores Flat and killed a prominent banker, William Cummings. A week after the robbery, the two returned to Frazee's house and remained hidden in the woods for two weeks. Crum met Dorsey and Collins at the American River below Folsom and furnished them with horses and the pair fled California.[2]

By the spring of 1880, Crum and Frazee had moved their operations to Yolo County and were joined by a young man from a good family named William Todhunter. During the next eighteen months, the gang, under Crum's leadership, stole more than two hundred horses from Tehama to San Francisco. The main camp for their stolen horses was an area in Stanislaus County called "the Pocket." Located about ten miles west of Modesto, it was so named because of a pocket of land that formed at the junction of the Tuolumne and San Joaquin rivers. The gang was considered the best organized and most desperate in California at the time.[3]

Like Miner, Bill Miller spent his early years in California. Miller's parents moved to a place near Grafton, in Yolo County, from Iowa when Miller was a child. On the night of May 5, 1870, Miller and his partner, Dwight Griffin, assaulted and robbed one Victor Aubrey near Woodland and were quickly caught and jailed by Sheriff Bullock. Apparently they stole a horse from Aubrey and were charged with grand larceny. On December 7 the two men escaped by picking the padlock to their cell. They were recaptured on April 14, 1871, in Jacksonville, Oregon, and returned to California on a requisition by the governor. Both men were tried, convicted, and sentenced to six years at San Quentin. Miller entered San Quentin on October 30, 1871, as convict No. 5017. On November 27, 1874, Bill Miller was pardoned and for the next seven years stayed out of trouble. Miller was described as an easygoing man with "no particular harm in him," but after continuous badgering and pressure from Miner and Crum, he finally agreed to join in the planned stage robbery.[4]

At 4 A.M. on November 7, 1881, Miner, Miller, Crum, and Stanton T. Jones held up the stage from Sonora to Milton ten miles west of Sonora. As the stage approached the Garibaldi mine, the four masked bandits stepped in front of the coach and commanded the driver, Clark Stringham, to stop. Without a word, Miner assigned the other three bandits to their tasks by simply motioning with his hands. One of the bandits took charge of Stringham while the other

Left: James Crum at the time of his arrest for the Sonora stage robbery in 1881. Courtesy of Wells, Fargo Bank History Room, San Francisco, California. *Right:* Bill Miller at the time of his arrest for the Sonora stage robbery in 1881. Courtesy of Wells, Fargo Bank History Room, San Francisco, California.

two ordered the three passengers out and made them stand with their backs to the stage and their hands behind them.

Stringham asked Miner, "Is there anything of mine you want?"

Miner replied, "No, the drivers of this line are all damned fine fellows, and I would rather give them something than take anything from them."

Having second thoughts, Bill laughingly said, "I guess I'll search you; you may have a revolver and might get mad and try to use it."

Finding the driver unarmed, Miner turned his attention to the express shipment. With a sledgehammer, the bandits broke open two Wells, Fargo iron-bound chests and an iron safe. To their delight, the robbers hauled out thirty-three hundred dollars in coin and gold dust. Then they began robbing the passengers.

When the stage had first been stopped, John Mundorf, a Sonora merchant, threw a bag containing five hundred fifty dollars into a gunnysack which also contained his lunch. Discovering the bag of gold dust inside the sack, Miner wisecracked, "This lunch will most suit us at this time of day," and threw it to one of his men.

Stringham, becoming impatient with the delay, called out, "Hurry up. I don't want to miss the train at Milton."

Miner responded, "All right. What time is it?"

The driver told him it was 5:30 A.M. Bill said, "Go ahead, I'm through," shook hands with Stringham, made some comment about the weather, and bid the passengers good morning. Before disappearing into the woods with his three companions, Bill Miner waved and called jauntily to the driver, "Ta-ta, my boy."

Three newspaper reports of the holdup illustrate the discrepancies that often occur when separate accounts of an incident are described. They also suggest that Miner and his gang had some compassion and that a lawman could jump to unwarranted conclusions. The *San Francisco Chronicle* reported that the bandits relieved another passenger, G. L. Osgood, of forty dollars, but when he whispered something to one of the robbers, the money was returned. Osgood's actions were so suspicious that Sheriff Ben Thorn arrested him as a confederate when the stage arrived in Milton. In the second version, carried by the *Stockton Daily Independent* and the *Sacramento Daily Record-Union,* the bandits took forty dollars from John Mundorf's son, and when he asked for some traveling money, the robbers gave it back.[5]

Sheriff Ben Thorn of Calaveras County happened to be in Milton when the plundered stage arrived and persuaded one of the passengers to accompany him in pursuit of the bandits. The two men immediately started on the trail but were unsuccessful in their search.[6]

News of the robbery quickly spread and law officers from the surrounding area made every effort to capture the bandits. It quickly became one of Northern California's most concentrated horseback manhunts. Numerous lawmen, including some of the best peace officers on the California frontier, joined the search. Participating in the hunt were Sheriff Ben Thorn of Calaveras County, Sheriff Thomas Cunningham and Deputy Sheriff Atwood of San Joaquin County, Sheriff George McQuaid of Tuolumne County, Sheriff Henry Rahm of Yolo County, Sheriff Henry McCoy of Yuba County, Sheriff Fulkerth and Deputy Sheriff McCabe of Stanislaus County, Chief Karcher and Officers William Arlington and Lee of the Sacramento police, Chief Orrin Langmaid and Constable James Brown of Stockton, Constable John Williams of Bantas, Constable Thomas Lane of Modesto, John Thacker and Charles Aull of Wells, Fargo & Company, and Capt. Peter Pumyea and Detective Martin R. Casad of the Oakland Police Department.[7]

In 1883 a reporter for the *New York Sun* visited San Quentin and interviewed both Bill Miner and Charles Aull, who was then captain of the yard. In his article, the reporter related Aull's version as to what led to the identification of Bill Miner as one of the bandits.

In early fall of 1881, Miner, as William Anderson, drifted into Chinese Camp in Tuolumne County. Sometime in October, he was taken ill with a high fever and chills. Miner's pleasant manner and charm reportedly won him many friends while he was recuperating. Following his recovery, Miner attended a dance at Angels Camp on November 6, the night before the stage robbery. During the evening, he became attracted to a young woman who at some point during their conversation remarked that she wanted some sheet music but could not obtain it. Miner told her he was going to San Francisco and promised to send her the music when he got there.

The day following the robbery, Capt. Charles Aull of Wells, Fargo & Company arrived at the scene of the holdup. After his investigation, Aull suspected that Bill Miner was involved in the robbery, although it was not known that he was in California at the time. Aull found out about Miner's dalliance with the young woman at the dance and his promise to send the sheet music. Two weeks later the music arrived and was intercepted by the officers.[8]

A more detailed account was written by a *Daily Alta California* reporter who interviewed Miner and Aull in 1886:

> It was also learned that some weeks prior to the robbery a rather dashing young man had stopped for a time at Chinese Camp, nine miles below Sonora. He was suffering from chills and fever, and placed himself under a doctor's care. His glib tongue and polished manners took the quiet population by storm. He gave the name of William Anderson. Anderson soon made the acquaintance of all the young ladies in the town, and one in particular he paid especial attention to. The officers soon determined that Anderson and Miner were identical.

Standing, left to right: A. W. Stone, San Francisco policeman; John Thacker, Wells, Fargo detective. *Seated, left to right:* San Joaquin County Sheriff Tom Cunningham; Calaveras County Sheriff Ben K. Thorn; Detective Harry N. Morse. Photo taken after the arrest of Black Bart in 1883. Thacker, Thorn, and Cunningham were involved in the capture of Miner, Miller, and Crum in December 1881. Courtesy of Wells, Fargo Bank History Room, San Francisco, California.

On the Friday night previous to the robbery John Curtin gave a ball at his new house, nineteen miles below Sonora, on the Knights Ferry road. Anderson was there, and, as usual, was the lion of the evening. Crum was also there, but kept discreetly in the background. At that ball Wm. Anderson agreed to send his young lady friend some

Ben Frazee at the time of his arrest for grand larceny. From John Boessenecker's collection.

music from the city. Some two weeks after the robbery that music arrived, and furnished the first definite clue as to the course pursued by the robbers.⁹

Following the robbery, the newspapers covered the story thoroughly, giving detailed accounts about the investigation and manhunt. In a report contrary to Aull's version, an Oakland newspaper provided what seems to be the most plausible account of how the bandits were identified:

The whereabouts of the gang was unearthed by Captain Pumyea, of this city [Oakland], and detective M.R. Casad, formally Marshal of Marysville. They learned in November that a "trick" was being planned in this city, but as there were five or six men in the gang, the officers thought a train robbery or a stage robbery was contemplated. After the Sonora stage was robbed, Pumyea and Casad began to work up their points. They found that the gang, including Miner, Ben. Frazee, Jim Crum, and Miller, all ex-convicts, had put up the robbery in Oakland, had returned here on the 17th and traded horses in this city, and two of them had new suits of clothes made at Moran's. On November [December] 1st Crum sent $400 by Wells, Fargo & Co. to his sister in Chillicothe, Ohio, using the name James Pratt. . . . Fletcher [Todhunter], the hackman [carriage driver for hire] left Oakland a short time since and was at the ranch owned by Miller, four miles from Cacheville in Yuba [Yolo] County. After getting their evidence fully prepared, Captain Pumyea telegraphed Detective Hume, Chief of Wells, Fargo & Co.'s detective force, and when the latter came to Oakland, told him where the gang could be found. Hume thought that Pumyea had been led astray, and would not go to the ranch of Miller, but got in communication with Sheriff McCoy of Yuba County, and he and some other officers were informed of the place Captain Pumyea believed the gang to be.[10]

After fleeing from the scene of the robbery, Miner, Crum, and Jones split up with Miller, who returned to Yolo County. Riding only at night, the trio rode through Livermore to Oakland and reached San Francisco five days later. Crossing to Oakland on the seventeenth, Miner soon satisfied his passion for lavish clothing by purchasing a fine eighty-five-dollar suit, black beaver pants, a flashy silk plush vest, and a double-breasted dark chinchilla frock coat. From a pawnbroker, he bought a gold watch and chain. After enjoying the pleasures of San Francisco, Miner and Crum left Jones in the city and started back for Chinese Camp, where Miner intended to resume his courtship. Arriving at the Pocket in Stanislaus County, the two bandits learned that officers were hot on their trail and quickly changed directions to escape capture.[11]

After two weeks of hard work, the officers now knew the identity of the bandits. Positive information had reached the officers that the robbers were hiding in the Pocket. On the evening of November 24, a large posse of lawmen, consisting of John Thacker and Charles Aull of Wells, Fargo, Sheriffs Cunningham and McQuaid, and six other officers raided the Pocket but found that the fugitives had been warned and had fled the day before.[12] The officers, twelve hours behind the robbers, tracked them through Stanislaus and Alameda counties to San Francisco, then back through Alameda, San Joaquin, and Sacramento counties to Yolo County.[13]

Pumyea's lead was correct and Bill Miner and two of his cohorts were in Cacheville (now Yolo) and had been hiding out at the ranch of Ben Frazee, Crum's associate in the horse-thieving business. On December 3, Detectives Thacker and Aull arrived at Woodland in

Yolo County, where they joined forces with Sacramento Officers Karcher, Arlington, and Lee. Together with Sheriffs Rahm of Yolo County and McCoy of Yuba County, they laid plans to continue their search for the stage robbers and to arrest Ben Frazee and his partner, William Todhunter.

Pumyea sent the telegram at 4 P.M. on the fifth and the next morning Thacker, Rahm, and McCoy set out for the ranch owned by Bill Miller's mother. When they were within three hundred yards of the house, they saw three men running out the back door, heading for cover. The officers had unexpectedly stumbled on Miner, Miller, and Crum. The startled officers immediately gave chase until they positioned themselves between the outlaws and their three stolen horses. Cut off from his horse, Crum jumped behind a tree and covered the officers with a double-barreled shotgun as Miner and Miller escaped into the brush. With their weapons trained on Crum, the three lawmen cautiously advanced until they were within four feet of him. The cornered bandit threatened to blow their brains out but Thacker shouted, "Don't you do it, Crum!"

Outnumbered three to one, Crum desperately attempted to draw a revolver with his left hand, but Thacker and Rahm quickly pounced on him. While McCoy trained his weapon on Crum, Thacker grappled with the outlaw until Rahm had him securely handcuffed. As the capture of Crum took a precious fifteen minutes, the officers postponed the search for Miner and Miller to go after Frazee. The lawmen proceeded to Frazee's ranch, where they captured both Frazee and Todhunter. Todhunter told his captors that he was a hack driver from Oakland and claimed that he had gone to Miller's ranch to get a pair of horses. The lawmen later learned that Crum's shotgun had been stolen by Todhunter in Oakland. The officers put irons on the three prisoners and took them to the county jail in Woodland.[14]

Aull and Arlington immediately started in pursuit of Bill Miner and Bill Miller. Throughout the night and all of the next day, the two officers futilely searched for the two bandits. Around 5 P.M. on the seventh, as Aull and Arlington were scouting on the west side of the Sacramento River about ten miles north of Sacramento, they suddenly came upon Miner and Miller on the levee. As soon as the bandits realized that they had been sighted, they drew their weapons. Heedlessly, the two lawmen made a dash for them. The fugitives lost their nerve, jumped a fence, and began running through the tules.

ARREST STAGE ROBBERS.

$1,800 REWARD!

On the morning of November 7th, 1881, the down stage from Sonora, in Tuolumne County, to Milton, in Calaveras County, was robbed about two miles from Stanislaus River, in Tuolumne County, by four masked men, and Wells, Fargo & Co.'s box rifled of $2,435 in coin, and $800 in dust; a passenger, John Mundorf, was also robbed of $550 in dust.

The State and Wells, Fargo & Co., have each a *Standing Reward* of $300 each for the arrest and conviction of such offenders.

It is now known that Jim Crumm, alias "Smith," alias "Davis," alias "Brown;" William Miller, alias "Barnes;" Billy Minor, alias "Anderson," and a man called Jim Brown, were the robbers. Jim Crumm was captured December 6th, at Miller's Ranch, about two miles from Cacheville, in Yolo County, the other three escaping to the brush.

DESCRIPTION:

BILLY MINOR, alias "Billy Anderson," sent to State Prison in 1871 for stage robbery from Calaveras County in company with James Harrington, alias "Alkali Jim," for 13 years; discharged in 1880; age now 34; height about 5 feet 10 or 11 inches; hazel eyes; hair dark brown; complexion light, thin face, slightly pockmarked; slim built; "UA" back left hand; star right forearm; mole on throat; native Michigan; long slender hands; large ears; is a good, fluent talker; fond of women. On October 26th bought in Oakland a fine suit of clothes for $85; black beaver pants, wide seams down the legs, silk plush vest, quite flashy, with variegated checks; *double breasted*, dark Chinchilla frock coat, wide binding, large flaps over pockets; bound same binding around wrists; 1 gold stem winding watch and oroide chain.

WILLIAM MILLER, alias "Barnes," native of Iowa, sent to State Prison October 30th, 1871, for robbery; discharged November 27th, 1874; age 33; about 6 feet; complexion fair; eyes blue; hair light, thin on top of head; light mustache; reddish chin whiskers; face thin and freckled; scar left forehead; has a drawling nasal twang to his voice, and always smiling when talking; a slouchy, stooped gait; rather slim built; is fond of playing poker, and talking about quarter horses; also, fond of whisky and fast women.

JIM BROWN, supposed to be an old convict; about 5 feet 7 inches; short black hair and mustache; round, full face; well built; 30 years old; not very talkative; a good carpenter.

It is believed that BILLY MINOR will try to make his way out of the State by railroad. Conductors are requested to keep a sharp lookout, as he can be easily identified.

If arrested, telegraph the undersigned at Sacramento, who will receive them at any jail on the Pacific Coast, and convey them to place of trial without cost to arresting party.

J. B. HUME,
Special Officer Wells, Fargo & Co.

SACRAMENTO, December 6th, 1881.

DON'T POST! These Circulars are for Officers only.

Wells, Fargo reward circular for the Sonora stage robbers. From William B. Secrest collection.

Aull, his shotgun ready, and Arlington, revolver in hand, immediately gave chase. Aull began peppering the air with buckshot at the two fleeing bandits. With buckshot whizzing around him, Miller threw up his hands and surrendered. He was secured by Arlington who immediately took him to Sacramento, leaving Aull alone to pursue Bill Miner on foot. After a grueling chase of approximately a mile, Aull began to gain on Miner, who, realizing the futility of his efforts, surrendered without resistance.

Aull procured a team of horses and headed for Sacramento with Miner in tow. Reaching Washington, Aull was met by Officer Arlington and Detective Hume of Wells, Fargo, who had started back to assist him in the chase for Miner. The officers continued on to Sacramento, where Miner joined Miller in the city jail. When captured, Miner and Miller had been armed with a shotgun and two revolvers each and one hundred rounds of ammunition. All three of the stage robbers had a considerable amount of cash on them when searched. Bill Miner was too well known to the arresting officers to deceive them by using the alias of William Anderson. The revolvers taken from Miner and Miller were of great interest to their captors according to the following article in the *Sacramento Daily Bee:*

> HANDSOME WEAPONS—The pistols, two each, taken from Miller and Miner last evening when they were arrested by Capt. Aull and officer Arlington, are handsome specimens of the Smith & Wesson brand. New, highly polished, nickel plated and self-cocking—the pattern used in the army, they are a dangerous weapon of offense or defense in the hands of an expert, and no toy to trifle with. They were admired at the station by old officers and men experienced in the use of arms, and pronounced to be as fine a weapon as ever defended honor or captured outlaw.[15]

On the morning of the eighth, Sheriff Cunningham of San Joaquin County and Deputy Sheriff McCabe of Stanislaus County brought Crum and Frazee to Sacramento and placed them in the city jail. The next day, Sheriff Cunningham, Captain Aull, Detective Thacker, and Sheriff McQuaid of Tuolumne County brought the five prisoners to Stockton by train. Frazee was charged on on an 1880 warrant with stealing a wagon. Both Frazee and Crum were charged with grand larceny. Todhunter was charged with cattle theft. On December 27, 1881, Frazee entered San Quentin for his second term after being convicted and sentenced to one year and six months for grand larceny. The three heavily ironed stage robbers were taken from Stockton to Sonora and jailed on the ninth by Aull, Thacker, and McQuaid.[16]

Stanton T. Jones, the fourth member of the robber band, was known to the officers as Jim Brown and was described as thirty years old, five feet seven inches tall, well built, with a round full face, short

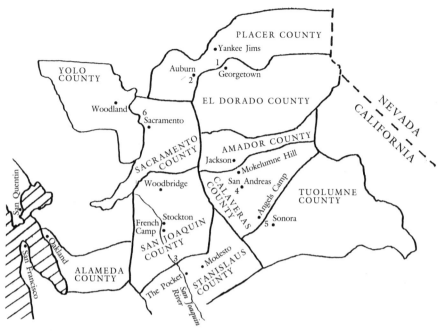

BILL MINER'S CRIMINAL CAREER IN CALIFORNIA, 1866–81
1 Illegal sale of two horses, early January 1866, Miner.
2 Robbery of merchant in Auburn and theft of horse, December 28, 1865; theft of horse, January 4, 1866, Miner.
3 Robbery of Porter near San Joaquin River, January 22, 1866, Miner and Sinclair.
4 Robbery of San Andreas Stage, January 23, 1871, Miner, Harrington, and Cooper.
5 Robbery of Sonora Stage, November 7, 1881, Miner, Crum, Miller, and Jones.
6 Capture of Miner and Miller, December 7, 1881.

black hair and mustache, and not very talkative. Fortunately for Jones, he had fled California before he could be apprehended. Reportedly, while en route to Ohio, he passed through Colorado, supposedly stole a horse, and was captured, tried, and sentenced to five years for the theft. This is incorrect and probably derived from the Sauguache County indictment against East, Jones, and Miner under his alias of Morgan. As East was convicted of grand larceny and sentenced to the Colorado State Penitentiary at Canon City, the identities of the two men were probably confused. Furthermore, there is no record of Jones's being imprisoned in Colorado or later in Ohio.

It appears that Jones was yet another victim of Miner's persuasive power, but unlike the others, he was lucky, escaping the clutches of the law and fading into oblivion.[17]

Upon their confinement in the Sonora jail, the three stage robbers were persistently questioned by Aull, who tried to get them to confess. Both Miner and Miller remained mute, but Crum, on the understanding that he would receive no more than a ten-year term, readily confessed to the stage robbery and implicated Stanton T. Jones as the fourth robber. As a result of Crum's confession, Miner and Miller finally admitted to their part in the robbery. The trio would cool their heels in jail until their trial commenced.[18]

CHAPTER 9

Home Again, San Quentin

BILL Miner knew that he was going back to the only home he had known for thirteen years of his life: San Quentin. On December 17, 1881, before Judge Rooney in Tuolumne County Superior Court at Sonora, Bill Miner, Jim Crum, and Bill Miller pleaded guilty to the charge of robbery. Charles Aull presented his plea to the judge in behalf of Wells Fargo that Crum receive no more than a ten-year sentence and on behalf of Miner and Miller, who also confessed, a sentence not to exceed fifteen years. Judge Rooney, a no-nonsense jurist, ignored Aull's plea and on December 19 sentenced Miner and Miller to a stiff sentence of twenty-five years each and Crum to twelve years' imprisonment.

In reporting the outcome of the case, even the *Calaveras Weekly Citizen* expressed surprise at the lengthy sentence the convicted bandits received after pleading guilty. On December 21, Miller, Miner, and Crum were delivered to San Quentin and registered as convict Nos. 10190, 10191, and 10192, respectively.[1]

Soon after the capture of the stage robbers, Charles Aull left Wells, Fargo and became captain of the yard at San Quentin. In 1882, James Crum furnished Aull with information regarding the 1879 stage holdup and murder in Nevada County, California, committed by Dorsey and Collins. Through Crum's information, Aull and another officer were able to track down the two killers and bring them to justice. In addition, Crum testified in the trial, and as a result, both men were convicted. Because of his information and testimony as well as his confessing to the Sonora stage robbery prior to trial, Crum was pardoned by Gov. George Stoneman on June 12, 1884, with the stipulation that he permanently leave the state of California. Ben Frazee also gave testimony at the trial. His sentence was commuted, and he was discharged from San Quentin on March 12, 1883.[2]

On March 11, 1882, less than three months after entering San Quentin, Bill Miller was transferred to Folsom Prison and issued convict No. 460. From 1888 through 1895, Miller made four separate applications for a pardon. In his fourth petition, Miller had the complete support of Charles Aull, who was now warden at Folsom. Aull, like other officials at the prison, did not consider Miller a criminal of the same class as Miner, and he cited Miller's exceptional conduct and exemplary work as a trusty at Folsom. In 1893, Miller's sentence was commuted to nineteen years. By 1897, however, his physical condition had so deteriorated as a result of tuberculosis that he was discharged on March 21 of that year. Miller died shortly after his release.[3]

Bill Miner made his third trip to San Quentin on December 21. It was then that false information about Miner began to emerge. To the San Quentin prison authorities he reported his age as twenty-eight and his birthplace as Canada. He facetiously gave his occupation as "shoemaker," a skill he had acquired in the prison shoe shop.[4]

During this prison term, evidence of Miner's ability to charm reporters and elicit favorable comments from the press also emerged. In 1883 a reporter from the *New York Sun* interviewed him for details regarding the Sonora robbery and his ultimate capture. The reporter was so favorably impressed with Bill that he wrote, "He is now thirty-seven years of age and not withstanding his many years of confinement is yet a handsome and graceful fellow, fluent of tongue and captivating in style." Captain Aull, however, saw Miner in a different light. In November 1882, Aull wrote Wells, Fargo Division Supt. S. D. Brastow that Billy Miner, behind San Quentin's walls, was the "inseparable companion" of noted criminals Buck English, Jack ("Black Jack") Bowen, and Frank ("Big Frank") Clark.[5]

Being a fourth- or fifth-termer, depending on the way the records are interpreted, Bill Miner had little hope of impressing the administrative heads of the state of California with his eloquence. Taking another approach, on May 14, 1883, Miner petitioned the State Board of Prison Directors to allow him to solicit money from convicts to employ a lawyer to challenge the constitutionality "of the indictment made upon information." Miner was challenging the district attorney's right to draw up a charge on information and issue an indictment without benefit of a grand-jury examination. Gaining nothing from his petition, Bill figured there was only one other way to get out of San Quentin.[6]

On the afternoon of April 17, 1884, Miner made an ingenious attempt to escape. He rigged up a dummy consisting of a stuffed shirt

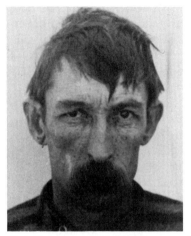 

Left: San Quentin Prison photograph of Bill Miner taken around 1888. Courtesy of the California State Archives, Sacramento. *Right:* Folsom Prison photograph of Bill Miller taken around 1888. Courtesy of the California State Archives, Sacramento.

and a pair of pants mounted on sticks with a face made of brown soap and painted flesh color. Miner's cell mate placed the dummy against the bunk to deceive the guards who passed by the cell at the time of lockup. The ruse failed and a search was made for Miner by Capt. A. C. McAllister and the yard officers. The officers found him hiding in a box that covered a large wheel in the sash-and-blind factory. The wily convict had intended to remain hidden until nightfall and then scale the wall and escape. On April 18 the prison board, finding Miner guilty of attempted escape, sentenced him to one day in the dungeon and revoked his nine years and nine months of credit time.[7]

Bill Miner's many exploits made him one of the best-known convicts in San Quentin, his notoriety second only to that of the prison pharmacist, Charles E. Boles, better known as Black Bart, California's most prolific stage robber. As Miner once boasted to reporters, "There's only one man I can take my hat off to, and that's the fellow down in the medicine shop, Black Bart."[8]

Miner was generally recognized as a leader of the convicts. This role was to lead him into further trouble with the prison authorities. A recurring complaint by the prisoners was bad food, and on September 23, 1886, Miner talked his comrades into doing something about it. Taking advantage of the fact that the State Board of Prison Directors was on the grounds for one of its regular meetings, accompanied by numerous visitors and newspaper reporters, Bill and a group of fellow prisoners, after their noon meal, refused to return to their jobs in the jute mill and door factory. With Miner in the lead, 150 convicts marched up to the yard to Captain Aull's office. Two civilians visiting Aull took one look at the scowling mob and fled to the front gate.

Aull, a strict disciplinarian who was generally hated by the convicts, stepped from his office and asked quietly, "Well, boys, what's wanted?"

There was no reply. For a moment it seemed as if Miner and his companions had lost their nerve.

"Don't any of you know what you want?" Aull snapped.

Although the crowd was full of murderers, robbers, and other desperadoes who could have killed the lone captain in an instant, each knew full well the penalty for their insubordination. Again Aull was met by lengthy silence.

"What do you men want here, for the last time?" he demanded. "If you have anything to say, speak up. You all know that you have no right to leave your work and come up here."

There was a sudden movement among the crowd, and Bill Miner hesitatingly stepped forward. "We want to see the Board of Directors."

"What for?" Aull demanded.

"Well, that's all right," Bill replied, now defiant. "We want to see the board."

"You cannot see the directors. You have come here in an unheard of manner, and I will not permit you to see the directors under any circumstances."

A low growl erupted from the convicts. By this time a squad of riflemen under Capt. Ned Reddy had scrambled into position on the gun rails, and Gatling guns in the towers were trained on the mob. Warden Paul Shirley now joined Aull and demanded, "What's the trouble?"

"I think the bread is bad," said Miner. "The meat and potatoes are good but the bread is bad."

Infuriated by the highwayman's impudence, the warden ordered the convicts to disperse immediately and return to their work. Captain Aull instructed two trusties to write down the convict numbers of each man in the crowd. Scenting the danger, many of the convicts lost their nerve and bolted for the prison shops before they could be identified. Miner tried in vain to stop them. Other convicts stood their ground as William Evans, a convicted robber, flung down his hat and shouted that he would never return to work.

Captain Reddy, from his position on the wall, trained his Winchester on Evans. "Pick up that hat."

Gazing at the gun muzzle, Evans slowly stooped down for the hat, then stood motionless as he considered the situation. Suddenly he turned and fled down the yard at full speed. At that, realizing the futility of the little mutiny, Miner slowly moved off, followed by the remaining members of the crowd.

Although in bygone years Miner and his comrades would have been flogged severely for such impudence, certain reforms had gradually crept into the prison administration, and instead he and eight other convicts lost their coppers in a hearing before the prison board. According to the minutes:

> September 27, 1886; Convicts numbers 12118 Henry Thompson, 11796 William Evans, 10191 William A. Miner, 9313 John Wilcox, 11512 Henry Mack, 11477 Charles Elliott, 11361 Chris Markle, 11436 Peter Smith, and 11857 Morris Wilson were brought before the Board charged with refusing to go to work when ordered to do so by the proper officer and inciting a revolt and insurrection among the other prisoners on the 23rd day of Sept. 1886. After hearing the statement of Capt. Charles Aull each of said convicts was found guilty of the offense as charged. It was therefore ordered by the Board on motion of Director Devlin (Director Sonntag voting no) that all credits of each of said convicts . . . earned to date of offence be declared forfeited.

In effect, Bill Miner received no punishment at all, since his time credits had been forfeited two years earlier.

Captain Aull knew Bill well, and he never believed the cagey outlaw was interested only in ridding the prison of bad bread. In his report to the warden, Aull wrote, "The attempted revolt was caused by the continued agitation of some of the very worst of the criminal element and is the result of a general belief on the part of the convicts that no punishment of any consequence will be meted out to the offenders." One of the participants admitted to Aull that the trouble had been stirred up "for a political purpose." Said this convict, "An election was coming on, and Miner and others who have lost all their credits, and hope for their restoration by change in the administration, got up the revolt to gain sympathy from the press representatives who were attending the meeting of the prison directors."[9]

Six months later, Bill Miner found his chance to redeem himself with the prison authorities. The San Quentin prison minutes reported:

> A communication was also submitted by the Warden and read, informing the Board that on April 5th 1887 about 2 o'clock PM, a fire was discovered in the drying rooms of the Door and Sash factory located about the center of the main shop building, but by the prompt action of the officers of the prison, aided by a large number of prisoners, the fire was subdued without any material injury to the building or its contents. Accompanying said communication was a report from the captain of the yard, with names of the prisoners engaged in extinguishing the fire, and recommending that all of the credits heretofore declared forfeited be restored to each, and in the cases of convict no. 5929 Jack Hays and 10191 William Miner whose credits were declared forfeited for attempting to escape, both of whom were conspicuous in their efforts to stop the fire the captain recommends that the attention of the Governor be called to their cases and that he be asked to commute their sentence in an amount equal to the credits hitherto forfeited for attempting to escape.[10]

On December 17, 1887, the prison board met to consider recommending to the governor that five years be taken off the sentences of Miner and Hays. But only two board members voted for the recommendation, so the motion was defeated and Miner and Hays gained nothing.[11]

Bill Miner may not have regained any credits, but he did gain some notorious publicity in the *San Francisco Examiner*. In the spring of 1889 the newspaper published an article depicting the lives of the most infamous convicts in San Quentin, which included noted stage robber Bill Miner.[12]

For two years following the fire-fighting episode, Bill attended to his assigned work and gave prison authorities no trouble. Nevertheless, in May 1889, trouble came to Miner. In almost every account of Miner's life, some mention is made of his being stabbed by another inmate named Bill Hicks, but the details have never been told. Hicks, convict No. 11971, was a dangerous man; he had served eight years for grand larceny, had been sentenced to life imprisonment for the July 4, 1876, murder of a railroad brakeman, and had been pardoned after serving seven years. In 1885, Hicks was sentenced to five years at

San Quentin for grand larceny committed in San Francisco. For some reason, hard feelings developed between Miner and Hicks, and the latter often threatened to "do up" Miner.

At 6:30 on the morning of Sunday, May 19, as the prisoners were returning from breakfast, Bill Hicks maneuvered himself into position directly behind Miner. As they reached the top of the cell-block stairs, Hicks slashed Miner across the throat from his windpipe to his right ear with a short-bladed shoe knife used for cutting strings in the jute mill. According to the *San Francisco Examiner:*

> Fearing that this would not be sufficient to produce death, Hicks jabbed the knife into the back of Miner's head. Hicks was immediately apprehended by one of the guards and locked up in the dungeon. Miner was conveyed to the hospital where his wounds were dressed.
>
> Dr. Durant, the prison physician, told an EXAMINER reporter yesterday that Miner wasn't hurt much, but the convicts say he is sure to die.
>
> Hicks declines to either admit or deny the stabbing, and refuses to talk about the matter.

On the nineteenth, the prison authorities telegraphed the news to Miner's mother in Sacramento. Miner's two sisters, then living in the state of Washington, evidently were visiting their mother and immediately left Sacramento by train, arriving at San Quentin on the morning of the twentieth. They told reporters their mother was too prostrated by the news to travel.[13]

On June 8, in a hearing before the prison board, Bill Hicks pleaded guilty to the charge of "cutting a fellow prisoner with a knife." The board ordered all Hicks's coppers, past and future, be forfeited. No more trouble occurred between the two convicts following Miner's recovery.[14]

The prison board's refusal to intercede with the governor to restore Miner's lost credits because of his aid in extinguishing the prison fire was a heavy blow to him. For five years his frustration mounted, and seeing no other way out, he planned another escape. Shortly after 5 A.M. on November 29, 1892, Miner and his cell mate, Joseph Marshall, made their bid for freedom. It was to end in a tragedy that made headline news in San Francisco's three major newspapers.

At the time of the escape attempt, Miner was a leather cutter in the shoe shop and Joseph Marshall, convict No. 12947, was in charge of the machine and repair shop. They were cell mates in cell 47 on the second tier of the old stone cell block built in 1854 at the southern end of the prison yard.

Joe Marshall, an intelligent and muscular man, had first entered San Quentin on December 2, 1878, for an eight-year term on two charges of grand larceny. Released in April 1884, Marshall was soon back in prison. On April 16, 1885, he was sentenced from Sacramento County to thirty years at Folsom on the charge of burglary. He forfeited all his credit time after an escape attempt in 1887 and was transferred to San Quentin on March 31, 1888.

About a month before the attempted break, Marshall approached Miner with the proposed escape plan, telling his cell mate he would do most of the work if Miner would not "blow" on him. Miner agreed because he had lost 117 months' coppers for his 1884 escape attempt and saw no other chance for freedom. They decided to make their move on Sunday night, November 28.

Marshall obtained some bailing rope from jute bags, a bent iron bar to use as a climbing hook, and a dark lantern, all of which they managed to smuggle into their cell. Marshall disassembled a ratchet drill, which he and Miner carried to their cell in two trips by concealing the parts under their shirts. It rained all day Saturday and Sunday, and the two men remained in their cells feverishly plaiting forty feet of rope. After lockup at 3 P.M. on Sunday, they discovered that the drill would not work and postponed the escape until Marshall could repair it.

On Monday afternoon they began drilling through the hasp controlling the bolts that locked the door. Removing the bolts, they took the plate off the cell lock and picked the lock. It took them until the early morning hours to open the lock. They hurriedly donned two old oilskin coats and put socks over their shoes to deaden their footsteps. Then Marshall cautiously peered out of the cell. Seeing no one on the cell block balcony, Marshall grabbed the hook and rope while Miner carried the dark lantern. The two convicts slipped out of their cell and headed for the steps at the corner of the building, intending to slip past a one-man guardhouse near the stairs.

Marshall was in the lead, and as he started down the steps, without any warning, the roar of a shotgun blasted into the stormy night. Marshall groaned and fell dead on the walkway with eleven buckshot in his head. As Miner turned and dropped to the platform in surrender, the shotgun roared again and a single buckshot tore through his left cheek, knocked out two teeth, and lodged in the right side of his face, knocking him senseless.

When the prison officials arrived at the scene five minutes later, they found blood and brain matter oozing from Marshall's head and Bill Miner writhing half-conscious on the platform. Marshall's body was taken to the prison morgue and Miner went to the prison hospital, where he quickly recovered after his wound was dressed.

Bill Miner had no aversion to talking to the newspaper reporters who flocked to the prison after receiving the news. Miner sadly told reporters from the *San Francisco Call* that he wished he were in the morgue with Marshall as it was "better there than here." To the *San Francisco Examiner* he gave a long and detailed account of the escape plan and the unexpected shooting. Bill said that if they had been given a warning, they both would have gone back to their cell immediately, "because it is no use to go up against buckshot."

The man who did the shooting was W. A. Alexander, a guard who had been hired in May 1891 on the recommendation of Sheriff Tom Cunningham of San Joaquin County. Alexander, in a statement to the *San Francisco Chronicle,* said he was stationed in a room directly across the court and on the same level as cell 47. He added that he knew he had two desperate characters to deal with and fired out the window without warning because he did not propose to take any chances with them.

Warden William Hale claimed that three months earlier he had received information from some of the convicts that an escape conspiracy was brewing and had hired extra men to watch special sections of the prison grounds. Hale admitted that Marshall and Miner were suspected and that Guards Alexander and Waters were cautioned to keep a special watch on cell 47. He defended Alexander's actions by stating lamely that Alexander was placed in the room, not to watch cell 47, but because his guards were stationed inside during bad weather. As for the escape conspiracy, Miner told the *San Francisco Examiner,* "There was nobody in with us, and I don't know anything about a general understanding that a break should be made by all the convicts in the place."[15]

At noon on November 29, Coroner Edward Eden impaneled a jury and held an inquest on the body of Marshall. The main witness

San Quentin Prison about 1890. The old stone cell block, built in 1854, is shown on right. The guards' dormitory building is across from it. The shots fired at Miner and Marshall from a window in the dormitory are to the right and out of view. California State Library, Sacramento.

1885 San Quentin photograph of convict Bill Hicks, who stabbed Bill Miner in a prison confrontation in May 1889. Courtesy of California State Archives, Sacramento.

was Alexander, and he implicated not only himself but also his supervisor, Capt. J. F. Birlem, in a cold-blooded murder:

> I was ordered to stay in that room until relieved. And I was also ordered to say nothing if I found any prisoner trying to escape, but to get as near to him as possible and then shoot into him. The man I killed was a dangerous one, and I see no reason why I should allow him to come near me. Anyway, I was carrying out my orders. The men were about fifty feet away when I fired. I could not have stopped him without shooting.

After testimony was taken from Warden Hale, Captain Birlem and other witnesses, the jury found

> that Marshall had died by a gunshot wound while endeavoring to make his escape, the gun being fired by one W. A. Alexander, while on guard and in the discharge of his duty, and we exonerate the prison authorities from all blame.[16]

On December 5 the prison board reported: "Guard Alexander is hereby exonerated from all blame and is commended for the faithful performance of his duty." The case had received so much bad publicity that evidently the prison officials wanted to whitewash the whole matter and, considering the wounding of Miner punishment enough, took no action against him for the attempted escape.[17]

The officials at San Quentin were not yet out of hot water. Marin County District Attorney Cochrane had received reliable information that the officers knew for several hours that Miner and Marshall were cutting through their cell door and could have confiscated the tools at any time. Instead it was decided to watch their cell and shoot them down when they emerged. On December 3, Guard Alexander was arrested; on the sixth, his preliminary examination was held before Justice of the Peace Dufficy.

Bill Miner was brought in to testify, and he described how he had been shot down without benefit of warning. Guard Waters, who was stationed with Alexander on the night of the shooting, testified with great reluctance. Their watch point was a blanket-covered bedroom window in the guards' dormitory, each guard taking a two-hour shift. Under the close questioning by Cochrane, Waters broke down and admitted that they were ordered by Captain Birlem to watch cell 47. When called to the stand, Birlem denied the whole thing in what was described as "a halting, hesitating manner that produced a most painful impression on those who heard him."

SHOT DOWN WHILE ESCAPING.

An Early Morning Tragedy Within the Walls of San Quentin.

TRAGIC DEATH OF A DESPERATE CONVICT.

John Marshall and William Miner Walk Out of Their Prison Cells and Are Greeted With a Load of Buckshot—The Ingenious Manner in Which They Pierced Their Iron Doors—The Verdict.

At an early hour yesterday morning W. A. Alexander, a guard in the San Quentin Penitentiary, fired upon two convicts who were attempting to escape, killing one of them instantly and wounding the other. John Marshall, the man who was killed, was serving a thirty-year term for burglary. The man who is only wounded is William Miner, at present in jail for the fifth time on a twenty-five-year sentence for robbing a stage in Tuolumne county.

Guard Alexander.

For nearly a month Warden Hale, on account of information received from some of the

Headline in the *San Francisco Examiner* announcing the shooting of Miner and Marshall. From John Boessenecker's collection.

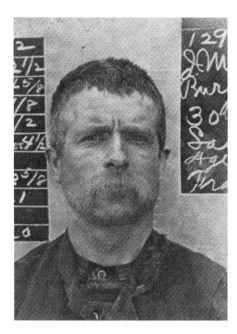

Convict Joseph Marshall, who was shot and killed while trying to escape with Bill Miner on November 30, 1892. California State Archives, Sacramento.

The proceedings were adjourned until December 8, and as soon as court reconvened, Guard Waters asked to be sworn in. Declaring that his previous testimony regarding Birlem was false, he stated that he must have been mistaken. Waters's denial prompted this caustic remark from the *Marin County Tocsin:* "Guard Waters' retraction was looked upon generally as a masterpiece of nerve." The *Tocsin* editor railed against the prison officers:

> A self-constituted judge and jury had passed the death sentence on Marshall and Miner and it was carried out as fully as the ability of the executioner could compass it. It was wholly unnecessary and wanton taking of human life.[18]

The examination was postponed until December 10, when Justice Dufficy ruled that it was not within the jurisdiction of his court to acquit or exonerate Alexander and bound him over on a charge of manslaughter for trial in Marin County Superior Court under five thousand dollars' bond. In its final statements regarding the affair, the *Marin Journal* pointed out that public opinion was equally divided, that many people believed Warden Hale and other officials at

San Quentin were justified in their actions. Whether or not Guard Alexander was ever actually brought to trial is unknown.[19]

The wounding of Miner and the manner in which it was carried out had a profound effect on the aging bandit, now nearly forty-six years old. His attitudes and actions changed dramatically, and from that point on he adhered strictly to the prison rules.

Four years later, on August 15, 1896, Miner's sister Mary Jane Wellman interceded for him and appealed to the prison board to restore his lost credits. Investigating the matter, the board refused to restore them, citing his dubious record since his confinement and his recidivism: "being a fifth termer."[20]

But Miner, a resourceful man, could not easily be defeated. In 1897, Gov. James H. Budd, who thirty years earlier had acted as his defense attorney, visited San Quentin. By chance he met Miner in the jute mill, where the old convict was at work. Never one to miss an opportunity, Bill immediately brought up his effort to regain his lost credits and managed to elicit a promise from the governor to use his influence with the State Board of Prison Directors on Miner's behalf.

Between September 1897 and November 1898, Miner wrote five letters to the governor reminding him of his promise. Alternately pleading, demanding, and whining, the letters show a true confidence man in action. Declared Miner, "I am existing in the extremest suspense. It is wearing me out. I have lived upon the hope founded upon your statement made to me during our conversation in the jute mill." Next the old bandit promised the governor he would reform. "Such action on your part will open to me a future, in which will be presented opportunities to lead a respectable career, for the balance of my days. A home is provided for me, where good influences exist."

Miner was even savvy enough to rely on the political makeup of the prison board. "When you promised me that you would have my credits restored you meant every word of it, and I know that you intend your wishes shall be complied with. Governor, I believe four of the Board are your appointees, and if you would write them a letter personally signed by you, certainly your desire would be at once complied with." Reaching back in the distant past, Bill played his trump card. "I also recall our conversation at the Depot in Stockton when you said to me that if ever chance appeared you would do all in your power for me." Much to the governor's chagrin, the cagey holdup man had recalled the promise Budd had made to him thirty years before.

But the governor did not live up to his promise and never exerted his influence on the outlaw's behalf. Wisely, he allowed the board to make its decisions about Bill Miner. The board members, fully aware of Miner's bad record and justifiably suspicious of his promises of reform, proceeded with great caution.[21]

Meanwhile, on October 9, 1897, the prison board again reviewed Miner's case for credit restoration and postponed action until the next meeting. On March 12, 1898, the board instructed the warden to investigate the matter and report his conclusions. On November 21, the board took some action by denying Miner's application for pardon but nothing was done regarding his restoration of credits until April 8, 1899, when the board again postponed a decision. At long last, on September 16, 1899, Miner was brought before the board to plead his cause, but again its members cautiously took the matter under advisement. Bill Miner's appeal dragged on until the next year, the turn of the century.[22] Finally, on February 10, 1900, the prison board took positive action. The minutes recorded its decision:

> In the case of Prisoner No. 10191 William Miner who had forfeited 9 years and 9 months credit time in April, 1884, for attempting to escape the Board has had this case under consideration for several months, and after hearing the statements of Capt. Edgar and others and it appears to them that his conduct has been good and that he endeavored to comply strictly with all the rules for several years past. On motion of Director Devlin the board restored to him 4 years 6 months of said forfeited credits and it was so ordered.

On December 8, 1900, the board restored an additional year of Miner's lost credit time.[23]

On June 17, 1901, after nearly twenty years in prison, the fifty-four-year-old con man and bandit was discharged.[24] This was the last time he would see San Quentin. The remarkable fact is that of his fifty-four years, Miner had spent exactly thirty-three years and six months behind bars, including time he spent in jail after arrest and awaiting trials. Never again would a prison hold him as well as had the old stone walls of San Quentin.

CHAPTER 10

No More Stages to Rob

FOR fifty-four-year-old Bill Miner, times had changed drastically during the nearly twenty years he had spent behind bars. The world into which the old bandit ventured must have filled him with awe. People were talking to each other from long distances on a device called the telephone or chugging along the roadways in a newfangled contraption called an automobile. There was even talk of a machine that would someday fly in the sky. One change taking place must have dismayed Miner, and that was the gradual disappearance of the horse-drawn stagecoach. One thing was certain, however: Bill Miner had had enough of California, and California of him.

Bill no longer had any family in California. Four months before he was released from San Quentin, his mother, Harriet Miner, had died. This is confirmed by the termination of her Civil War pension on February 24, 1901.[1]

The next two years of Miner's life are shadowy, but at least he stayed out of the clutches of the law. After he left San Quentin, he headed for Samish Flats, near the town of Bow, Washington, where his oldest sister, Harriet, was living. His other sister, Mary Jane Wellman, and her husband, Louis, were living in nearby Whatcom. Louis Wellman had left Colorado in November 1882 for Washington Territory and had located a homestead the following March at Whatcom, now a part of Bellingham. Mary Jane Wellman had left Colorado in May and joined her husband in Bellingham on June 18, 1883. Reportedly they were the first family to settle there.

But it was not family ties that enticed Bill Miner to the bay area of Washington. He saw none of his family for more than two years.[2] While imprisoned at San Quentin, Miner had made friends with his cell mate, Jake Terry, commonly known as "Cowboy Jake," a smuggler and counterfeiter from the Bellingham-Sumas area of Washington. It was likely through Terry's influence that Bill decided to go to Washington, and here the two resumed their friendship following

Terry's release from San Quentin in 1902. This relationship would have a profound impact on Miner's future.[3]

Arriving in the bay area, Bill Miner went to work as superintendent of an oyster bed in Samish Bay. He was remembered as a friendly man who was always courteous and mannerly.[4] He spent the summer of 1903 in and around Whatcom, and during this time he began a friendship with a fresh-faced, seventeen-year-old youth named Charles Hoehn, who was living in Equality Colony, Sagit County, Washington. Hoehn, a native of Ohio, had come to Equality Colony in 1898 and during the summer of 1903 had spent some time in jail at Mount Vernon, Washington, for petty larceny. Once again using the alias Bill Morgan, Miner promised Hoehn a trip to Mexico, where they could make a lot of money and could live well. It can be safely assumed that Miner's interest in the gullible youth was more than simply paternal.[5]

That summer, Bill made a trip south to Oregon to the Farr Brothers lumber camp near Goble at the request of another former convict he had known at San Quentin, forty-three-year-old Z. G. ("Gay") Harshman. Claiming that he had been cheated by the railroad, Harshman had been contemplating holding up a train to get even and was on the lookout for confederates he could trust. Harshman approached Miner, who readily agreed. After having spent two frustrating years at honest labor, Bill missed his old trade. Now that the stagecoach was passing into oblivion, here was an opportunity to return to his "profession" with a new twist: train robbery.[6]

Like Miner, Gay Harshman was a habitual criminal. He had arrived in Oregon in the early 1880s, married, and farmed until he killed a man in a jealous rage. Although he was never brought to trial, Harshman was not well regarded, being a quarrelsome man always at odds with his neighbors. In the early 1890s, Harshman moved his family to Washington, where he became involved in counterfeiting, for which he spent two terms in prison, the second as a federal prisoner at San Quentin. After his release in May 1902, Harshman returned to Oregon and worked in various logging camps until meeting Miner during the summer of 1903.[7]

The major problem with their scheme was that neither Harshman nor Miner knew the first thing about robbing trains. Nevertheless, the two men made their initial plans, and after informing Harshman that he could get a third reliable man, Miner returned to Sagit

County, Washington. Up to his old tricks, Bill Miner enlisted the naive Hoehn in the scheme, and on August 17 the two left for Oregon.

At Goble, Miner and Hoehn met Harshman, who was using the alias John Williams. The three men worked briefly at a lumber camp piling wood while daily discussing the planned robbery. Passing word that they were going to open a coal mine near Nehalem, the trio went by wagon to an abandoned cabin on Government Island about sixteen miles below Goble. Returning the wagon to Goble, the three spent the next several days at the cabin. Hoehn later said he first learned about the robbery plan on Government Island and claimed he had been controlled by Miner and forced to participate in it.[8]

On the night of September 19 the three would-be train robbers attempted to stop the Oregon Railway and Navigation Express. Miner picked the town of Clarnie, ten miles outside Portland, to stage the holdup. He reasoned that after the robbery they would be close enough to Portland to return to the city and disappear quickly.

When they arrived in Clarnie, Hoehn went down to the tracks with a set of red stop signals to await the approaching train while Miner and Harshman stationed themselves on a high bank ready to fire upon the train after it stopped. Hoehn, unfamiliar with train signals, was on the wrong side of the track when the train approached. Consequently the engineer ignored the red lights and sped on.

The trio had brought along twenty pounds of dynamite, probably stolen from the lumber camp where they had worked, for blowing open the express-car door. Miner, seeing that the train was not going to stop, ordered Harshman to light a stick of dynamite and toss it onto the express car as it passed. Harshman refused because he was afraid the explosion might injure the passengers. Miner and Harshman quarreled on top of the embankment as the train roared past, carrying away their booty, with Hoehn below vainly waving the red signals.[9]

Patching up their differences, Miner and Harshman hit upon a new plan. Hoehn was sent to Goble to purchase a boat, which he bought for twenty dollars from a local fisherman. Hoehn then floated the boat down the Columbia River to Corbett, twenty-one miles east of Portland, where he cached it and caught a train back to Goble. On the twentieth, Bill Miner bought whiskey, sugar, coffee, and other provisions. On September 23 the three men left Govern-

Artist's drawing of Charles Hoehn *(left)* and photograph of Gay Harshman *(right)* after their capture for the attempted robbery of the Oregon Railway and Navigation Fast Express on September 23, 1903. Mark Dugan's collection.

ment Island and went downriver by rowboat. Reaching shore, they walked to Troutdale. As soon as they arrived, Hoehn was sent three miles up the track to Corbett with instructions to await the arrival of the train.[10]

At 8:15 that night, the Oregon Railway and Navigation Fast Express No. 6 left Portland heading east. When the train paused at Troutdale, Miner and Harshman, who were masked with black cloth and carrying several sticks of dynamite, climbed into the blind baggage car just behind the engine tender. Finding a tramp named Robert Bryden in the car, they searched him for weapons and then ordered him into the coal box with a warning to stay put or they would kill him. As the train left the station, the two robbers climbed over the tender to the engine where they covered the engineer, Ollie Barrett, and the fireman, H. F. Stevenson, with revolvers. Ordering them to stop the train at the twenty-one-mile post at Corbett, the bandits told the cowed trainmen, "If you obey orders no harm will come to you, but if you attempt any trickery work, death will be your reward."

When the train was halted, the two crewmen were ordered off by Miner and Harshman, who told them to lead the way to the express car. One of the bandits called out to Hoehn, who emerged from the side of the tracks carrying a rifle. Reaching the express car, they forced Barrett to order the express messenger, Fred Korner, to open the door. Making no reply to the bandits, Korner told the express helper, Solomon Glick, "Put out the lights." For several minutes Miner and Harshman discussed the situation and decided to dynamite the door.

Lighting the fuses of the dynamite sticks, which were tied to long poles, Miner and Harshman placed them against the express-car door which was completely shattered by the explosion. Glick, who was on the rack above the door, was badly shaken by the blast, but Korner was hiding in the dark interior of the car and immediately fired his shotgun at the bandits. Harshman, who was in front of the others, was hit in the right side of his head and tumbled headlong into a ditch along the track siding. A stray slug also caught engineer Barrett in the shoulder. With this unexpected turn of events, Hoehn immediately fled over the bank to the spot where the boat was cached on the Columbia River. Miner, after checking on the condition of Harshman, also realized the futility of the attempted robbery and took off after Hoehn, leaving his fellow bandit behind.[11]

The *Oregon Daily Journal* added some amusing highlights to the scene after the conductor warned the passengers of the holdup:

> Watches, purses, tickets, and jewelry were stowed away in all conceivable places. Men paled and women grew hysterical. Some of the male passengers had revolvers, but no thought of going out to do battle with the bandits was entertained or even suggested. One man, it is said, even hid his revolver.

Even the description of the escaped bandits, especially Miner, was inaccurate:

> [Hoehn] Age 24; 5 feet 8 inches in height; weight 175 pounds; dark hair; light brown moustache; brown eyes, dark clothes, badly worn; black slouch hat; two weeks growth of beard.
> [Miner] Age 30; taller and more slim than other man; wore gray suit badly worn and with one sleeve out at elbow; dark complexion.[12]

News of the attempted robbery was sent to Portland immediately, and a special train was ordered to bring a posse to the holdup site.

Delayed for two hours until Multnomah County Sheriff William Storey could be located, the train finally reached the robbery scene about 12:30 A.M. with Sheriff Storey and his posse, along with Capt. James Nevins, the superintendent of the Pinkerton Detective Agency, and his men. They found Harshman badly wounded, face down in the ditch where he had fallen. Harshman and Barrett were placed under medical care on the train, which immediately returned to Portland.

Meanwhile the posse dispersed in groups between Bridal Veil and Portland in search of the fugitives. Near Bridal Veil, one group picked up the tramp, Robert Bryden, who said he had stayed hidden in the coal box until the train got to Bridal Veil. Bryden was held, pending identification of the robbers. Word was sent to Sheriff Biedecker on the Washington side of the river, and a search was begun there. A suspect named W. R. Frulock was arrested and turned over to Sheriff Storey. Frulock was held in the Multnomah County Jail overnight, grilled the next morning by the district attorney, then released. Because no trace of the robbers could be found, rewards were issued in the amount of $1,300 for each of the fugitives.

Harshman was taken to Good Samaritan Hospital in Portland, where he was expected to die at any time. He gave his name as Jim Conners but would give no other information. Refusing all food and drink, he had to be force-fed, and he was sullen and morose, refusing to speak to anyone.[13]

When Bill Miner left the scene of the robbery and reached the cached boat, he told Hoehn that Harshman was dead, and they quickly crossed the river to the Washington side. From there, they went to Government Island and burned their hideout cabin. The two then split up, agreeing to meet in Tacoma, Washington. By walking and hopping freight trains, Hoehn reached Tacoma only to find Bill Miner there ahead of him. The two made their way to Samish Flats. Hoehn, using the name of Charles Morgan, took a job in a shingle mill near Bow; Miner again went to work on the oyster beds. There being no leads to their identities or destinations, Miner and Hoehn avoided capture for a time.[14]

About October 2, Capt. James Nevins of the Pinkertons obtained a lead on Hoehn from a young boy in Portland who knew him. Enlisting the boy's aid, Nevins took him to Bow to work in the shingle mill alongside Hoehn. He was to watch Hoehn to see if Hoehn would lead the detectives to the third bandit.[15]

Finally, two weeks after the attempted holdup, the officers got their first break. While Harshman remained in the hospital under guard, officials sent descriptions of him statewide for positive identification. On October 6 the Tacoma Police Department identified him as Gay Harshman.

Receiving this information, Sheriff Storey, who had been hunting the fugitives in Oregon and Washington, returned immediately to Portland and confronted Harshman in the hospital. With his identity now known, Harshman broke down and related the details of the robbery, naming his confederates. His story was partly fabricated. He claimed that five men had been involved in the robbery: himself, Bill Morgan [Miner], his nephew Charles Morgan [Hoehn], George Underwood, and Jim James, a supposed relation of Jesse James. The rest of his confession was accurate, including the information that the Morgans could be found at Samish Flats in Washington.[16]

After Harshman's confession and identification of the other robbers, Captain Nevins promptly ordered Hoehn's arrest via Sagit County Sheriff Risbell. On October 7, Risbell rode the fifteen miles of railroad track to Bow on a velocipede and made the arrest. Hoehn was taken to Mount Vernon, Washington, and jailed. Two days later, Hoehn confessed to the attempted robbery, stating, like Harshman, that five men were involved. Sheriff Risbell and posse began searching the Samish Bay area for Miner.[17]

Bill Miner had left his job on the oyster beds on October 1 and headed for Whatcom to see his sister, Mary Jane Wellman, whom he had not seen since she visited him in the prison hospital in 1889. While there, Miner evidently learned of Harshman's confession and the arrest of Hoehn. Fearing his own arrest, Miner told his sister he was going to Anacortes, Washington. On October 9 he disappeared, leaving his overcoat, which was stained with Harshman's blood.[18]

Sheriff Storey left Portland and arrived at Whatcom on October 10, the day after Miner had fled. Having obtained the information from Hoehn or the Pinkertons that Miner had a sister in Whatcom, Storey obtained a warrant and went to the Wellman home, where he discovered the bloody overcoat.

Bill's sister told Storey that her brother's true name was Allen E. Miner and that until his recent visit she had not seen him in four-

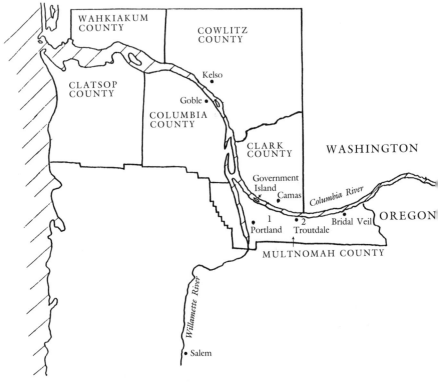

BILL MINER'S CRIMINAL CAREER IN OREGON, 1903
1 Attempted robbery of the Oregon Railway and Navigation Express, September 19, 1903, Miner, Harshman, and Hoehn.
2 Attempted robbery of the Oregon Railway and Navigation Express No. 6 and the wounding and capture of Harshman, September 23, 1903, Miner, Harshman, and Hoehn.

teen years. She also informed Storey that her brother had left for Anacortes.

Not following the lead given by Miner's sister, Sheriff Storey proceeded to Mount Vernon where, on October 11, he and Captain Nevins took Hoehn into custody and left for Portland. Arriving the next morning, they placed their prisoner in the Multnomah County Jail. On the same day, Harshman was released from the hospital and lodged in jail with Hoehn. Both Harshman and Hoehn finally admitted that there were only three men involved in the robbery attempt. Harshman added that Miner was known as Jim James as well as Morgan.[19]

During the week of October 12 a vagrant named James Fenning was arrested in Everett, Washington, as Bill Morgan, the third member of the train robbing crew. When the news reached Portland, the *Oregon Journal* picked up the story and reported:

> In the first place the detectives say Feeney [Fenning] does not correspond with the description of the fugitive robber given by Harshman or Hoehn. . . .
> Furthermore it is stated that Feeney was in jail at Everett, serving a term for vagrancy at the time the attempted robbery took place. . . .
> Harshman, the other bandit under arrest, is too ill to make the trip to the Washington town for the purpose of identifying Feeney. But from a description of the latter, Harshman does not hesitate to say that he does not believe the prisoner is Morgan.

Sheriff Storey, desperate to arrest the third bandit, had Fenning held in jail at Everett until requisition papers were drawn up. On the nineteenth, Storey picked up Fenning in Everett, brought him back to Portland, and locked him in the Multnomah County Jail. The whole episode was a travesty of justice, and Fenning was released on November 10 by order of the district attorney. Sheriff Storey later admitted that Harshman, when brought face to face with Fenning, said the man was definitely not the third bandit.[20]

During their investigation of the robbery, the Pinkertons gathered information regarding Bill Miner's habits. The old bandit's association with young Hoehn led to the first public disclosure of his bisexuality. A reward poster for Miner's arrest issued by the Pinkertons on October 27 stated, "[Miner] is said to be a sodomist and may have a boy with him." The reward poster described Bill further:

> PECULIARITIES AND MARKS—Slight squint in right eye. India ink marks at base of left thumb [VA]. Projecting ears. Dancing girl in India ink on right forearm. Face somewhat pitted; badly wrinkled at base of nose and on cheeks about eyes. High cheek bones. Flesh mole on left shoulder blade. Mole on breast near point of right shoulder. Walks erect.
> Miner's usual system of working is to locate himself in a cabin in a secluded place near a stage line, on a pretense of prospecting or following some lawful occupation. He then selects a time and place for robbery, and after committing a crime leaves the country by avoiding the highways, and does not appear again in the vicinity where the robbery was committed.[21]

/25. $1,300.00 REWARD

The following rewards are offered for the arrest and conviction of A. E. MINER, alias WM. A. MINER, alias WM. MORGAN, alias OLD BILL MINER, who in company with GAY HARSHMAN and CHAS. HOEHN (the two latter are now in custody), held up O. R. & N. Co. Passenger train No. 6 at mile post No. 21, near Corbett, Oregon, on the night of September 23rd, 1903.

$500.00 by the Oregon Railroad and Navigation Co.
$500.00 by the Pacific Express Co.
$300.00 by the State of Oregon

Miner was liberated from prison at San Quentin, Calif., June 17th, 1901, where he had served a sentence of 25 years for stage robbery, less his good time allowance.

Miner's usual system of working is to locate himself in a cabin in a secluded place near a stage line, on a pretense of prospecting or following some lawful occupation. He then selects a time and place for robbery, and after committing a crime leaves the country by avoiding the highways, and does not appear again in the vicinity where the robbery was committed.

HIS VICTIMS ARE ALMOST INVARIABLY STAGE LINES, although he may again participate in a train or other robbery. He is likely carrying a Winchester rifle and a Colts revolver.

We have sufficient evidence to convict Miner of the O. R. & N. Co. train robbery.

Above is a photograph of A. E. MINER alias WM. MORGAN, and the following is his description:
RESIDENCE—Sammish Flats, Wash.
NATIVITY—Canadian.   COLOR—White.
OCCUPATION—Shoemaker.
CRIMINAL OCCUPATION—Stage and Train Robber
AGE—50 years; looks to be 55.
HEIGHT—5 ft. 9½ in.
WEIGHT—About 145 pounds. Slim build.
COMPLEXION—Medium Dark.
COLOR OF HAIR—Quite Grey. Original color, brown and brushes it back from temples.
EYES—Brown.   NOSE—Long.
STYLE AND COLOR OF BEARD—When last seen (October 1, 1903,) was smooth shaven.
PECULIARITIES AND MARKS—Slight squint in right eye. India ink marks at base of left thumb. Projecting ears. Dancing girl in India ink on right forearm. Face somewhat pitted; badly wrinkled at base of nose and on cheeks about eyes. High cheek bones. Flesh mole on left shoulder blade. Mole on breast near point of right shoulder. Walks erect. Is said to be a sodomist and may have a boy with him.

If located, arrest and notify by wire at our expense the undersigned at the nearest office listed above, when arrangements will be immediately made to have the authorities of Multnomah County, Oregon, request his detention and send an agent for him, with necessary requisition papers.

PINKERTON'S NATIONAL DETECTIVE AGENCY,

Or
JAMES NEVINS,
Res. Gen'l Supt.

303 Marquam Building,
PORTLAND, OREGON.

PORTLAND, OREGON, October 27th, 1903.

Reward poster for the arrest of Bill Miner for the Portland train robbery on September 23, 1903. Issued by the Pinkerton National Detective Agency on October 27, 1903. Furnished to Mark Dugan by Robert Olson of Pico Rivera, California.

Harshman and Hoehn were kept in jail without bond until November 13. On that day in Multnomah County Court, Harshman pleaded guilty to two charges: assault with a deadly weapon and attempted train robbery. Still suffering from his wound, Harshman had to be assisted to and from the courtroom. Hoehn pleaded not

Oregon State Prison photographs of Charles Hoehn *(left)* and Gay Harshman *(right)*. Courtesy of the Oregon State Penitentiary, Salem.

guilty to the charge of attempted robbery even though he had confessed his guilt earlier. Nevertheless, on the thirteenth the young bandit was found guilty by Judge Cleland and sentenced to ten years' imprisonment. On November 24, Harshman was returned to court and sentenced to twelve years' imprisonment by Judge Cleland, five years on one charge and seven years on the other.[22]

Hoehn was delivered to the Oregon State Penitentiary at Salem on November 16 and registered as convict No. 4792. Because of petitions submitted by residents of Washington state, citing his youth and gullibility at the time of the attempted robbery, Hoehn's sentence was commuted by Gov. George E. Chamberlain and he was released November 14, 1907.[23]

Gay Harshman entered the Oregon State Penitentiary on November 28 as convict No. 4796. Contrary to earlier predictions, Harshman survived his wound and, after serving more than eight years of his sentence, was discharged March 28, 1912.[24] If train robbery was not

Harshman's forte, counterfeiting certainly was. Within two years he was caught at it again and sentenced to another prison term.

As for Bill Miner, it was the first time, after being identified, that he evaded capture. Although Oregon and Washington law officers continued to pursue him, he eluded them, leaving no clue as to his whereabouts. He had mastered the art of outfoxing the hunters, but not without help from his old San Quentin cell mate, Jake Terry. The next four years, spent in association with and under the influence of Cowboy Jake, would be the most successful of Miner's entire criminal career.

CHAPTER II

Canada's First Train Robbery

FROM his sister's home in Whatcom, Bill Miner made his escape into Canada with the aid of Jake Terry, presumably using the obscure smuggling trails that crisscrossed the border. Adopting the alias George W. Edwards, Miner made his way to Princeton, British Columbia. Claiming to be a southern gentleman in search of peaceful surroundings for the winter, Miner found lodging at the Schisler farm on Bald Mountain near Princeton.

The following spring, Miner told the Schislers he needed to visit his gold mine in South America. He left his belongings in their care, stating that if he did not return they could have them. He returned in a few weeks and moved in with Jack Budd, who had a farm a few miles from the Schislers.

A grey-headed, bent little man who had been attracted by the Granite Creek gold rush, Jack Budd had migrated to British Columbia, supposedly from Texas, during the mid-1880s. He traded horses around Douglas Lake and Aspen Grove until he took up homesteading near Bald Mountain. In 1900, Budd went into partnership and began a livery stable in Coalmont, but when that failed, he returned to his homestead.

Budd's claim to have known George Edwards in Texas gave Miner an excuse to move from the Schislers. Years later, after Budd's death, the residents around Princeton received information that Bill Miner and Budd were actually brothers.[1] This, of course, was not true; both of Miner's brothers were long dead. Regardless of the relationship, Miner settled in at the Budd ranch and made a host of friends in the area while prospecting and running a few cattle near Aspen Grove.[2]

The blundered robbery at Portland in no way daunted Miner. He needed willing accomplices and soon cultivated a friendship with William J. Dunn, a stocky character known around Princeton as "Shorty." Dunn, whose lawful name was J. William Grell, was born April 15, 1869, in Milwaukee, Wisconsin, of German-American Catholic parents. Nothing more is known regarding his life before he emigrated to Canada. Dunn had prospected in the area, but at the time he met Miner, he was working in a sawmill near Princeton. To gain control over Dunn, Miner showered him with gifts, including a watch and a new gun. As the relationship developed, Miner took Dunn on several hunting trips and cattle drives to the coastal areas.³

Bill Miner also kept in contact with Cowboy Jake Terry, who had been released from San Quentin in the summer of 1902. Terry, one of the most notorious smugglers on the United States–Canada border, had begun smuggling while working as a railroad engineer, combining the two careers for several years. This earned him two trips to a federal prison. He also had been a policeman until he became mixed up with a counterfeiting ring near Seattle, which landed him back in prison, this time in San Quentin, where he became Bill Miner's cell mate. Because of his vicious nature, he was also known as "Terrible Terry." On one occasion, alone and unaided, he terrorized and held an entire town at bay for a week, yet he remains relatively unknown. Terry was unequivocally a desperado's desperado.⁴

Jake Terry's major contribution to the world of crime, however, was engineering Old Bill Miner's most famous train robberies without gaining the tarnished laurels for himself. The combination of Miner and Terry proved to be, at least in a criminal sense, a winning one. Their personalities, on the other hand, were completely opposite. Where Miner was affable, Terry was brash and cocky; where Miner was evasive and shadowy, Terry was outspoken and visible; where Miner could be violent, Terry, at times, was extremely vicious. Yet the careers of Miner and Terry were similar in that neither was successful until they joined forces, and when they did, they became major problems for law officers on both sides of the border. As might be expected, when their association ended, their success ended with it.

During his frequent absences from the Princeton area, Bill Miner joined Terry in smuggling Chinese aliens and opium across the border. According to the *Bellingham Herald*,

> Miner has not only been a train robber, but with Terry he was engaged in the smuggling business for a number of years. He operated on the Canadian side while Terry was the man who did the work on this side of the line.⁵

Miner and Terry began planning a train robbery, this time to be staged on the Canadian side of the border. Terry's expertise as a rail-

San Quentin mug photo of Jake Terry. Courtesy of Dick Nelson, San Quentin Museum Association.

road engineer with extensive knowledge of train routes, shipment schedules, and timetables, as well as his smuggler's knowledge of virtually every hidden trail across the border, made him Miner's prime choice as organizer and planner. In 1904, after recruiting Dunn into the scheme, Miner and Terry set their plans in motion.[6]

Sometime during the summer of 1904, Bill Miner, possibly accompanied by Dunn, drove a small herd of cattle along the Hope Trail to Chilliwack, selling them at a good price and also making many new friends. From there Bill went to Vancouver, telling his new acquaintances that he wanted to see the sights. In reality he was scouting the territory from the Hope Trail to Vancouver for an escape route he could use after the planned train robbery.

In September 1904, Miner and Shorty Dunn left the Princeton area, supposedly on another hunting trip or cattle drive. Instead they headed south toward the border, their objective being to rob the Canadian Pacific Railway outside Vancouver. With Jake Terry's ex-

Princeton, British Columbia, around 1900. Miner lived in and around Princeton from 1903 until 1906, using the alias George Edwards. Courtesy of British Columbia Provincial Archives, Victoria.

pertise to aid him, Bill Miner did not intend to make the same mistakes as he had during the fiasco at Portland the previous year. Somewhere near the United States–Canada border, Miner and Dunn rendezvoused with Jake Terry.[7]

About 9:30 on the night of September 10, 1904, the three bandits boarded the Canadian Pacific Railway's Transcontinental Express No. 1 at Mission Junction (now Mission City), forty miles east of Vancouver. Dense fog covered the area, and the three were not detected when they climbed aboard at the water tower or when they secreted themselves in the blind baggage.

As the train pulled away from the water tower, the engineer, Nathaniel J. Scott, was startled by a hand placed on his shoulder and a soft-voiced command: "Hands up!" Two masked bandits were armed with revolvers; the third held a rifle on Scott and the fireman, Harry Freeman. Miner softly told Scott, "I want you to stop the train at Silverdale crossing," adding, "Do what you are told and not a hair of your head will be harmed." Scott quickly responded, "I am at your service." Nothing more was said until the train stopped five miles west of Mission Junction.[8]

During their initial scouting of the area, the bandits had learned that a consignment of gold dust on the way to the United States Assay Office in Seattle would be in the express safe. Reminiscing many years later, ninety-year-old former lawman Jack Parberry stated that Bill Miner got this information by tapping the wires. This is probably incorrect; Miner had no experience in telegraphy. Jake Terry, as a former railroad man, presumably had experience using the telegraph, and probably it was he who tapped the wires. Cowboy Jake also knew that it was railroad policy to keep the express safe locked between stations. On the day of the robbery, the bandits again tapped the wires and, implying that the message came from headquarters, telegraphed the agent at Mission Junction that the combination to the safe was lost and ordered him to leave the safe unlocked. As a result, the express safe was easy prey for Miner and his companions.[9]

At Silverdale, Miner ordered fireman Freeman to go with him and one of the other robbers back to the express car. As soon as the train stopped, the brakeman, Bill Abbott, stuck his head out of the car and came face to face with Miner, who told him, "Get back inside unless you want your head blown off, and be quick." Abbott obeyed immediately but soon managed to escape and make his way back to Mission Junction. There he reported the holdup to the agent, who foolishly refused to believe his story.

When Miner and Freeman reached the express car, the messenger, Herb Mitchell, opened the top portion of the car door. Mitchell spotted the fireman through the fog and thought the fruit cars were being sidetracked. He closed the door, unaware of the impending robbery. Miner ordered the fireman to uncouple the express car from the rest of the train. After this was completed, the bandits returned to the engine. "Go to the Whonock mile post and stop in front of the church," Miner ordered Scott with the warning, "Do as you are told and no one will get hurt." When the train stopped, Miner left Terry to guard the fireman, and with Dunn took Scott back to the express car. In 1944, Herb Mitchell, recalling the events of the robbery, gave a riveting account:

> Then a rock came at the door; hit the outside. I looked out of the window and saw Nat Scott, the engineer, with a torch in his hand. I asked him what he wanted. He said, "Open up the door or the car

will be blown up." I said, "Who's going to blow it up?" He says, "Those fellows here." I opened up the door and one of the fellows poked a rifle under my nose. He ordered me to put up my hands and come down. As I lit on the ground one of the fellows grabbed me around the waist, and took my gun from me. Then he ordered me back in the car. Bill Miner was holding my own gun at the back on my ear, and Shorty Dunn was standing about ten feet [away] with a rifle, hammer cocked, lined on the point of my nose. Bill Miner said to me when I was in the car that all I had to do was do as I was told, and "[we] won't hurt a hair of your head," and "it is not your money I want."

There were two safes in the express car, a large combination safe which had been left unlocked and a smaller one bound for Vancouver. Approaching the larger safe, Miner ordered Mitchell, "Now, open up that safe." It was empty. Mitchell was then ordered to open the smaller safe which contained four thousand dollars in gold dust that was consigned to the United States Assay Office in Seattle, two thousand dollars in gold dust for the Bank of British North America in Vancouver, and one thousand dollars in cash.

After the safe was plundered, Miner meticulously went through the express car gathering up the registered mail and putting it into satchels. Into these satchels went $50,000 in United States bonds and an estimated $250,000 in Australian securities, which later would have a great impact on the old outlaw's future. As their final act, the bandits threw out the fireman's coal shovel to hamper feeding the engine, thus delaying the train and news of the robbery. The holdup had been executed in thirty minutes.

As Miner was leaving, Scott remarked to him, "Happy journey." To this Bill Miner politely replied, "Be careful when you are backing up that you don't meet with some accident." Scott reportedly added, "You fellows have your nerve with you," to which Miner retorted, "Yes, and we have something else." With this, the old bandit and his two companions quickly disappeared into the fog. Bill Miner had accomplished two things that night. He committed his first successful train holdup and, whether he was aware of it or not, pulled off Canada's first train robbery.[10]

As soon as the train reached Vancouver, the British Columbia Provincial Police and the Canadian Pacific Railway Police interrogated the train crew who stated that the three robbers were professionals and had American accents. This being Canada's first train holdup, the British Columbia police called in the Pinkerton Detective Agency in Seattle, which immediately dispatched agents throughout the area around the border. The government of British Columbia and the Canadian Pacific Railway offered large rewards totaling $11,500.

Several arrests were made but proved false. Tracks of three men were found after the discovery of an abandoned boat near Whonock. The trail was followed until it was lost near Sumas, Washington. Superintendent James Dye of the Pinkertons arrested a man named B. R. Davies near Sumas, who later proved to be a detective working on another case in the area. When all leads were exhausted, the British Columbia police and the Pinkertons returned to their posts, having gone without food or sleep for several days. Superintendent Dye, after thoroughly going over his records, was convinced that the Canadian Pacific robbery had been committed by Bill Miner.

During the manhunt a skilled tracker found and followed the tracks of three men that led into the mountains over Hope Pass but lost the trail after a long search. Inconceivably, after receiving this information, the British Columbia police completely discredited it, choosing to believe the robbers had escaped across the border to the United States.[11] What the British Columbia police had discredited was exactly what the robbers had done—gone over the Hope Pass and returned to Jack Budd's ranch near Princeton. Miner, under the guise of congenial George Edwards, continued to play the part of the southern gentleman around Princeton and was never suspected by the inhabitants of being a notorious train robber.

Bill proved a great favorite with the children in the area. He would take them to the outskirts of Princeton and give them free rides on his horse, Pat, or sit around for hours with them telling stories or showing off the fine points of his pistol, which they always wanted to see. He was welcomed into the homes of all the residents, who had nothing but good things to say about him. Kind, friendly, good natured, he was a favorite to all who knew him.[12]

One incident demonstrates Bill Miner's compassion and kindness for the children of Princeton. As a young girl, Mrs. Maisie A. C. Armytage-Moore, had lived in isolated Nicola Valley. During the winter of 1905, Miner, as George Edwards, discovered that she had no children her age to play with. He spent two days clearing a field and flooding it from a nearby stream to make a pond for her to skate on. Mrs. Armytage-Moore recalled: "It was a kindly thoughtful act and helped to break the monotony of long dreary winter days."

Another act of kindness was credited to Miner during this time.

He frequently came to the town of Landers and while there would leave his horse at Joseph Jordon's livery stable. One day Miner was driving a buckboard and had one of the Jordon children with him. There was an accident, and the little boy was hurt. Feeling responsible for the accident, Miner sat up the entire night nursing the child.[13]

The loss of $250,000 in Australian securities and $50,000 in United States bonds was a staggering blow to the Canadian Pacific Railway. To avoid public embarrassment and the resulting loss of confidence of their customers, the railroad attempted to suppress news of the loss. Nonetheless, bolstered by the offer of $11,500 in rewards (suggesting that something of greater value than seven thousand dollars in gold dust was missing) rumors became rife.

The CPR was responsible for the return of the bonds and securities because they had been lost in transit, and should the makers be unable to cancel them, the railroad would be forced to make them good. Their face value, $300,000, was an enormous sum in those days, equal to more than five million of today's dollars. This was a huge financial loss as well as a public-relations disaster. The return of these bonds and securities became the chief concern of the railroad, which in those days wielded tremendous influence in the Canadian government.

Although the stolen bonds and securities appear to have been negotiable, they would soon convert into another value as great as their monetary worth to Bill Miner: bargaining power. Miner fully recognized their face value, but he realized that if he attempted to cash them he could easily be traced. One of the bonds was reportedly an eighty-thousand-dollar bearer bond and Miner knew that no bank would be likely to cash such a large item unless it knew the bearer and knew he was acting in the regular course of business. Also, the bond was probably too large for a fence to handle, as even a sophisticated dealer in stolen goods would have much trouble passing it.

Unable to cash the bond himself or to sell it to a fence, the canny old outlaw figured another way to solve his dilemma: he would rob his comrades as well as the railroad. Perceiving that the bonds and securities would come in handy in the future, Miner evidently convinced Terry and Dunn that they were too large and too risky to negotiate and thus were of no value. Later events showed that Miner then hid them where even his partners could not find them.

It was not long before Bill Miner learned that he was the prime suspect in the Mission Junction robbery. He liked Canada and wanted to stay there, so the crafty highwayman soon cooked up a scheme that he hoped would create a refuge from U.S. lawmen. Unable to negotiate with the railroad for the return of the bonds and securities without exposing himself to capture, he contacted Jake Terry and struck a deal with him to act as an intermediary. Miner wanted immunity for the Mission Junction holdup and presumably agreed with Terry that he would demand a finder's fee from the railroad, which the two holdup men would then divide.

Bill believed that if the Canadian Pacific wanted the booty badly enough, it could arrange, through judicious use of political pressure and by bribing the appropriate officials, a safe haven for him in Canada. If this could not be accomplished, Bill surely felt that the railroad would pay dearly to get the bonds back.

Following the robbery, Terry returned to his old haunts around Sumas and Bellingham, Washington, using the name Brown. Terry was not yet a suspect in the robbery, and after being contacted by Miner he dropped the Brown alias and publicly declared that he was to be Miner's emissary in any negotiations with the Canadian Pacific Railway. Of all the criminals who moved in and out of Miner's career, Jake Terry was the nerviest and most calculating. Realizing that they had nothing to lose and much to gain, he brazenly admitted his close friendship with Miner and freely acknowledged that the old bandit was guilty and that the only way that the entire amount of stolen bonds and securities would ever be returned was to negotiate through him. But neither the railroad nor the government would yield to such blatant blackmail—at least not yet.[14]

This is the way things stood until the last of September 1905, when Bill Miner and Shorty Dunn made another of their frequent trips to the coastal area of British Columbia.[15] On October 1, Jake Terry was in Bellingham and reportedly left there for Portland.[16]

At 9 P.M. on October 2, the eastbound Great Northern Overland passenger train was robbed just north of Seattle near Ballard and Ravenna Park, an area well known to Terry, who had worked there in 1889. Although Bill Miner and Jake Terry were never officially charged with the Seattle robbery, newspaper reports identified them as the bandits.[17]

Miner, Terry, and Dunn worked their way south to Seattle, where they picked up a one-horse spring wagon. The horse and wagon had been stolen by James ("Lem") Short, a small-time crook from Seattle who had probably been hired by Terry to steal it. Short drove the stolen wagon north where he turned it over to the three robbers. The bandits cut the telephone wires between Kirkland and Medina, then drove the wagon furiously around Lake Washington until they reached a point five miles north of Ballard. Here, Terry and Dunn got out. Miner drove the wagon south to Interbay, where he abandoned it.

Bill Miner, fully masked, boarded the train at Interbay, climbing into the blind baggage. He ordered two hoboes in the blind baggage, Alfred Frankie and Roland Gibbs, to lie flat on the tender and keep out of sight. Miner made his way over the tender to the engine where, with two drawn revolvers, he forced the engineer, Caulder, and the fireman, Julette, to keep the train rolling until they came within sight of a campfire beside the railroad tracks. There Miner ordered them to halt, and as the train stopped at the signal fire, Cowboy Jake boarded the engine.[18] Julette later described the robbery:

> There were only two of them . . . and they were old hands at the business. They were as cool as ice and what they didn't know about handling the train crew was not worth knowing. They called each other "Bill" and "Tom." One of them, the larger, had a pronounced stoop to his shoulders. He did all the work. The other was a small man and did the directing. The tall man with the stoop shoulders was "Bill." The short fellow was "Tom."
>
> After they got into the car they opened the way safe first and found nothing in it. "Damn the luck," said Bill, "this is bad as ———," and he mentioned the name of another railroad which I did not catch. Then they went at the through safe and that's where they made use of me. They made me tie a blue handkerchief across my face and they did the same with engineer Caulder.[19]

What Julette meant by "they made use of me" was that the bandits forced him to place dynamite on the safe and light the fuse. They jumped off the express car, but the blast failed to blow open the safe. Julette was ordered to dynamite the safe again, but upon reentering the car, they found the safe still undamaged. Terry then set the third detonation himself. This time the blast shattered the safe, and Julette was ordered to remove the loot.

Meanwhile, Bill Miner periodically jumped down from the express car and stepped from one side to the other, shooting down the sides of the train to cow the passengers and keep them inside. After Terry had looted the safe, the two bandits fled north along the tracks. The

Mission Junction, British Columbia, and Canadian Pacific Railway's engine No. 251 in 1909. This is the site where Bill Miner committed Canada's first train robbery in 1904. Courtesy of National Archives of Canada, Ottawa, Ontario.

interior of the express car was a complete shambles, and all the express matter was destroyed.

The holdup ended on a slapstick note. Frankie and Gibbs, the two tramps on the blind baggage, went from the tender through the train and took collections from the passengers, claiming they had been robbed and needed money to get to Spokane. Many passengers were so nervous and upset that they thought the two hoboes were members of the gang and forked over their money. After the train reached Everett, the two were arrested and fined one hundred dollars in police court for vagrancy and were held in jail pending further investigation. They admitted going through the coaches taking money but denied any knowledge of or association with the actual robbers.

What part Shorty Dunn played in the robbery is uncertain. Fireman Julette claimed that there were only two robbers, whereas the passengers said that they saw more than two men involved. Since lights on the shoreline had been seen from the train, Dunn may have been posted at that point to protect the boat that reportedly was

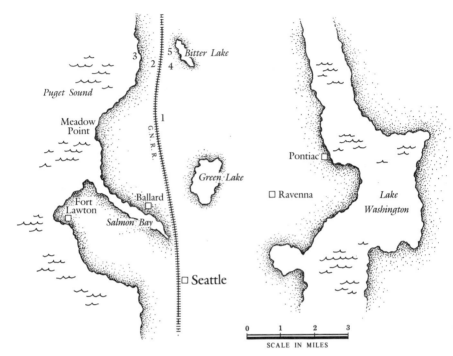

BILL MINER'S CRIMINAL CAREER IN WASHINGTON, 1905
1 Empty buggy seen going north at 2:45 A.M., October 3, 1905.
2 Robbery of the Great Northern Overland passenger train, October 2, 1905, Miner and Terry.
3 Lights on shoreline spotted by train crew and passengers during robbery.
4 Abandoned buggy found at 7:00 A.M., October 3, 1905.
5 Empty canvas bag stencilled "$36,000" found by farmer, November 1905.

used in the bandits' escape. The outlaws' flight was successful, and Terry was back in Sumas the next day.[20]

During the robbery a night watchman for the Great Northern Railroad had observed the crime and fled by boat to a nearby residence, where he telephoned the news to the railroad company's office. Another train, manned by railroad police officers, was dispatched quickly, but by the time it reached the scene of the robbery, the bandits had vanished. The Pinkertons were called in but made no investigation. They said they would play a waiting game, believing that sooner or later they would find a stool pigeon willing to talk.[21]

Despite the fact that Julette's description of the two bandits matched the characteristics of Terry and Miner, Terry was able to prove an alibi through friends in Sumas. On October 5, Terry brazenly gave an interview to the *Seattle Post-Intelligencer,* and in his usual brash way he verbally goaded the lawmen investigating the case:

> They [the officers of the Great Northern Railroad] lie when they say I did it, and they know they lie. The Canadian Pacific started that story for reasons of its own. It's like that bunch of stiffs, but they can't get me that way. . . . It makes me laugh to think of that bunch of incompetents chasing me and Bill Miner through the brush of this state with a lot of bum bloodhounds. They ought to know better than that. I had nothing to do with it, and if they want me here I am, or if they will wire me I'll go down to Seattle and they can operate on me there. They can have me all right enough, but if they want Bill I guess they will have to find him. Bill's up here all right, and I guess he knows even more than I do about that work Monday night, but I'll leave that for Bill to tell. If you want to talk to him, just run up across the line and you'll find him sitting there in the woods. Bill likes the woods.[22]

Because a letter belonging to Lem Short was found near the scene of the robbery, he was arrested in Chehalis in mid-November. For two weeks, Short was grilled constantly by the Seattle officers, but he adamantly refused to divulge any information. The police ended up having to be satisfied with charging him with the theft of the horse and wagon used in the robbery.[23] This was the last official charge or arrest pertaining to the train robbery, and the crime remained officially unsolved.

The actual amount stolen in the robbery is unknown. The railroad, inclined to minimize losses, claimed it did not exceed one thousand dollars, but rumors at the time brought the figure up to thirty-six thousand dollars, most of which was reported to be in gold bars in transit from the United States Assay Office. Later an empty canvas bag was found on the property of a farmer near Bitter Lake. Stenciled on the bag was the figure "$36,000," and punched into the bag were two frayed holes indicating that it had been carried by two men with a stick pushed through the holes. Undoubtedly Miner and Terry, and perhaps also Dunn, buried the gold, intending to return for it when pressure died down. When that time came, only one man would retrieve it.[24]

CHAPTER 12

Fifteen-Dollar Fiasco

AFTER the Seattle robbery, Jake Terry made his headquarters at Port Townsend, Washington, where he continued smuggling. In December 1905, Cowboy Jake was again in trouble. In Sumas he accidentally met his former wife, who had remarried, and he lost no time courting and bedding her. He physically threw her husband out of their house, moved in with her, and embarked on a spree in which he terrorized the whole town for a week. Finally he was jailed at Whatcom for assault and robbery. Strangely enough, this proved fortunate for Terry: it prevented him from joining in a new scheme planned by Miner.[1]

Bill Miner and Shorty Dunn had returned to the Princeton area, resuming their residence at the Budd ranch. During this period, Miner worked for the Douglas Lake ranch and continued to run cattle around Aspen Grove. Neighbors later recalled that he was never without money.

During the latter part of 1905 or early 1906, a stranger showed up at the Budd ranch. He was Louis Colquhoun, a twenty-eight-year-old former bookkeeper from Gifford, Ontario. Colquhoun had contracted tuberculosis and as a result came west to Calgary for his health. There he first worked in a warehouse and later became a surveyor. From Calgary, Colquhoun drifted to Vancouver and then to the United States, first to San Francisco and then to the state of Washington, where he was arrested and sentenced to two years at Walla Walla Penitentiary for petty theft. After serving his sentence, he returned to Canada, where he worked at various jobs until he reached Budd's ranch. He was an easygoing, good-looking man with nice manners but lacked ambition. He fit well into the easy life at Budd's ranch and also into Bill Miner's plans, because Terry was now cooling his heels in the Whatcom County Jail.[2]

For two months in early 1906, Miner, still calling himself George Edwards, stayed with Alonzo Roberts, a farmer at Aspen Grove.

Roberts remembered Miner as a decent, likable man who loved riding, hunting, and boasting of his mines in Argentina. Miner was never without cash and often displayed ten- and twenty-dollar gold pieces. During a prospecting trip, Roberts noted that the old bandit frequently ate opium pills, which he called his "poppy root." Roberts also recalled that Miner was a heavy smoker and used "black strap" tobacco in his pipe.[3]

How or when Bill Miner picked up the opium habit is unknown, but hop heads (a slang term for opium users) were not unusual among the criminal class. Opium was not illegal in the United States during the early 1900s, but by 1897 import duties were as high as six dollars per pound. Miner likely picked up the habit in San Quentin, where the drug was smuggled in by prisoners and crooked guards. He also had access to opium during his smuggling activities with Jake Terry and may have frequented the Chinese opium dens common in towns and cities on the West Coast. Rather than causing violent behavior, opium had a calming effect, giving the user strong feelings of euphoria.[4]

In March 1906, Dunn and Colquhoun showed up at the Roberts farm and, with Bill Miner, told Roberts they were going out to prospect the creeks between Merritt and Princeton. Miner and Dunn visited the McFadden ranch near Princeton and told the rancher they were going on a prospecting trip near Kamloops and would return in three weeks. The rancher generously lent them two pack horses.

One day in April, Bill Miner stopped at Rosehill, nine miles southeast of Kamloops. It was a Sunday and services were being held at the schoolhouse. For some reason, the preacher had failed to appear. Informed of this, Miner stabled his horse at Milton's barn and, according to a commonly accepted report, preached a fine sermon to the congregation. It is doubtful that the irony of the scene was lost upon the versatile old highwayman.

On April 29, Miner, Dunn, and Colquhoun appeared at Ducks, now known as Monte Creek, sixteen miles east of Kamloops. Here they stocked up on supplies, told the local residents they were prospectors, and camped in the area until the night of May 8.[5]

Around one o'clock the next morning, as the Canadian Pacific Railway's westbound Imperial Limited No. 97 pulled out from a routine stop at Ducks, the engineer, J. Callin, was surprised by a man wearing goggles and a handkerchief over his face standing on the tender with a gun pointed at him. It was Bill Miner, who had boarded

Bill Miner after his capture on May 14, 1906, near Douglas Lake, British Columbia, for the robbery of the Canadian Pacific Railway's Imperial Limited No. 97 on May 10, 1906. Courtesy of British Columbia Provincial Archives, Victoria.

Shorty Dunn *(left)* and Louis Colquhoun *(right)* after their capture near Douglas Lake, British Columbia, for the robbery of the Canadian Pacific Railway's Imperial Limited No. 97 on May 10, 1906. Both were captured along with Bill Miner. Courtesy of British Columbia Provincial Archives, Victoria.

the train unnoticed at Ducks. Bill warned him, "Don't do anything foolish, and you won't be hurt. Stop the train at Mile Post 116." Forcing Callin and the fireman, A. Radcliffe, to leave their posts, Miner commanded them to uncouple the engine and the first car from the rest of the train. Returning to the engine, the old bandit told Callin to pull ahead about two miles and stop. Then Dunn and Colquhoun, carrying dynamite wrapped in a newspaper, scrambled aboard the train and joined Miner.

The three bandits, with the engineer and fireman under guard, proceeded to the attached car and ordered the two mail clerks, A. L. McQuarrie and W. M. Thorburn, to climb out. The clerks offered no resistance and were thoroughly searched for weapons by the cautious bandits. Miner, forcing McQuarrie ahead of him, boarded the car and commented, "You are somewhat ahead of your time. We didn't expect you for another hour." McQuarrie explained that during the summer, trains ran in two sections and this was the first section. Searching for the registered mail, Miner demanded, "Where is the shipment for San Francisco, the registered mail for Frisco?" The mail clerk replied that there was no mail for San Francisco. In frustration, Miner exclaimed, "This isn't the express car, it's the baggage car!" For some reason the express car with the safe in it had been switched with the baggage car and was left behind with the passenger cars.

Instantly realizing his blunder, Bill unloosed a stream of oaths and shook his head violently. That was his second mistake. His mask became dislodged, giving McQuarrie a good look at him. Regaining his composure and readjusting his mask, Miner groused, "We must have left the express car back with the rest of the train. Well, let's see what's here." Making the best of the situation, Bill ripped open registered-mail sacks and rifled the contents. Spotting a package of catarrh pills, he broke the package open and pocketed them. Unknowingly, the unlucky outlaw passed up several small packages on a shelf which contained forty thousand dollars in bank notes. Miner ordered the engineer to pull ahead another two or three miles, and there the three bandits jumped off. Miner called out cordially, "Goodnight, boys. Take care of yourself." The total take, besides the catarrh pills, was $15.50.[6]

By daybreak, the British Columbia Provincial Police were out in force. Constable William L. Fernie, with the help of Indian scouts, took to the trail of the robbers. At the holdup site, Fernie found the dynamite, wrapped in a Kamloops newspaper, which the trio had

Bill Miner after his arrest for the train robbery at Ducks, British Columbia, in May 1906. Courtesy of British Columbia Provincial Archives, Victoria.

British Columbia Provincial Police and posse involved in the capture of Miner, Dunn, and Colquhoun on May 14, 1906. *Left to right:* Tracker Alec Ignace, Constable William Fernie, Constable E. Pearse, tracker Michel Lakama, Ernie Carter, Constable Young, E. LaRoux, Douglas Lake Ranch manager Joe Greaves, Louis Campbell, and tracker Philip Thomas. Courtesy of British Columbia Provincial Archives, Victoria.

abandoned. He also discovered three sets of tracks leading away from the railroad as well as the camp where the bandits headquartered before the robbery.

Because a forest fire was raging north of Ducks, Fernie concentrated his search southward toward Douglas Lake. Hastily following the tracks of the two pack horses, Fernie came across a second campsite at Campbell's Meadow. Evidently the posse's approach had startled Bill Miner and his men: in their haste to flee, they had abandoned their two pack horses and all their provisions. Now on foot, the fugitives were at a great disadvantage.[7]

On May 11 the Royal North-West Mounted Police were called in to take part in the search. Figuring that the train robbers were heading for the U.S. border, Sgt. J. J. Wilson, in charge of a detachment of four Mounties—Sgt. P. G. Thomas, Cpl. J. C. Stewart, Cpl. C. R.

The Royal North West Mounted Policemen who captured Miner, Dunn, and Colquhoun on May 14, 1906, for the robbery of the Canadian Pacific Railway train at Ducks, British Columbia, on May 9, 1906. *Left to right, front row:* Constable J. H. Tabuteau, Sgt. J. J. Wilson, and Cpl. C. R. Peters. *Left to right, back row:* Sgt. P. G. Thomas, guide Jim Benyon, Sgt. T. M. Shoebotham, Cpl. J. C. Stewart, and Constable J. T. Browning. Courtesy of Royal Canadian Mounted Police Museum, Regina, Saskatchewan.

Peters, and Constable J. H. Tabuteau—was dispatched from Calgary to Kamloops that afternoon. At Morley and Banff, Sergeant Wilson picked up two more Mounties, Constable J. T. Browning and Sgt. T. M. Shoebotham. Arriving at Kamloops at 3 P.M. on the twelfth, they obtained fresh horses and by six o'clock that evening were heading south in a driving rain in search of the holdup men.[8]

Prior to this, at five o'clock on the morning of the eleventh, Constable Fernie discovered a third abandoned camp. Following tracks that disappeared periodically, Fernie slowly plodded through the driving rain. On the morning of May 14 near Douglas Lake he unexpectedly came face to face with the trio of bandits. Fernie being dressed in civilian clothes, the robbers showed no sign of apprehension. Miner questioned the officer about the route to Quilchena and, after a few more pleasantries, Fernie walked on. As soon as he was out of sight of the robbers, Fernie quickly made his way to the Graves ranch, obtained a fresh horse, and raced on to Chapperon Lake, arriving there at noon. Here the constable found Sergeant Wilson and his Mounties and told them of his encounter with the three strangers.

Wilson sent Sergeant Thomas up the mountain to see if he could spot the three men and ordered their guide, Jim Benyon, Constable Tabuteau, and an Indian trailer to track them from the area where they were first seen. Guided by Fernie, Wilson and the remaining four Mounties quickly made the seven-mile ride to the spot where Fernie had encountered the trio. The officers spread out and searched the brushy terrain. After scouting about for a mile and a half, Corporal Stewart discovered campfire smoke. Waving his hat, Stewart signaled the others to come ahead.[9] Sergeant Wilson's official report offers a firsthand account of what happened next:

> We all dismounted, leaving the horses standing, went into the brush and found three men eating dinner. I asked them where they came from. The eldest man, who afterward gave the name of Edwards, said, "Across the river." I asked them where they were before that. Edwards

Site of the capture of Miner, Dunn, and Colquhoun on May 14, 1906. The site, which is near Douglas Lake, was called Salmon River at that time. Photographed by Daryl Drew of Victoria, British Columbia, in 1982.

said "From over there." (Pointing towards Campbell's Meadow). I asked how long since they had left there. Edwards said, "Two days." I then asked them what they were doing. The one who afterwards gave the name of Dunn, answered, "Prospecting a little." I said then, "You answer the description given of the train robbers and we arrest you for that crime." Edwards said, "We do not look much like train robbers." Just then Dunn rolled over and said, "Look out boys, it's all up," and commenced to fire his revolver. I immediately covered Edwards. Corporal Peters was standing close to Colquhoun, who was reaching for his revolver, and he covered him and ordered him to put up his hands, at the same time snatching away Colquhoun's revolver. Sergeant Shoebotham, Corporal Stewart and Constable Browning ran after Dunn, firing as they went, he returning the fire as he ran. After some twenty shots had been exchanged, Dunn fell into a ditch and threw up his hands, saying, "I am shot." The men ceased firing and took two revolvers from Dunn. On taking him out of the ditch it was found he had been shot in the calf of the leg, the bullet going right through. I told him he had done a foolish thing as he might have been shot in the head instead of the leg. He said, "I wish to———you had put it through my head, but you couldn't blame me could you?" I then had Dunn's leg bandaged up and sent a messenger to get a rig to convey the prisoners to jail.[10]

A search of the prisoners yielded a small arsenal, including three automatic pistols, a Colt .44 revolver, an Iver Johnson .38 revolver, a Smith and Wesson .38 revolver, and a Winchester .44 carbine. The goggles Miner wore during the robbery were found, plus the bottle of catarrh pills taken from the mail car. Miner had twenty-six dollars in his pockets; Dunn and Colquhoun only had some small change. The Mounties bound the hands of Miner and Colquhoun, and when the rig arrived, the officers and their prisoners headed for Kamloops. After nearly five years of freedom, Bill Miner was back in the clutches of the law.[11]

The Mounted Police went to the Douglas Lake ranch, borrowed a spring wagon to transport their prisoners, and proceeded to Quilchena, where Dunn's wound was tended. Late in the afternoon of May 15, they arrived at Kamloops in a torrential downpour. A crowd of one thousand spectators braved the rainstorm to catch a glimpse of the outlaws. As they drove into town, the Mounted Police, garbed in yellow slickers, surrounded the rain-drenched train robbers seated in the spring wagon. Miner was conspicuous, being wrapped up in a blanket and shivering in the cold. According to Frank W. Anderson, the *Kamloops Standard* reported:

Four of the handguns the Canadian Mounties took from Miner, Dunn, and Colquhoun after the train holdup at Ducks, British Columbia. At top left is Miner's .32-caliber Colt, a Model 1903 hammerless automatic. Courtesy of Royal Canadian Mounted Police Museum, Regina, Saskatchewan.

New Westminster Penitentiary photos of Shorty Dunn *(left)* and Louis Colquhoun *(right)*, 1906. Courtesy of Pinkerton's, Inc., Van Nuys, California.

The first to go through of the officials was the old man George Edwards, who took his medicine with utmost nonchalance. He is rather a striking looking fellow with grizzled hair and moustache, erect and active and does not appear to bear within the weight of age which the prison records now credit him with. He claims to be 62, looks like a man of 50, and moves like one of 30. He answered all the questions put to him coolly, but sometimes hesitatingly, evidently considering his answers well. He was asked point blank by one man whether or not he was Bill Miner and his answer was, "Can't be seeing that I never heard of the man."

By the next evening, despite the old outlaw's insistence that he was George Edwards, Bill Miner's identity had been established. His description had been furnished to the Mounties by the Pinkertons, and his photograph was positively identified by the mail clerk, McQuarrie, as that of the bandit whose mask had come off during the train robbery. Reportedly, Warden Kelly of San Quentin Prison came to Kamloops to identify Miner. After confronting the warden, Miner remarked airily, "I'll shake hands with you all right, but I don't know you."

The prisoners were lodged in jail, and at ten o'clock on the morning of May 17, Kamloops Mayor Gordon held their preliminary hearing. Attorney General Fulton handled the prosecution, and Alex D. McIntyre conducted the defense. All five of the Mounted Police officers testified, and the evidence was so conclusive that the three prisoners were bound over for trial. The $11,500 reward offered by the CPR for the Ducks train robbers was paid to Sergeant Wilson, Sergeant Shoebotham, Corporals Stewart and Peters, Constable Browning, and William Fernie of the Provincial Police. The lawmen were justifiably proud of having captured one of the most wanted outlaws in North America.[12]

On May 28 in Kamloops, amid immense publicity and fanfare, Justice P. A. E. Irving presided at the trial of the three defendants. Deputy Attorney General McLean now conducted the prosecution with McIntyre still acting as defense attorney. Justice Irving was convinced that the three defendants were guilty, but not so the jury, which could not agree on a verdict. The sixty-five-year-old foreman, J. Morrill, who bore a resemblance to Miner, held out for acquittal, believing that a poor man should not be sent to prison.

A new jury under foreman A. McGregor was impaneled on May 31, and the trial was held on June 1. Throughout the proceedings in the packed courtroom, Dunn could be heard periodically emitting a ner-

$11,500.00 REWARD

The Canadian Pacific Railway Coy.

... offers a reward of $5,000 (Five Thousand Dollars) for the capture, dead or alive, of the three robbers who held up train 97 between Ducks and Kamloops on the morning of the 9th inst., or $1,000 (One Thousand Dollars) for the capture, dead or alive, of any one of the robbers.

The Dominion Government

Also offers $5,000 (Five Thousand Dollars) on the same terms as the above.

The Provincial Government

Offers One Thousand Five Hundred Dollars (Five Hundred Dollars for each man) for capture and conviction.

DESCRIPTION.

LEADER: About 5 ft. 7 in. in height, slim build, about 50 years of age, wore a grey stubby moustache, face and hands very much sun burnt, eyes somewhat inflamed, wore glasses, tattoo mark on back of right hand, wore a black slouch hat and a blue-black overcoat.

SECOND MAN: About 5 ft. 7 in. in height, medium build, weight about 170 lbs, black hair, dark complexion, very clear and distinct voice, with slight Cockney accent, wore an old blue sweater.

THIRD MAN: Age about 40 years, about 5 ft. 10 in. in height, light or reddish moustache and thin face.

By Order.

Reward poster issued by the Canadian Pacific Railway for the Ducks train robbery of May 9, 1906. Courtesy of British Columbia Provincial Archives, Victoria.

vous and hysterical laugh while Colquhoun remained quiet except for an occasional hacking cough. Miner sat out the proceedings in indifferent and unconcerned silence. On the evening of the first, the jury brought in a verdict of guilty for all three men.

Because of Bill Miner's previous record at San Quentin and because Dunn had fired on the police, Justice Irving sentenced them to life imprisonment. Colquhoun was given a tough sentence of twenty-five years. The court ordered all three men to serve their terms in the penitentiary at New Westminster, British Columbia.[13]

On June 2 a large crowd gathered at the Kamloops depot to witness the three heavily manacled prisoners escorted to the train. Appearing to be in good spirits, each was given a handful of cigars as he passed through the sympathetic crowd. Sighting Albert Ducks, one of the Crown witnesses, among the throng of people, Miner remarked in droll humor, "If I'm ever in the area, I'll look you up."

The consensus of many Canadians at that time was summed up in a popular joke: "Oh, Bill Miner is not so bad, he only robs the CPR once every two years, but the CPR robs us every day." Mrs. Maisie Armytage-Moore recalled the feelings of the people around Prince-

Kamloops, British Columbia, in 1906 about the time of the trial of Miner, Dunn, and Colquhoun for train robbery. Courtesy of British Columbia Provincial Archives, Victoria.

Miner, Dunn, and Colquhoun being brought to Kamloops, British Columbia, after their capture by the Royal North West Mounted Police near Douglas Lake, British Columbia, on May 14, 1906. Miner can be seen conspicuously wrapped up in a blanket. Courtesy of British Columbia Provincial Archives, Victoria.

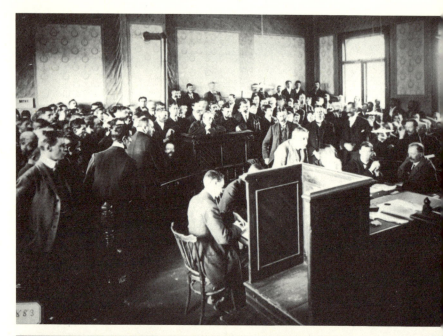

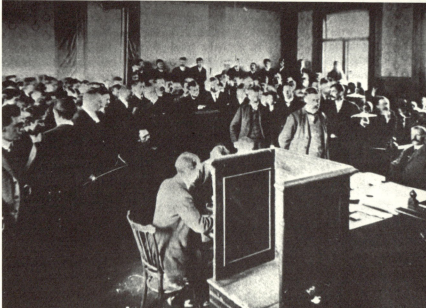

Two scenes during the trial of Miner, Dunn, and Colquhoun at Kamloops, British Columbia, on May 28, 1906. The three men were convicted of robbing the Canadian Pacific Railway's Imperial Limited No. 97 on May 10, 1906. Miner and Colquhoun can be seen seated in the center of the photographs, while Dunn, because of his wound, was seated below and to the right of Miner. Courtesy of British Columbia Provincial Archives, Victoria.

FIFTEEN-DOLLAR FIASCO

ton: "After Bill's arrest, Dad Allen rode from Aspen Grove to Lower Nicola to plead with me not to judge our old friend too harshly. He was just one of those socialist fellows, who took from the rich and gave to the poor."

Such opinions were prevalent throughout British Columbia, prompting a huge crowd to gather to greet Bill Miner and his partners at the New Westminster depot. This caused the officials to take them off the train at Sapperton. Their efforts to deliver the prisoners unobserved, thus avoiding any publicity sparked by public sentiment, came to no avail. Unexpectedly, a large crowd had also gathered

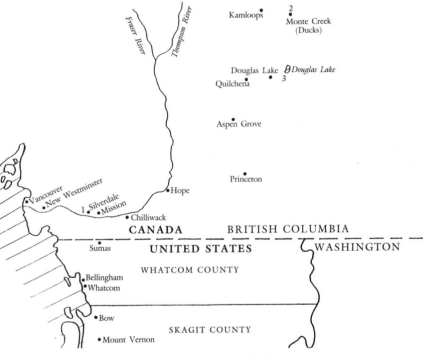

BILL MINER'S CRIMINAL CAREER IN CANADA, 1904–6
1 Robbery of the Canadian Pacific Railway's Transcontinental Express No. 1, September 10, 1904, Miner, Terry, and Dunn.
2 Robbery of the Canadian Pacific Railway's Imperial Limited No. 97, May 9, 1906, Miner, Dunn, and Colquhoun.
3 Capture of Miner, Dunn, and Colquhoun by the North West Mounted Police, May 14, 1906.

at Sapperton, with cries of "Hello, Bill" and "How are you, Bill?" When the train passed through Mission Junction, one of the crowd reportedly called out, "Hello, Bill! Here you are again," causing Miner to grumble to the guard next to him, "At Kamloops I was called Mr. Edwards, but down here even the dogs seem to take me for Bill Miner." The officers had no choice but to continue their trip to the penitentiary through the clamor.[14]

As he had done at San Quentin, Bill Miner gave the prison officials false information, claiming he was born in Ohio in 1840. He did, however, correctly report his birthday as December 27. Miner was registered as convict No. 980, Dunn as 981, and Colquhoun as 982. Miner stated stoically that since he would not live much longer, he might as well be in the penitentiary as anywhere else.[15]

But Old Bill Miner was not yet through, and neither were his criminal escapades. The securities and bonds stolen during the Mission Junction train robbery were soon to prove the most invaluable loot he had ever stolen.

CHAPTER 13

"No Prison Walls Can Hold Me"

THE penitentiary at New Westminster was virtually a prison without walls. It was protected only by a wooden wall that enclosed a wooden fence, both of which occasionally collapsed. The prison seems to have been badly run by an incompetent administration that provided no definite operational policy, which resulted in low morale among the guards.

After his conviction, Bill Miner had told the court, "No prison walls can hold me." As a consequence, he was kept in close confinement and was put to work in the shoe factory. However, the prison officials soon forgot his quiet boast and allowed him visiting privileges. One person in particular became much interested in the notorious outlaw. She was Catherine Bourke, daughter of the deputy warden, and her object was to proselytize and reform the old bandit. Bill's charm and apparent sincerity impressed her, and in turn she persuaded her father to relax the tight security over him. For Miner, it seems that one of the few discomforts he suffered in prison was looking daily upon the tracks of the Canadian Pacific Railway, which ran directly in front of the penitentiary. The trains and express cars that rumbled by must have been a tempting but frustrating sight to the aging holdup man.

Catherine Bourke was not the only visitor allowed to see Miner. His defense lawyer, Alex D. McIntyre of Kamloops, was granted permission to visit any time Miner wanted to see him. Bill also was granted special privileges, including letting his hair grow out, writing more than the one letter a month allowed each prisoner, talking to visitors without a prison officer present, and having the freedom to leave the prison interior to mingle with "short-timers" in the brickyard. The most flagrant breach of regulations occurred when prison officials allowed Miner to hold unauthorized visits and meetings at the penitentiary. The reason? Authorities were secretly negotiating with him for the return of the missing bonds and securities.

135

The penitentiary at New Westminster, British Columbia, in 1900, scene of Bill Miner's escape on August 8, 1907. Courtesy of British Columbia Provincial Archives, Victoria.

The meetings began on June 12, 1906. Miner was taken to Warden J. C. Whyte's office for a confidential interview with McIntyre. The meeting was held in the warden's presence. On January 12, 1907, J. H. Stanton of Portland, Oregon, met with Miner in the presence of prison officials. The important session occurred on February 9, 1907, when Miner met with Warden Whyte, attorney McIntyre, Detective R. E. Bullock of the Canadian Pacific Railway, and, incredibly, his old train-robbing partner, Cowboy Jake Terry. Bullock lamely explained that he brought Terry to the meeting to see if Terry knew Miner. The detective later admitted there had been talk of a pardon for Miner if the securities were located. On May 28, G. R. Murray of Victoria held a meeting with Miner in the guardroom, and on June 27, Chief Constable McIntosh and Miner's captor, Sgt. J. J. Wilson, visited the old outlaw. The last reported visit was in July, when Inspector Dawson of the Inspectors of Penitentiaries Office in Ottawa met with Miner.[1]

Nearly a year before the February meeting, Terry had jumped bail in Whatcom County and fled to Canada to avoid prosecution. It was common knowledge that Cowboy Jake was a suspect in the train robberies, but evidently there was not enough evidence to charge or arrest him.[2] The *Bellingham Herald* clearly pointed this out:

The second time he [Terry] came out of the "pen" [San Quentin] he was a little more careful and took to train robbing. That he was mixed up in the C.P. holdup at Mission three years ago, there is no doubt. That he was involved in the holdup only eighteen months ago [Seattle], many believe.

Jake Terry was in for a surprise if he thought that Bill Miner would honor their bargain. The *Bellingham Herald* also outlined Terry's role in the negotiations:

> It was announced that he [Terry] was negotiating with the Canadian Pacific Railroad for the return of $300,000 worth of bonds that had been taken from an overland train in a holdup two years previous. It was claimed that Terry and the famous Bill Miner, now doing time in Canada for train robbery, turned the trick. Jake returned to Sumas, B.C. [*sic*] broke. At the time he wanted to betray Bill Miner, his pal, for consideration, but the authorities would not listen to him. . . .
> He claimed that Bill Miner, who is serving a life sentence across the line, did him "dirt" and that is why he tried to betray him.[3]

In a later edition, the *Herald* elaborated further:

> Terry . . . claimed that Bill Miner played him "dirt" and he tried to "peach" on his former pal, but the officers took no stock in his story.[4]

Now that Bill Miner was in prison, he was no longer interested in getting immunity or money in exchange for the bonds. He wanted something much more basic: his freedom. Because he was behind bars, Miner no longer had any need to use Jake Terry as an intermediary. He could deal with the railroad himself. Too, he knew that Terry's desire for a finder's fee would unnecessarily complicate negotiations. So Miner double-crossed his pal and cut him out of the deal.

After the meeting at the penitentiary, Terry, not knowing where the bonds and securities were hidden, truthfully accused Miner of having done him dirt and futilely attempted to tell all he knew in exchange for reducing or dropping the charges in Sumas. With Miner behind bars, his statements fell on deaf ears; the officers and authorities obviously did not trust him. They knew that if Terry knew where the booty was, he would have absconded with it long ago.

At this same time, Shorty Dunn was visited at the penitentiary by a Pinkerton detective trying to negotiate the return of the $50,000 in U.S. bonds. Like Terry, Dunn obviously had no idea where the bonds were hidden and could not cooperate.

During the meeting at the warden's office, the CPR detective, Bullock, verbally offered Miner a pardon for the return of the missing bonds and securities. But the cagey old bandit demanded the Canadian Pacific's written guarantee of a full pardon. This the railroad detective could not promise, for even in those days of widespread corruption, such a blatantly illegal agreement would cause a scandal if it became public. Bill Miner refused to return the bonds and securities.[5]

But Miner knew there was more than one way to skin a cat. Evidently, so did the officials of the Canadian Pacific. It would take a year, but his release from the prison was carefully and quietly arranged.

On the afternoon of August 8, 1907, Bill Miner was working at the drying kiln in the brickyard. His job was to alternate with other convicts in delivering bricks in a wheelbarrow to the drying kiln. After each trip, Miner would stop and rest against the yard fence. Three other convicts—Albert F. McClusky, serving seven years for robbery; George Clark, a forger with a three-year sentence; and Walter John Woods, also serving three years—were alternating with Miner. They, too, would rest against the fence after each trip. According to later reports, the four men were digging an escape hole under the fence.

All this was accomplished, presumably, undetected by the two guards, John Doyle, who was supervising the work, and Alex McNeil, who patrolled every two minutes from the 150-foot watchtower. When McNeil went into the guard room in the tower, the four convicts reportedly scrambled through the hole into the compound between the inner fence and the 12-foot outer wall. McClusky broke the padlock on a work shed with a pickax, grabbed a ladder, and all four disappeared over the outer wall.

Outside the wall, Bill Miner uncharacteristically split up with his companions and fled in a different direction. Guard Doyle soon spotted the discarded wheelbarrows and the escape hole and fired a warning shot with his revolver. The escape bell clanged loudly, and the guards, after securing the other prisoners, began the pursuit. Deputy Warden D. D. Bourke boasted, "I will have Miner and his three companions behind prison walls within twenty-four hours." He was partly right, for just at dusk, McClusky, Clark, and Woods were reportedly recaptured, but no trace of Old Bill Miner could be found.

At the time of his escape, Bill was suffering from sore feet. On August 1 he had displayed his feet to Deputy Warden Bourke and asked

Reward poster for Bill Miner issued by the Dominion Police at Ottawa, Ontario, after Miner's escape from the penitentiary at New Westminster, British Columbia, on August 8, 1907. Courtesy of Vancouver Public Library, Vancouver, British Columbia.

to be put to work in the fresh air. The request was granted, and Miner was assigned to the brickyard. After Miner escaped, the officials claimed to be confident that he could not get far in his dire condition but expressed concern that he would make for his old haunts near Princeton, where he had many friends who would shelter him. The *Seattle Post-Intelligencer* pointed out that lawmen considered Miner dangerous: "Detectives expressed the opinion that they will unlikely be able to take Miner alive."

At 5:00 A.M. on August 9 a special bloodhound in company with its keeper, Bradford Lanton of Vancouver, was set on Miner's trail. The dog easily picked up the scent and followed it in a northerly direction. This raised fears that Miner would reach Burrard Inlet, where he could obtain a boat or jump a train for the interior. Guards were stationed at every road leading out of New Westminster, and boats were manned with prison guards on the Fraser and Pitt rivers. But no trace of Bill Miner could be found; it was almost as if he had vanished into thin air.

From the beginning, Miner's escape aroused suspicion, which was duly reported in the *Seattle Post-Intelligencer:* "It is probable that the men had assistance from the outside, as some suspicion has been attached to some visitors in the neighborhood of late."[6] The *Post-Intelligencer* of August 13 expressed further doubts about the escape in the following statements:

> Sheriff Williams who has returned from Blaine, said that Bill Miner had an easy task in making his escape from prison. He reports that one of the guards informed him that Bill had more than an hour to tunnel under a high board fence.
>
> During all the time they were never more than 500 feet away from the tower in which was perched an armed guard. He evidently failed to see the escape purposely or was asleep at the time, according to the penitentiary officials with whom Williams talked.

Commented the *Post-Intelligencer* two days later on Bill's prison break and the ensuing manhunt:

> Not the least interesting feature of Bill Miner's remarkable escape is the public sympathy being extended to him. Many on Vancouver streets declare openly that they hope Bill Miner will never be recaptured, and that he will live long to enjoy his freedom.
>
> There is probably no doubt but that Miner received aid from the outside.... Miner is credited with having close to $20,000 tucked away in different places to secure freedom.
>
> The single bloodhound available next morning traced the tracks for

a mile and a quarter where Miner seemed to have left his companions and started by himself into the underbrush. His footprints were noticeable because he wore a special kind of shoe.

Many people believe that Miner is being sheltered in some house in Westminster or Vancouver, and that he will be kept there until he has succeeded in getting across the Fraser river and south of the international boundary line, where he knows every foot of the country, and is perfectly at home in the woods, like the hunter he is.

The "man hunt" so far has been a farce. Prison guards and policemen have worked over the wooded district between Vancouver and Westminster.

Deputy Warden Bourke and his well-intentioned daughter were greatly embarrassed by Bill's escape as reported in the *Post-Intelligencer* of August 15:

> It was by the clever ruse of shielding behind a mask of piety, a craving for religious literature and illness that Bill Miner enjoys liberty, according to Miss Katherine [*sic*] Bourke, daughter of the prison keeper, who on more than one occasion displayed interest tending to the welfare of the prisoners. She is one of the most disappointed of all concerned in this wholesale escape because it shattered hopes that she had entertained that her efforts would eventually lead to making a better man of the notorious bandit.
>
> "Why, only last week, Bill said he was resigned to his fate and was satisfied, did not care to get away, and would do anything to merit a happier home in the other world," said Miss Bourke.
>
> "We all felt sorry for Bill when we realized that he had to spend all of his life in prison and we took much interest in him. He pretended to have become highly interested in religion and asked for religious works, and he had been so good lately that he was fast getting so that he could be regarded as an ideal prisoner. But my! It's different now."[7]

Catherine Bourke was not the only one who believed in Bill Miner. Sympathy and support abounded for him from people of all walks of life around Vancouver. A reporter who conducted several interviews wrote, "It is interesting to note the feelings of a majority of people, including prominent Vancouver businessmen, toilers with brain and brawn, men and women, heads of families. No less than twenty-five this morning when asked if they had seen anything of Miner replied that they had not and if they had, they surely would not tell the authorities and would aid Bill in his plight." A Vancouver resident commented, "Not only would nine-tenths of the people of the Nicola and Similkameen not betray Miner were he there, but they are proud of the fact that there is wide-open welcome for him, good at any time and under any circumstances, with what amounts to practical protection from the police. He is regarded as a Robin Hood in these latter days of steam railways, and indeed if all that is said about him is true, he has some of the qualities which endeared to the public the old highway robber of Sherwood Forest."

The editorialists responded with disdain. Wrote one: "As men admire contrasts, these foolish ones admire Miner. He is clever, they are not; he is possessed of a certain courage; they know they have not got it; he can conceive a plan and carry it through to completion; but these men know that they could not do such a thing to save their lives."[8]

Because of Warden Whyte's illness at the time Miner escaped, Deputy Warden Bourke took charge and immediately telegraphed the Inspectors of Penitentiaries Office in Ottawa about the escape of the four prisoners. The next day, Bourke again telegraphed Ottawa, reporting that Bill Miner was one of the escapees. Strangely, Bourke received no answer for several days. After Inspector Dawson of the Ottawa office started his investigation, he berated Bourke for addressing the telegrams to him personally when he was out of town and claimed that this caused the investigation to be delayed. Bourke maintained that he did not address Dawson personally and provided copies of the telegrams to prove his point. The address had been changed on the telegrams but it was never determined who had altered them.

The escape of Bill Miner became a controversial issue in Canada, and eventually it embroiled both Parliament and the prime minister. A series of investigations ultimately was begun, and eighteen months after the escape, British Columbia newspapers began to report the details. First, most of the detectives and police officers who inspected the escape hole in the prison fence agreed that it was too small for a man to crawl through. They were of the opinion that the convicts went out through the main gate with the help of friends and that the hole had been dug as a ruse. Too, they also found it difficult to believe that a partly crippled sixty-one-year-old man, without help, could elude the intensive manhunt while his three younger companions were captured hours after the escape. Despite these suspicious circumstances, Inspector Dawson concluded his investigation and reported to the minister of justice that there had been no collusion in the prison break. A year and half later, the dam broke.

On January 28, 1909, piqued because of a recent dispatch from Ottawa implying that discipline at the New Westminster penitentiary was lax during his tenure, former Deputy Warden Bourke threatened to open the Pandora's box and let out the secrets behind Miner's escape. On January 29 the *Montreal Gazette* reported that Bourke stated that unless justice was done to him, he would "open up a new field for moral reformers by telling the world the truth about the escape of Bill Miner," adding that the disclosures were spreading that the Canadian Pacific Railway had arranged for Miner to make his successful escape in return for the stolen Australian securities. The burgeoning scandal soon attracted the attention of Parliamant.[9]

The bombshell landed on February 11, 1909, in the House of Commons in Ottawa. J. D. Taylor, MP (Member of Parliament) from New Westminster and managing director of the *Daily Columbian*, brought up rumors that the penitentiary gate had been left open so Miner could escape, that one of the guards had passed money to Miner, and that detectives had been allowed to visit the old bandit at the penitentiary. Taylor added that only an impartial inquiry could clear the matter up. The *Montreal Gazette* reported on February 12, "If Mr. Bureau [the solicitor general], with some of his customary tact, had treated the matter seriously, instead of endeavoring to put off Mr. Taylor, the matter might have ended differently." As a result, Taylor conducted a long and blistering cross-examination of the solicitor general, who eventually made a number of damaging admissions.

When Bureau claimed he knew little about Miner's escape, Taylor caustically replied that the matter was too serious to be dismissed lightly and added that Bureau had deliberately concealed the facts from the House of Commons. Bureau lambasted Taylor for his accusation and concluded with the ridiculous statement that he had not given all the facts because of his lack of command of the English language, which brought loud laughter from his constituents.

Opposition leader R. L. Borden tried to heal the breach by declaring that Bourke's statement had no credibility at the present time and that the former deputy warden should be summoned before a committee of Parliament and compelled to tell the truth. Minister of Justice Aylesworth then jumped into the fray and impassionately defended his department and its officials against Bourke's accusations, dismissing them as completely unfounded.

After this bitter harangue, Bureau finally admitted that one of the guards had been caught taking notes from Miner and had resigned. The *Daily Columbian* added:

> The solicitor general gave the thing away by the admission that detectives had held intercourse with Miner on many occasions and that they were in search of Australian securities taken from the train held up near Mission and possession of which the Canadian Pacific Railway company was most anxious to regain. This admission, extracted from Mr. Bureau after prolonged cross-examination, supplied the key to the whole situation. There was, it appeared, motive for securing the release of Miner; emissaries of the persons having that motive were permitted access to him; and his release did occur.[10]

On February 17 the question of Bill Miner's escape was brought up again in the House of Commons by Mr. Meighen of Portage la Prairie, who asked Minister Aylesworth to give more details regarding the visits Miner received while imprisoned. Aylesworth gave the dates and particulars of all meetings, and the *Montreal Gazette* added these comments:

> Mr. Aylesworth added that the penitentiary regulations authorized wardens to permit members of a convict's family to visit them at regular intervals. All other persons have to secure the consent of the minister of justice. In admitting McIntyre, Bullock and Terry, the warden [Whyte] acted on his own reponsibility. For the other interviews the deputy warden [Bourke] was responsible. Permission had not been asked from the minister or officials of the department. The minister said no one knew of these visits until after Miner escaped, and no authority for the interviews had been given by any official of the Justice Department.

In response to Meighen's question of when the Justice Department became aware that the purpose of the visits was to secure information about the missing bonds and securities, Aylesworth admitted that Detective Bullock stated that Miner was promised a pardon if the securities were located. The minister also reported that Inspector Dawson received confirmation from Bullock that Miner was promised a pardon. The *Gazette* concluded, "But since the escape of Miner no steps had been taken to ascertain whether these bonds had been located."

The *Gazette* also held this interesting interview with Sgt. J. J. Wilson of the Royal North-West Mounted Police:

> Speaking of Miner's escape, Sergt. Wilson said it was hard to see how he could get away in broad daylight, and past two lines of guards.

Continuing, he said: "There has been some talk that he had been allowed to go if he gave up the C. P. R. bonds he stole at Mission Junction, and promised not to hold-up trains anymore, and there has been none of them stopped since."

Wilson added, "He [Miner] did not have much idea that he was going to get away, as a few days before he gave me an order for his automatic gun, saying he did not expect to have any more use for it."[11]

Within two weeks, newspaper headlines shouted: "EX-WARDEN BOURKE MAKES DEFINITE CHARGES ASSOCIATING COUNSEL OF CONVICT AND C. P. R. DETECTIVE WITH COMPLICITY IN ARRANGING ESCAPE." Bourke detailed the meeting involving Miner, his lawyer, CPR Detective Bullock, the warden, and Jake Terry, stating that Miner was offered a pardon for the return of the securities. Bourke explained how the negotiations fell apart when Miner demanded a written promise of pardon. Bourke also accused Inspector Dawson of attempting to cover up the scandal and implied that Dawson had participated in the escape scheme.

On March 2, Miner's escape was again brought up in the House of Commons. The *Gazette* described it as "the stormiest and most exciting scene of the session, which at one time threatened to develop into something more ugly." The session started with the opposition urging the government to institute a full inquiry. J. D. Taylor and Minister Aylesworth again crossed swords when Taylor accused the minister of whitewashing Inspector Dawson's involvement when it had been established that the inspector never reported his interview with Miner to the Justice Department. Taylor then brought up Bullock's promise of a pardon to Miner if the securities were located, and carried the confrontation further by raising the question of why the Justice Department had made no effort to contact the Australian government to determine whether the securities had been returned.

Having stirred up this hornet's nest, Taylor soon changed his tune and attempted to direct suspicion away from the CPR. Perhaps he had run afoul of the heavy hand of the railway, for Taylor said to his fellow MPs:

> I propose to read an extract from the Vancouver *Province,* a most influential and independent newspaper published at Vancouver, a paper I may say of the highest respectability and responsibility and which I am sure would not publish a paragraph of this kind except on the most unquestioned authority. I read from the Vancouver *Daily Province* of the 12th of February this statement. . . .

"An official who is in a position to speak authoritatively on the subject of Bill Miner's escape from the penitentiary at New Westminster this morning made the following statement for publication:

"'At the time of the investigation into the escape made by Inspector Dawson, I could have told him, had I been called upon to testify, that Bill Miner did not escape from prison by crawling under the fence through the hole through which it was alleged he went. No man ever crawled through that hole for two good reasons. The first was that the hole was not large enough; the second because the hole was made only for the purpose of covering the letting out of Mr. Miner. The story of the loss of $50,000 worth of bonds or money by the Canadian Pacific Railway or anyone else in the robbery and that it had been cached by Miner was an invention in the interests of the robber himself. No one ever lost that sum; no bonds were ever stolen. Miner's friends on the outside called on him and conducted fake negotiations for his so-called escape and the securing of the cached money. Certain persons made it possible for Miner to escape, apparently on the understanding that he would divide up on the booty. These facts can easily be proved if the government makes an investigation.'"

This account clearly implicated the prison guards in the escape by accusing them of releasing Miner in exchange for a share of the stolen loot.

The *Gazette* gave this report of the minister's reaction: "Mr. Aylesworth, who has been kept informed by Messrs. Graham and Bureau of the principal points made by Mr. Taylor, started off by throwing polished sneers across the floor at the want of foundation in the case as framed against the department by the member from New Westminster." Although Aylesworth did admit that no inquiry had been forwarded to the Australian government to ascertain whether the stolen securities had been returned, he quickly made a feeble effort to shift the blame by accusing Taylor's newspaper of distorting the facts in the case. The minister claimed that a dispatch had been telegraphed to the *Columbian* that he had stated Chief Constable McIntosh had informed the department that Miner had been promised his release for the return of the securities, when in reality it was Instructor McKenzie who informed the department. Taylor, with the support of R. L. Borden, opposition leader in the House of Commons, successfully defended himself by proving that this report had been taken from other newspapers.

Aylesworth then assured the legislators that Inspector Dawson's investigaion had been thorough and that there was no truth whatsoever to the rumors. "He had not heard of any communication with

Miner from the outside," reported one newspaper of the minister's findings. "In fact, he was sure that there had not been any. And the story of the search for securities as an incentive to secure Miner's release he dismissed as shadowy and without foundation." The minister added that the Justice Department had received a letter from former Deputy Warden Bourke to the effect that he had nothing to add to his testimony, and that the department had no part in any quarrel between Dawson and Bourke.

Opposition leader Borden retorted, "What is the meaning of the extraordinary apologetic attitude assumed in this House by the Minister of Justice towards this man Bourke? He [Bourke] has been charging that officials for whom the Minister of Justice is responsible in this House have connived in that escape." Martin Burrell, MP from Yale-Cariboo, rejected the investigation by Inspector Dawson and demanded an impartial inquiry into the scandal:

> The capture of this convict was a credit to the police system of the country and his sentence strenghtened the confidence of the public in the administration of justice in Canada and now that he has escaped . . . and in view of the unrest in the public mind about the circumstances of the escape of this notorious criminal, is it not time that we should have an impartial inquiry, not an inquiry at the hands of Inspector Dawson who is hopelessly mixed up in it, but a thorough inquiry conducted by some impartial tribunal.

In his own defense, Aylesworth said lamely, "No person in this country can regret the fact of his escape more than I do. . . . What is to be done about it? What can be done? Every exertion that I was able to think of was made at that time to capture the man. . . . At any moment, any day, Miner may be recaptured." Although there was now strong evidence that the CPR was deeply mixed up in the escape, several legislators came to the defense of the railroad and Minister of Justice Aylesworth by lambasting Bourke.

Canada's prime minister, Sir Wilfrid Laurier, expressed his outrage in a speech to the House of Commons:

> The question which interests the country . . . is whether there has been any connivance on the part of anybody in the escape of Miner. No more dangerous criminal, I think, was ever in the clutches of Canadian justice. It was a fact for which we took some credit that when one of these American desperados came to Canada, thinking to play with impunity in this country the pranks he had been playing on the other side of the line, he was arrested, tried and convicted. It was a

shock when we heard, and we heard it with a good deal of shame also, that he had subsequently been allowed to escape from the penitentiary.

But even the prime minister bowed to the pressure when he declared that vague rumors were not grounds for investigation and that nothing had been known to warrant further inquiry.

The debate ran hot and heavy between the members of Parliament until 10 P.M. In the end, the *Gazette* said it all when it reported: "Government Flatly Refuses to Institute a Full Enquiry."[12]

CHAPTER 14

A Gentleman of Wealth and Leisure

BILL Miner was never caught in Canada, and no impartial investigation of his escape was ever made. In the only punishment meted out, prison guard Alex McNeil was fired and Deputy Warden Bourke was forced to retire on a pension. It seems that they were but scapegoats offered up to protect those who evidently engineered Miner's escape: the Canadian Pacific Railway and the Office of Inspectors of Penitentiaries Office.[1] This disreputable affair even became news in the United States, and four years later the leading newspapers in Georgia plowed up the details afresh while reporting Miner's escapades in the Deep South.[2]

On the day Bill Miner escaped from New Westminster, Shorty Dunn also had been working in the brickyard. He was aware that Miner was escaping but was too far away to join in without drawing attention to what was occurring. When asked later if he had prior knowledge of the escape plan, Dunn was resolute in his denial. The Pinkerton detective who had been visiting Dunn in regard to the return of the missing U.S. bonds suddenly ceased his visits after Miner's prison break.

Shorty Dunn was a model prisoner throughout his term and on December 4, 1913, his sentence was reduced to fifteen years. He was paroled on May 25, 1915, with orders to report to the New Westminster chief of police every month until October 1918. In the spring of 1916, Dunn received a proposition from a man named Allison to go into partnership in a prospecting venture. Dunn requested permission from the minister of justice in Ottawa to alter his monthly parole reports. On July 16, 1916, he received permission to report every three months and from then on Dunn spent the remainder of his life prospecting.

After his release from prison, Shorty Dunn remained law abiding and later decided that he wanted to become a Canadian citizen. Through the years, the ex–train robber, now using his lawful name,

William Grell, had become friends with Andy Fairbain, a corporal in the British Columbia Provincial Police stationed at Telkwa. It was through Fairbain that Dunn appealed for help in seeking citizenship. Dunn informed Fairbain of his participation in the train robbery and subsequent imprisonment. Nevertheless, Fairbain interceded for Dunn because of his exemplary record since his release from prison. After studying his case and application, Judge F. McB. Young of Prince Rupert granted Dunn citizenship under his real name, William Grell.

Shorty Dunn continued to prospect throughout the area and in 1927, while on a trip from Whitesail to Ootsa, he drowned when his canoe overturned in floodwaters. His body was found a year later by a band of wandering Indians. After identification, Dunn was buried by Constable G. A. Johnson in a clump of spruce trees near the Tatsa River Forks.[3]

Louis Colquhoun was not as fortunate as Shorty Dunn. At the time of Miner's break, he was in the prison hospital with tuberculosis. He seemed pleased when informed that Bill Miner had escaped but told prison authorities he knew nothing about the escape plan. Through the years his condition worsened, and he died in prison at New Westminster on September 22, 1911.[4]

For two years following Miner's escape, many conflicting reports circulated concerning his movements and actions. One version is that Bill successfully escaped across the border into the United States and worked for a time in mining. He then allegedly robbed a train in Oregon and went to Europe on the proceeds. Supposedly, while in Europe, Miner got into trouble with banking officials and had to flee back to the United States. He also was credited with single-handedly robbing a Portland bank of twelve thousand dollars in June 1909, but no report of a bank robbery in Portland can be found in the local newspapers of that year.[5]

On December 7, 1908, however, a bank robbery was committed in Portland. At 5:45 in the evening, three armed and unmasked men entered the East Side Bank on the corner of Grand Avenue and East Washington Street and told President H. H. Newhall, his son Roger Newhall, and the bookkeeper, B. D. Coulson, "Hold up your hands." Not wasting any time, the leader vaulted through the teller's window and within two minutes had scooped up all the cash in sight. Climbing back through the teller's window, the leader told his confederates, "Come, get out of this quick." The trio then fled down East

Washington Street with $14,745 in loot to a waiting buggy and disappeared. The buggy had been rented from Anderson's stables by a man giving the name of J. Lawrence and was found abandoned on the evening of the robbery.

From the descriptions of the robbers by the employees and eyewitnesses, it is highly unlikely that Bill Miner was involved. All were described as between thirty-five and forty years old and of medium height. Two had dark hair and dark complexions, and the third was blond or light haired with a light mustache. Although the theory was that the bandits probably were disguised, Miner, now nearly sixty-two years old, would have had difficulty hiding his age.[6]

On June 22, 1909, a CPR train was held up near Ducks, but no loot was obtained. Bill Miner was immediately suspected, but this theory was discounted after several photographs of Miner were shown to the train crew. It turned out that the bandits were brothers, Bill and Dave Haney. On the evening of June 29, Dave Haney and Constable Isaac Decker of the British Columbia Provincial Police killed each other in a shootout near Ashcroft, but Bill Haney escaped and was never caught.[7]

Immediately after Bill Miner's escape from New Westminster, there were several reported sightings of him. On August 9, Miner and another man, incorrectly believed to have been McClusky, one of the escapees, supposedly appeared at the Jackson Stark farm outside Ashcroft. That evening, Stark gave the two men supper and let them sleep in the barn overnight. The next day, the two men arrived at the Abel Johnson farm around noon. Johnson gave them bread and butter and let them pick some apples from his orchard. Both men were reported armed, and they remained in the vicinity until they boarded a freight train as it slowed down at an incline.

On August 12 the *Seattle Post-Intelligencer* reported another sighting of Miner:

> Bill Miner, the notorious train robber who escaped from the British Columbia penitentiary at New Westminster Thursday, was seen near Georgetown yesterday by a Seattle woman who exacted a promise from the police that her name would be withheld in connection with the convict. The woman was coming towards Seattle in an automobile shortly before 6 o'clock last evening when she met Bill Miner on the road. She had known him in years gone by and declares that she could not be mistaken. She at once informed the police.
>
> A squad of detectives in charge of Sergt. Frank Bryant went at once to the place where Miner was said to have been seen, and clews were

found that convinced the sleuths that Miner had passed that way. People living in that vicinity had seen a man closely answering the description of Miner, but when night came on all trace of the escaped convict was lost.

Undoubtedly this report was true: Miner probably was heading for the buried plunder from the Seattle train robbery. The Seattle police also held to this theory and believed Miner was trying to obtain assistance from friends in the Seattle area.[8]

Presumably, after Miner crossed the United States border following his escape, the securities and bonds were returned to Canadian Pacific Railway officials. The only fear Miner might have had was retaliation by Cowboy Jake Terry. But this fear was put to rest one month before Miner's escape. Obsessed with his former wife, Terry boldly crossed the border into the United States. Again he bullied her husband, Gus Linday, but the inoffensive little man had had enough and shot Terry to death.[9]

Was it fate or planning that Miner's escape occurred one month after the dangerous Jake Terry was eliminated? Regardless, the old bandit was in sole possession of the buried spoils.

There were many conflicting stories which described Miner's

Bill Miner, convict No. 980, as he appeared when he entered New Westminster Penitentiary in 1906. Courtesy of Pinkerton's Inc., Van Nuys, California.

movements after the prison break. While imprisoned later in Georgia, Miner related an experience which, if it took place at all, occurred at this time:

> I came to a small Oregon town on the eve of Thanksgiving with a large amount of dust. I stepped into a store and bought a cigar. A nicely dressed man came in and began ordering a large amount of groceries. My curiosity was aroused, and I inquired for whom he was buying so many eatables. He stated he was a member of the relief committee of his town, buying groceries for a dinner to the place's poor for Thanksgiving. I pulled out my bag of dust, and scraping a small amount into a tobacco sack, handed the remainder over to the grocery man, and said, "Here pardner, take this and give the poor people all it'll buy."[10]

Many years later, J. M. Everly of Snoqualmie, Washington, recalled a strange meeting with Bill Miner:

> In the fall of 1907 I was on the extra list of the NPRR as telegraph operator. They sent me to Welch's Spur to relieve the regular operator for a couple of nights while he and his wife took a trip to Butte. They were green as far as the west was concerned, the woman, in her thirties, sporty, and much older than her husband who was dumb. They had a strange friend who was introduced to me as Mr. Edwards. He was a hard-bitten westerner, middle-aged, plainly after the woman. He acknowledged the introduction, but not another word. He went with them to Butte and returned, still silent as far as I was concerned. . . . I was immediately suspicious, and years afterward I saw his picture in a magazine—Bill Miner.[11]

In August 1913, just before his death, Miner related the so-called story of his life to the warden while imprisoned at the Milledgeville prison farm in Georgia. Much of what he said was fictitional, but in some cases, such as the following, he gave truthful accounts. Bill Miner stated that after his escape from Canada he made his way to the Midwest and lived a fashionable but uneventful life on his loot. After spending the winter of 1909–10 in the South and running out of money, he made his way north. Later, Miner proved to have acquired a remarkable amount of knowledge of the railway schedules and roadways throughout the South, a fact which tends to corroborate his story.[12]

There is also sufficient evidence to show that Bill Miner had told the truth about spending much of this time in the Midwest. The *Denver Republican* reported that he made his headquarters in Denver, where, dressed in "fashionable clothing of noisy design" and wearing diamonds of unusual size, he associated with other lovers of fashion, playing the part of a gentleman of wealth and leisure. This report adds confirmation that Miner did indeed retrieve the hidden loot from the Seattle train robbery and freely spent it as fast as he could. There being no evidence that he committed any crimes during this period, he must have had a stockpile of money to support such a lifestyle.

Interestingly, while in Denver, Miner became romantically involved with a woman, and during one of his absences from the city he wrote her a letter saying money had been used in some way to aid his escape from New Westminster. This fact came to light on March 1, 1911, when a reporter from the *Atlanta Constitution* interviewed Miner, who was in jail in Georgia. After the reporter confronted him with evidence of the letter's contents, Bill angrily replied, "That's a damn lie."[13]

After living it up for nearly three years, by the spring of 1910, the old bandit was broke. Bill Miner may have been a socialist, but he had no qualms about living the life of a capitalist during those years. Nevertheless, he was now in need of money which meant, of course, another train robbery. He also needed comrades to augment his plans, and with this in mind the aging outlaw left the southland and headed north.

CHAPTER 15

Last of the Old-Time Bandits

IN the spring of 1910, Bill Miner returned to his home state of Michigan, where he met thirty-one-year-old Charles Turner, alias Charley Hunter. Miner, now using the alias of George Morgan, persuaded Hunter to accompany him to Pennsylvania. Leaving his wife and children, Hunter traveled with Miner to Pennsylvania, where they worked in the coal fields. From there, the pair made their way south through West Virginia, laboring in various coal mines throughout the state.

Each day after work, the two would sit and talk, the oily-tongued bandit filling Hunter's head with tales of easy money to be made by holding up a train in the South. Like many others before him, Hunter fell prey to Miner's persuasive powers and finally agreed to the plan. By October 1910 the pair had worked their way to the Blue Ridge Mountains of Virginia, where they took jobs in a sawmill. Miner was now using the aliases of George Anderson, John Luck, George Morgan, and George Budd, the last possibly as a vindictive jibe at former California Gov. James H. Budd for refusing to honor his alleged promises and grant Miner a pardon in 1897.[1]

While working at the sawmill, Miner and Hunter made the acquaintance of a fellow worker, Jim Handford, whom Bill decided to recruit into the train robbery scheme. Thirty-three-year-old Handford, whose true name was Charley H. Couch, was originally from Royal, Nebraska. He had been an itinerant worker throughout the country for ten years prior to coming to Virginia and did not have a previous criminal record. Later, Handford was to describe Bill Miner's ability to exert his will and control over him:

> [T]hey stayed at the mill and talked with me for about two weeks and finally convinced me to enter the gang as the third man. . . . George Anderson was an unusual person and had an unusual personality. He could over persuade most anyone, and being myself only a common laborer with few advantages in life he naturally picked me out as a vic-

155

> tim. At first I was able to repulse his advances and had no trouble in declining to enter his scheme, but he held onto me staying near me and talked interestingly and convincingly of his plans, and finally I saw myself yielding to him and his plans. They seemed so plausible and he pictured them to be so easy and pictured great wealth and luxuries to me and compared these things with the hard life and meager existence I was then living and finally had me so completely under his influence that I simply could not resist him at all. It was more like being hypnotized than anything else.[2]

Miner further convinced Hunter and Handford of the feasibility of his plans by displaying his impressive knowledge of the railroad lines and wagon roads throughout the South. Bill had equipped himself with maps and railroad schedules and could trace on the maps all railroad lines with ease. For weeks they discussed the planned robbery. Finally, Miner pulled out a map, and after tracing lines all over it, decided that Georgia was the best possible place to stage the holdup. They settled on the Southern Railway as their target. Hunter and Handford reverentially began calling Miner "Captain." In December, after working two months at the sawmill, the three men headed south.[3]

They leisurely traveled to Knoxville, Tennessee, and from there took a train to Blue Ridge, Georgia. Now traveling on foot, Bill and his two comrades made their way deeper into the mountains to Winding Stairs Gap, where they spent the night at the mountaintop home of a family name Tipton.

Crossing the mountains, they continued south until they arrived at Dahlonega, Georgia on the afternoon of Sunday, February 12, 1911. The trio had supper at Watson's Stand, a local restaurant, where they told the proprietor, A. E. Watson, that they were miners from the West and would be looking for gold in the mountains of Georgia. That night they took lodging at the Dahlonega Hotel, which was owned and operated by John F. Sargent, sheriff of Lumpkin County.[4] Sargent noticed the three men in his hotel that night and later recalled:

> I went to their rooms that night that they stopped at my house and had a full description of the men and inquired as to what they were doing in that section and their answer was that they were prospecting for gold mines. They left my hotel early the next morning and was seen by Bill Tobert [U.S. Mail driver between Dahlonega and Gainesville, Georgia] in Gainesville Tuesday morning following. This dis-

Left to right: Charley Hunter, Bill Miner, and Jim Handford. Composite photograph of the three Georgia train robbers compiled by photographer W. J. Ramsey of Gainesville, Georgia. The three photos were taken by Mr. Ramsey on February 23, 1911, when the three bandits were brought to Gainesville after capture. From Mark Dugan's collection.

closed the fact to me that they were not prospecting and that they were not gold miners.[5]

On Tuesday morning, February 14, the residents of Dahlonega saw Miner and his two companions heading south, instead of north toward the mountains. Reaching Gainesville on the morning of February 14, the three took lodging for the night with a Mrs. McAfee. The next day, they holed up in a deserted cabin by the railroad tracks near White Sulphur Springs, between Gainesville and Lula. On the sixteenth, Charley Hunter went to Atlanta, where he hocked Miner's watch at a pawnshop on Decatur Street for fifteen dollars. Hunter used the money to buy several bottles of whiskey and a dark lantern and then returned to the cabin at White Sulphur Springs.

On the afternoon of the seventeenth, Bill Miner went to a store in White Sulphur Springs to purchase kerosene. The store was managed by Mrs. J. McCracken, wife of the Southern Railway agent at White Sulphur Springs. While purchasing the fuel oil, Miner questioned Mrs. McCracken in great depth about the surrounding countryside. Returning to the shanty, Miner and his two companions waited until the early hours of the eighteenth.[6]

Southern Railway's Fast Mail No. 36 left Atlanta at 2:15 A.M. on the eighteenth, with engineer David Fant pushing to make up several minutes of lost time. At 3:12, as the train reached a point two miles north of White Sulphur Springs, Fant spotted a red signal ahead. Approaching the signal, the engineer saw that a man was flagging the train with a red lantern. Suspecting that an obstruction was on the tracks ahead, he brought the train to a complete stop.[7]

Having successfully flagged the train, Charley Hunter kept the engineer's attention by informing him that the rails were out ahead and were being repaired. At that point, Miner and Handford, both masked, boarded the engine and held engineer Fant and fireman Rufus Johnson at bay with revolvers. Leaving Handford to guard Fant, Miner forced Johnson at gunpoint to walk back and uncouple the engine and the express car from the rest of the train. Johnson was unable to uncouple the cars and, for some unknown reason, Miner sent him down the tracks and the fireman managed to escape into the woods. Bill Miner returned to the engine within fifteen minutes and, with Handford, forced Fant to go back with them to the express car.

When the train stopped, conductor Walter T. Mooney and flagman C. H. Shirley were in the day coach. Believing there was an obstruction ahead, both men stepped off the coach and upon reaching the engine spotted Hunter with the red lantern. Approaching Hunter, Mooney asked him what was wrong but received no answer. Becoming irritated, Mooney again demanded to know what the problem was and again received no answer. Hunter was shielding his face with his arm and Mooney angrily pulled his arm down only to find himself and Shirley covered by a revolver in the hands of a masked man. Hunter remained calm and good-naturedly told the two railroad men, "Everything's all right. Just climb back up in the train and be good, and you won't get hurt." Realizing that there was nothing they could do, both men returned to the train. Shortly afterward, Shirley managed to escape from the back of the train and made his way to White Sulphur Springs to spread the alarm.

At the express car, Bill Miner told the engineer to get the expressman, William B. Miller, to open the door. When Miller refused to comply, Miner went in through a side door which negligently had been left unlocked.

"Throw up your hands!" Bill barked. He ordered Miller to open the safe, but the messenger told him he could not open it.

"Give me the keys," Miner snapped.

When Miller claimed he had no keys to the safe, Miner shrugged, "I'll blow it open."

Bill was well prepared with six sticks of dynamite. He set one stick under the large stationary safe, unaware that it contained some sixty thousand dollars. Putting a match to the fuse, Miner and the expressman leaped from the express car. A deafening roar ripped through the coach, and when the smoke cleared Bill climbed back into the car, only to find the safe undamaged. Frustrated, he called out to one of his men, "Push that messenger back up here."

As Miller climbed back into the car, the bandit leader demanded, "Which safe has got the most money?"

"I don't know," the frightened expressman exclaimed, "They all have got sealed packages."

"I will try this one," replied Bill, and placed two sticks of dynamite on the smaller safe and ordered engineer Fant to hand him two shovelfuls of dirt which he tamped around the dynamite. Lighting the fuse, Miner again jumped from the car. This time the explosion was so tremendous that it blew a hole in the roof of the coach, shattered all the windows, blew out the ventilating system, and completely shattered the smaller safe.

The three bandits had previously agreed to call one another by numbers, with Miner as "Number One," Handford as "Number Two," and, to confuse the trainmen of the actual size of the gang, Hunter as "Number Four." After lining the train crew in front of the express coach door, Bill reentered the car, seized an express pouch, and called out, "Number Four, open this bag."

As Hunter vainly tried to break the seal, the agitated old outlaw exclaimed, "No, cut the thing open."

Whipping out a knife, Bill sliced the bag open himself. He and Hunter stuffed the contents of the safe into canvas bags while keeping their eyes on the crew. The take was $770 in Mexican currency, around $1,000 in U.S. currency, $442 in British gold coins, assorted foreign silver coins, women's jewelry, various stock certificates, letters, and mortgages, all of which were thrown into the canvas bag.

Two curious passengers, who had left the coach, approached the bandits, but Handford fired a shot at them. The bullet whirred inches past them, sending the terrified pair scrambling back into the car. Miner then called in Number Two to help finish loading the bags. Climbing down from the express car, Bill told engineer Fant that he could leave. The three bandits disappeared down a ravine into the woods and headed east toward the Oconee River. The whole operation had taken less than forty minutes.[8]

As soon as the telegraph operator at Gainesville received news of the robbery, he sent word to county lawmen. A hastily assembled posse under Deputy Sheriff W. A. Little of Hall County left immediately for the scene of the robbery. The officers discovered the shanty where the robbers had holed up before the robbery and inside found a Southern Railway track wrench, an expensive corduroy coat, a pair of overalls, a safety razor, and a shaving brush. Near the tracks where the robbery occurred, the officers found the remains of a campfire, several discarded foreign coins, and an old overcoat that the bandits had left behind. Not finding any visible clue with which to track the bandits, the officers soon had bloodhounds from the convict camp at Buford, Georgia, on the trail. Although at least five other train robberies had previously been committed in Georgia, this robbery was by far the most sensational ever executed in the state.[9]

The Southern Railway immediately posted a reward of one thousand dollars for the bandits' capture and quickly sent a posse of railroad detectives to the area to join the search, including Detectives Tom Hanie, W. F. Terrell, and H. A. Terrell; Special Agent Partee from North Carolina; and Detectives C. W. Burkee, O. M. Sadler, and H. M. Duncan of South Carolina. Also joining the search was United States Marshal B. B. Landers. On the evening of the eighteenth, Georgia Gov. Joseph M. Brown offered an additional but paltry reward of one hundred dollars each for the robbers. Every officer involved agreed that the robbery and escape were well planned, as that wild and uninhabitable section of the country offered the fugitives excellent cover for their getaway.[10]

But making a getaway was exactly what Bill Miner and his two confederates did not do. After traveling about a mile from White Sulphur Springs, they stopped and hid out in the woods, burying the canvas bag filled with documents, stocks, and mortgages under a log. Before the robbery they had purchased snuff and red pepper in Dahlonega, and these the canny Miner now put in their shoes to throw the dogs off their tracks. Later that morning the robbers split up the money and valuables, each taking $255 in Mexican currency and $340 in other currency. They divided the foreign coins by weight, Miner taking the bag of British gold coins and a gold watch.[11]

Throughout the day the three fugitives waited in the woods, periodically hearing the posse and dogs that were hunting them. At nightfall they decided to leave the area by the same route that brought them in but could not find the road back toward the mountains. To get their bearings, they were forced to go back through Gainesville, where they barely escaped capture by a party of men in town. Finally, Bill and his men found the right road and, after crossing the Gainesville bridge, hastily retreated toward the mountains. On the morning of Sunday, February 19, hunger impelled Miner to obtain breakfast at a farmhouse. After his meal, he returned with enough food for both Handford and Hunter.

After spending the intensely cold Sunday night in the woods, the trio made their way the next day to Briar Patch, six miles from Dahlonega. To escape the cold weather, they spent the night of February 20 in an outhouse on the farm of Pete Carmichael. The three bandits remained hidden in this unpleasant refuge until the afternoon of the twenty-first, when hunger again forced them to move on. Because of the many patrols throughout the area, they decided to split up and meet at Winding Stairs Gap. Handford and Hunter headed northeast toward the Fannin County line leaving Old Bill Miner on his own.

The old bandit took a meal at the home of W. H. Earley, then walked to Dahlonega where he bought some canned goods and a box of snuff before heading toward the mountains. At six thirty that evening, he stopped and was granted lodging at the home of Elbert Kendall, seventeen miles northwest of Dahlonega.[12]

When Lumpkin County Sheriff John F. Sargent received news of the train robbery and the descriptions of the bandits, he immediately suspected that the three men who had spent the night in his hotel were the guilty parties. He promptly telephoned residents throughout the county to be on the lookout for the trio. Pete Carmichael, spotting the three fugitives holed up in the old outhouse near his home, telephoned Sargent with the information. The sheriff later recalled:

> I went immediately to the old outhouse and got on the trail of the men and tracked them through the woods and along the road to where I discovered that two of them had gone in one direction and the old gentleman in another. I followed the old gentleman and tracked him into Dahlonega. I then followed him through Dahlonega and found he had gone out of Dahlonega in the same direction that he came to my hotel on the Sunday night before. I followed him seventeen miles north of Dahlonega to the home and passed the home of Jim Davis, ex-sheriff of Lumpkin County, and on to the home of Elbert Kendall.[13]

The Kendalls periodically took in lodgers for the night, so no one was suspicious when Miner asked for lodging. Exhausted, Bill soon retired to a bed in the loft. At midnight Sheriff Sargent, accompanied by former Sheriff Jim Davis, Davis's son Joe, and a posseman, Walt Walters, arrived at the Kendall home. Told that the suspect was asleep in the loft, the posse hurriedly rushed upstairs to make the arrest.

The apprehension of Miner turned out to be one of the most bizarre yet comical captures on record. Petty jealousies and greed for the reward money overcame the lawmen, and Miner, still half asleep, had to suffer the brunt of their avarice.

Former Sheriff Davis was the first to reach the sleeping bandit, and he immediately handcuffed one of Bill's wrists. Sheriff Sargent and Walters came in behind Davis, and Sargent demanded the prisoner. Davis adamantly refused to give him up. Sheriff Sargent then handcuffed Miner's other wrist, and the two men began pulling the groggy old bandit back and forth between them while heatedly arguing over who was to get the reward. Walters stepped between the two men and told them to stop arguing, reminding Davis, "No trouble about it, Sargent is Sheriff and turn him over to him." Davis reluctantly relinquished the bewildered outlaw to Sargent.

Miner's .44-caliber revolver was found under his pillow, and a bag containing $442 in British gold coins was taken from his coat. Davis wanted to keep the money until it was decided whether the prisoner was guilty or not, but the sheriff foolishly ordered Davis to return it to Miner. Scattered under the bed was an additional $2.44 in silver. The gold watch was not found until the next morning. With their prisoner in tow, the captors then left the Kendall residence.

Davis wisely expected that Miner would try to dispose of the evidence. About a mile from the Kendall home, Miner furtively tossed the bag of gold coins into the brush. Davis's keen eye caught Bill's trick, and after a short search Walters retrieved the bag. Before heading back to Dahlonega with his prisoner, Sheriff Sargent asked his three possemen to be on the lookout for the other two bandits. Arriving at Dahlonega about four in the morning, Sargent locked Miner in the Lumpkin County Jail and telephoned the Southern Railway detectives, informing them of the arrest.[14]

Meanwhile, after separating from Miner on the twenty-first, Hunter and Handford headed in the same general direction Miner had taken. That night the two fugitives found refuge from the cold in a deserted farmhouse. In an effort to evade pursuers, they periodically backtracked over previously covered ground and by late afternoon on the twenty-second had traveled only fourteen miles from Dahlonega.

Residents of the Nimberwill district had observed the suspicious movements of the two men making their way through the fields and woods and subsequently reported this to former Sheriff Jim Davis. Davis, his son Joe, Walt Walters, and Robert Long started in quick pursuit and after traveling a short distance from Davis's house, saw the two fugitives near a sawmill on the public road from Dahlonega. The exhausted train robbers were completely surprised by the four armed men. Collapsing by the roadside, they meekly surrendered.

"Looks as if they've got us, pard," Hunter said dejectedly.

"Shut up, fool!" shouted Handford.

But Hunter talked, saying remorsefully, "It was a sorry day for us, that Saturday. I guess you've got us now, and we had just as well out with it."

Hunter readily confessed to the robbery but refused to reveal his name or the names of the others involved. As he began to hand over the stolen money, Handford reluctantly did the same. Besides having a .44-caliber revolver each, they had fifteen hundred dollars in gold and silver stuffed into their hats, shoes, stockings, and every pocket of their clothing. When they were informed of the capture of the other robber and heard his description, they readily identified him by the aliases of John Luck and George Anderson, stating that he was the leader of the gang.

The two prisoners were taken back to Davis's house where they spent the night under guard. The next morning they were delivered to the sheriff's office in Dahlonega and locked up in the Lumpkin County Jail. The three prisoners were kept separated in the jail, and even though Hunter and Handford had identified Miner under two of his aliases, Miner adamantly refused to talk. No one in Georgia knew who he was, and Bill Miner wanted to keep it that way.[15]

CHAPTER 16

"It Was No Harm to Rob an Express Car That Was Robbing the People"

BILL Miner was destined to become a folk hero in Georgia, just as he already was in Canada, and would capture the hearts of southerners through the attention of the press. The Georgia newspapers, from the time of the train robbery until Miner's death, kept his story alive and conducted interviews with him.

The press was attracted to Bill Miner for a number of reasons. The old highwayman brought back the bygone days of the Wild West—the days of Jesse James and the romance of the dime novel—to the heart of the South. That the Southern Railway train had been robbed by a sixty-four-year-old relic of that colorful era added spice to the story. Miner's engaging and gentlemanly manner thoroughly charmed the Georgia press. In turn, Bill was flattered by the attention and willingly talked to newspapermen for the first time in his career. Thus he inadvertently revealed insights into his character, his beliefs, and his ideals which, when pieced together, would present an overall portrait of the man himself.

Even though Bill did not reveal his identity, he allowed reporters to interview him in the Dahlonega jail. From the start the newspapermen focused their attention on Miner while generally ignoring Hunter and Handford. The *Atlanta Journal* reported:

> It is said that the older prisoner told the people of Dahlonega that he liked the jail very much and that he had been very comfortable there, although he did not know whether he would ever come back or not. He gave his pistol to the jailor's son and told him he could buy a gun like that anytime he wanted to from a Chicago firm!

Handford was reported to have told an officer, "Any man could hold up a Southern railway train with a toy pistol."[1]

The *Dahlonega Nugget* also interviewed Bill Miner during his incarceration at Dahlonega and reported the following:

The old man who was arrested and lodged in jail here for about two days before he was carried off for robbing the Southern train, talked very intelligently upon any subject that was brought up, and proved that he had traveled a great deal. When spoken to about the offense with which he was charged, stated that he had never been guilty of robbing a widow or orphan, but said it was no harm to rob an express car that was robbing the people, although he would not say that he was guilty of robbing the Southern express.

Preacher Elgin visited the stranger and conversed with the old man on religious matters, who informed the divine that he believed in only a part of the Bible, yet he was willing to come face to face with his God at any time.

Bill also demonstrated his knowledge of mining and said that mining prospects in Georgia were very favorable. He explained that is was best to follow western mining policy: after a mine is "pinched out," or spent, it should be dug deeper to locate larger and richer veins of ore.

Bill Miner became acquainted with a young prisoner in the Dahlonega jail named Mark Crane. Miner told Crane that he had hidden nine hundred dollars in two places and drew a map of the locations on the stove in the jail. Miner said ruefully that the money would do him no good, but it might help the boy and his family. Crane immediately told the officers that he would reveal the location of the loot for 20 percent of the find. The lawmen agreed. Several went to the area and found the location but discovered that the money was not there. They reported that someone had beaten them to it because there were tracks all around the hiding places. The whole thing may have been another one of Miner's wild tales.[2]

Before his removal from the Dahlonega jail, Miner presented his meerschaum pipe to A. E. Watson. The restaurant owner tagged it and placed it in the show window of his business, where it remained for many years.[3]

On the morning of the twenty-third, General Manager J. B. Hockaday, Detective Tom Hanie, and R. H. Duncan of the Southern Railway, accompanied by Pinkerton Detective Henry W. Minster, arrived at Dahlonega to take the three bandits to Gainesville. Sheriff Sargent and Detective Hanie bundled Miner into an automobile. As the old outlaw was driven into Gainesville, crowds of people lined the street to catch a glimpse of him. Bill jokingly remarked, "They must think I'm a bear."

That afternoon, Handford and Hunter were taken separately to

"IT WAS NO HARM TO ROB AN EXPRESS CAR..."

Pipe belonging to Bill Miner. Miner gave the pipe to A. E. Watson of Dahlonega, Georgia, in February 1911. The pipe was obtained by Georgia historian James C. Bonner of Milledgeville, Georgia. The pipe was given to Mark Dugan by James C. Bonner, Jr., in December 1987. From Mark Dugan's collection.

Gainesville. Upon their arrival, the three prisoners were photographed by a local photographer, W. J. Ramsey. While being photographed, Hunter broke down and cried.

Miner was lodged in the Hall County Jail, while Hunter and Handford, who were now willing to talk, were taken to a local hotel, where they were questioned by the detectives and identified by some of the train crew. Hunter even extended his hand to engineer Fant, saying, "No hard feelings, I hope." The two finally admitted their true names, and Hunter sold his revolver to General Manager Hockaday for five dollars. That evening the detectives took Hunter and Handford to White Sulphur Springs to locate all the missing documents and valuables. Most of the material had been treated roughly and was damaged and torn. On returning to Gainesville, Hunter and Handford were placed together in a cell and kept separate from Miner.[4]

After his confinement in the Hall County Jail, Bill Miner settled right into his new lodgings, as reported by The *Gainesville News:*

> They are all intelligent, and Anderson when seen in the jail, a short time after he was put in jail, was sweeping his cell and getting things in shape to suit himself in his new surroundings, and appeared to be perfectly contented as he filled his pipe with tobacco and offered those standing by some of his smoking tobacco.[5]

At noon the next day, the twenty-fourth, the three prisoners were taken to the Gainesville courthouse for preliminary examination under Judge George E. Sims, justice of the peace for the Gainesville district. Hunter and Handford waived their right to a hearing but Miner, as George Anderson, demanded a hearing through his attorney, B. P. Gilliard.

Throughout the afternoon, the following witnesses testified: engineer Fant, expressman Miller, Sheriff Sargent, and former Sheriff Davis. Handford and Hunter, when questioned by prosecuting attorney Howard Thompson, gave full details of the robbery and related information pertaining to their background. Miner admitted

Above, left to right: Engineer David Fant, flagman C. H. Shirley, and conductor W. T. Mooney, who were all trainmen on the Southern Railway's No. 36 when it was robbed by Miner at White Sulphur Springs, Georgia, on February 18, 1911. From the *Atlanta Constitution,* February 19, 1911.

"IT WAS NO HARM TO ROB AN EXPRESS CAR..."

Bill Miner and his captors in photos taken on February 23, 1911, in Gainesville, Georgia, by W. J. Ramsey. *Top and bottom left:* Sheriff John F. Sargent, Miner, and Southern Railway Detective Tom N. Hanie. *Bottom right:* Former Sheriff Jim Davis. From the *Atlanta Journal,* February 24, 1911.

nothing, saying only that his name was George Anderson and that he was from Virginia. The defense asked no questions. After hearing all the evidence, the judge ordered the three men to be tried during the next court term and remanded them to jail under ten thousand dollars bond each.[6] The *Atlanta Journal* covered the hearing and described Miner in court:

> The older man, Anderson, is game in the full sense of the word. He sat in the midst of the hundreds of people gathered about him, without a flinch or change of expression in his face and countenance.[7]

The next day at Toccoa, Georgia, Superior Court Judge J. B. Jones ordered the three men to be tried in a special term of Superior Court scheduled for March 3, 1911, in the Hall County Courthouse. The *Gainesville News* reported that Hall County Sheriff W. A. Crow "has sent the pictures of Anderson to the rogue's gallery in Washington, and further information concerning the man may result." The sheriff also made arrangements for the jail to be guarded around the clock to prevent Miner's escape. As evidenced by the following article in The *Gainesville News*, these new developments apparently began to worry Miner:

> The two younger men rest easy in their cells and sleep well at night, but Anderson is restless and sleeps but little, moving about in his cell very nearly all night. He is vehement in his cursing of corporations and says that all of them should be put out of business.[8]

Bill Miner after his capture on February 22, 1911, by Sheriff John F. Sargent of Lumpkin County, Georgia. This photograph was taken on February 23, 1911, in Gainesville, Georgia, by photographer W. J. Ramsey. *Left to right:* Sheriff Sargent, Miner, and Southern Railway Detective Tom N. Hanie. From the *Atlanta Constitution,* February 24, 1911.

"IT WAS NO HARM TO ROB AN EXPRESS CAR . . ." 171

On February 27, Bill's fears became a reality when news was released by the Pinkertons that he had been identified as A. E. ("Old Bill") Miner. Pinkerton Detective Henry W. Minster, who had been working on the case in Georgia, found that the numerous marks and scars on Anderson tallied exactly with those of Miner. Miner's distinguishing marks had altered since they were first recorded at San Quentin in 1866. Pinkerton's file carried the following description of him:

> Miner's distinguishing marks are on his forearm and were made by a tattooing needle and Indian Ink when he was a youngster; carries a tattoo at the base of thumb of left hand [information in the San Quentin Prison Register states that the letters "VA" were tattooed on Miner's left hand]; also a heart pierced with a dagger; a ballet girl is tattooed on his right forearm and also a star; both wrist bones are large; has a mole in center of chest; mole under left breast and another on his right shoulder; another star tattooed on outside of calf of left leg; a discoloration on left buttock; a scar on his left shin; a scar on his right knee. A mole on his left shoulder blade. Two small scars on his neck. His face is pitted and he wears both upper and lower false teeth.[9]

The *Sacramento Daily Bee* was quick to pick up the news from Chicago about the notorious California bandit and duly reported it under the headline "Jesse James Rival Again Under Arrest":

> That "Old Bill" Miner, second only to Jesse James in notoriety as a train robber, was one of the White Sulpher, Ga., bandits arrested at Gainesville, Ga., last Thursday was asserted by the National Detective Agency here today.
> Miner was famous for a decade as one of the "bad men" of the Northwest. He was sentenced to life imprisonment several years ago at Vancouver for train robbery but escaped prison.
> Unless the Dominion authorities seek Miner's return, he will be tried for the White Sulpher robbery.[10]

Following Miner's identification, it was not long before the newspapers in Atlanta received the story behind his Canadian escape, which they immediately played up. Reported the *Atlanta Georgian and News*, "At the time he escaped it was said he knew the hiding place of papers which meant a large sum to a corporation and that the corporation aided him to escape." The *Atlanta Constitution* reported the same basic story, although neither newspaper named the Canadian Pacific Railway as the corporation in question.[11]

When the news reached Canada that Bill Miner was in custody in

Georgia, the government of British Columbia sent a telegram to Georgia Attorney General Hewlette Hall in Atlanta:

> Victoria, British Columbia
> To Attorney General, Atlanta, Georgia
>
> Understand that Bill Miner is now being held in Gainesville. He is an escaped life convict from here for train robbery, and we are most anxious to have him back. Will you consent to his surrender? If you have any doubts as to his identity the officials at San Quentin Penitentiary, California can give you an accurate description, including tattoo and other body marks.
>
> W. J. Bowers
> Attorney General
> March 1, 1911 [12]

In response to the Canadian request, Attorney General Hall refused deportation of Bill Miner on grounds that "a State has the right to hold a prisoner and give him trial, and if convicted he shall first serve sentence before being turned over to foreign authorities." This ended any further attempts by Canadian officials to have Miner returned, although they did send law officers south to make positive identification.[13]

The news that Georgia had the notorious Bill Miner created a stir among lawmen on the West Coast and in the Pacific Northwest. The *Atlanta Constitution,* in an article headlined "Fearless and Desperate Miner Defies Detectives," reported:

> Miner's Identity Fully Established. Detectives from the Pacific slope and from British Columbia now here have recognized him beyond all doubt. Photographs of past years trace his criminal career through half a dozen states and two nations. Birthmarks, scars and India ink figures shown in half a dozen circulars, are all found on the prisoner. But as the prisoner shows these marks without hesitancy to the searching officers, he declines to talk. His only response to questions as he is confronted with evidence is a quiet, hissing laugh. About the only remark he has made since being brought here is, "You seem to know so much, you can find out the rest, damn you."[14]

Bill Miner, realizing that he was trapped and not knowing what lay in store for him, made a futile attempt to escape. Just prior to his trial, he had somehow obtained a smuggled saw and hid it in the seam of his pants. When alone in his cell, he frantically began sawing the bars off the jail window. Just when he was almost finished, he was discovered and his escape thwarted. Said The *Dahlonega Nugget*, with more truth than it realized, "He is an old rooster and it is going to be hard to keep him anywhere."[15]

The train robbery trial opened on March 3 with Judge J. B. Jones presiding. The Gainesville courtroom was so congested that Sheriff Crow had to move people back. "I'm sorry that the court house is not large enough to accommodate all the people who desire to hear this trial," said the sheriff, "but this is the best we can do for you."[16]

Although all three men were on trial, Miner was the center of attention. Even though he had been identified as Bill Miner, he was charged and tried under the alias George Anderson. The trial was well covered by reporters from the leading newspapers. One reporter, E. C. Bruffey from The *Atlanta Constitution*, keenly observed Miner's actions in the courtroom that day:

> Beside the old man sat B. P. Gilliard, a young and hard fighting attorney of the Gainesville bar, retained by Anderson. But whether the aspiring attorney, with an excellent flow of language, got a fee from his client no one knows, as he declines to say. The two kids [Hunter and Handford] were wiped off the slate of attention when they announced they were ready to accept any sentence imposed by the judge. Quickly all interest centered around the old man.
>
> As the younger men announced their guilt, Anderson, the old man, was sitting in a low chair, behind his attorney. The two younger prisoners were behind him. As they arose the old man, knowing what their plea would be, turned quietly and easily in his chair until he was brought face to face with them. Resting an elbow on the back of his chair and laying his right cheek in the palm of his hand, he looked the two kids squarely in the face. It was an eye to eye battle between companions in crime, and the elder man made the younger man drop their eyelids and end that duel. There was not a tremor in the old man's face. Stolid and indifferent he appeared. Apparently what he was to hear was wholly and absolutely new to him, as though he had not in the slightest, anticipated what he was sure to hear. Then as the kids dropped back the old man turned his face towards Judge Jones, and there his eyes remained until he was asked to plead to the indictment.
>
> "We plead not guilty, your honor," said Attorney Gilliard.
>
> Though a total stranger in Hall County, Anderson had more to do with selecting that jury than did his attorney. He scrutinized every face as the proposed juror arose, and then when the full twelve men had been secured he dropped back at rest in his chair until the dozen men came to their feet to qualify.
>
> When the witnesses went upon the stand he gave little heed to what they said. Occasionally he glanced at the occupant of the witness chair as though he had been aroused from a pleasant dream to an un-

pleasant fact. Then the lids would droop over those penetrating grey eyes set in an old head. To Enigineer Fant's story of the hold-up, to Express Messenger Miller's recital of the safe blowing, he apparently paid no attention—and yet he probably heard every word they uttered.

But when the lady from Pensacola [Bessie Lindenstrut], who had shipped the beaded purses North, went on the stand the old man became actively interested. He not only listened to recital, but smiled occasionally as she told of lodging the package with the express company. And when that witness manifested her anxiety about the package after she had learned that the train on which it might have been was held up, the old man's face changed from a smile to an apparently regretful mood—regretful that he might have caused a lady worry and anxiety.

There was a contrast between the attention he gave the Pensacola lady and the man [Julius Levy] who shipped a watch from Mobile to New York on that train. Both the watch and the purses were found in the possession of the prisoners. To the man's loss he gave no thought. He was a man and could take a man's part in the world. But she was a woman and was not to be treated the same way. That was an inference to be drawn without trouble from the manner in which the old man listened to those two witnesses.

Something of resentment in the old man was apparent to even the most casual observer in that courtroom. The old man dreamed in his chair as his attorney made his opening address. It was though he knew nothing could be said to influence that jury. Mr. Gilliard, in presenting his case, claimed no evidence of his client's guilt had been presented, apart from what self confessed outlaws had given. It was a clever outline the defendant's attorney made within fifteen minutes and it was an effective piece of oratory on the large assembly.

It was once only that his face showed any feeling during the argument and that was when Howard Thompson, one of the attorneys for the express company, was addressing the jury. Impassively he heard Mr. Thompson arraign him as an outlaw, a convict, an escaped convict and a man whose criminal career would embrace the catalogue of crimes. He gave no heed to Mr. Thompson when that attorney said that murder was not too bad for anyone who would use dynamite—that deadly weapon. But when Mr. Thompson said:

"Think not of the lives of the men who were endangered when this old criminal, this man, steeped in crime, set off that dynamite. But think of the women and children back in those coaches who might have been blown into eternity without a second's warning."

It was then that the old prisoner leaned forward and threw a most vengeful, glaring and hateful glance at the speaker.

As the jury filed out of the courtroom at 5:45, the old prisoner dropped back in his chair as though relieved.

But the old man's rest was short for within five minutes after the jury had gone out, Sheriff Crow, of Hall County, came in to carry the prisoners back to jail. So stubbornly had Mr. Gilliard fought the case and so cleverly had the prisoner disguised his feelings that there was an impression that the jury might take hours to deliberate. Hardly had the sheriff reached the county jail with his prisoners, however, before he was advised that a verdict had been found. Flanked on both sides of the sidewalk, the prisoner with a chain about his wrist, walked back to the courthouse.

He heard his doom without the slightest change in his expression, but when the judge pronounced the twenty years, a smile spread over the old prisoner's face, and, it seemed involuntary on his part. He broke in with—"Thank you, Judge."

There was nothing of bravado in his tone or his bearing. It seemed to come direct from his heart. It seemed as though he was getting less than he expected.

When the judge had completed his allotment of time to the three prisoners, the old man turned to his left, where there was a great bank of ladies and college girls, and with a sweep of his hat, remarked:

"When one breaks the law one must expect to pay the penalty. I am now old but during all my life I have found the golden rule the best guide to man in this world."

It was as a philosopher he spoke and when he had his say he smiled over the assembly and sat down to await his transfer to jail, where he will remain until finally disposed of.[17]

In all, there were nine witnesses for the prosecution, one of whom was train robber Charley Hunter. He was the only one of the three bandits who testified.[18]

In Handford's and Hunter's cases, Judge Jones took their plea of guilty into consideration. He sentenced both men to serve fifteen years' imprisonment.[19]

The trial had been dramatic and sensational. Spectators and newspapermen were fully aware that they would never have another chance to see a real outlaw of the Old West. As reporter Bruffey concluded observantly, "It is doubtful if Georgia or any other southern state had a case anything like this one."[20]

CHAPTER 17

"He Will Go Hurtling through Georgia History"

JIM Handford and Charley Hunter were kept in the Hall County Jail until March 10, when they were taken to the Newton County Convict Camp at Covington to work out their sentences on the chain gang. On August 29, 1911, Charley Hunter mysteriously escaped and was never recaptured. The news of Hunter's escape was not broadcast, and no reward or governor's proclamation was offered. Hunter simply disappeared.[1]

While working on the chain gang, Jim Handford was regarded as a model prisoner and was made a trusty in January 1914. During two separate escape attempts by convicts Ham Shaver and Mose Williams, Handford was put in charge of the bloodhounds and allowed to leave the prison camp and assist in the recapture of the fugitives. In June 1917 a parole application was filed for Handford, supported by Warden C. T. Thornton of the Newton County Convict Camp. A year later, on July 4, Handford was paroled and released from prison the next day.[2]

During his trial, Bill Miner had declared, "Robbery is robbery, but this is another case." This proved to be true, much to his chagrin. He was not allowed to accompany Hunter and Handford to the prison camp, but was held in the Hall County Jail. The *Gainesville News* reported the reasons behind Miner's extended stay in jail and also gave a somewhat dramatic but otherwise excellent account of Miner's true character, motives, beliefs, and convictions:

> Anderson, now self-confessed train robber, makes the statement that in all his career, checkered and base as it has been, he has never been guilty of lying.
> While the other two men were carried to Covington to work out their sentences on the roads of Newton County, Anderson was kept in jail by order of the state prison commission, with the intention of obtaining information which will be of value in throwing light upon other robberies which have been committed and which had not been cleared up.

This was done upon request of Superintendent Smith of the Southern Express Co.

Money which Anderson had taken had been hid in the mountains of Lumpkin County. He told Sheriff Crow where the money was placed.

"I believe you are lying to me," said the sheriff.

With a flash of eye, that looked hatred and vengeance, and the movement of his body like a wild-cat, the robber replied, "I have never yet told a lie, sir, you will find the money just as I tell you."

Sheriff Crow did find the money, about five hundred dollars one time, and about three hundred dollars another.

Anderson says it is an easy matter to rob a train, or a bank, and that he has never yet had any trouble in carrying out his plans; that he has not found it necessary to resort to means that would result in physical hurt to any person.

He tells of robbing a bank of an enormous sum and settling debts of a gloomy friend, who had failed in business.

Col. B. P. Gilliard deserves much credit from the viewpoint of a defending attorney, for the skill he exemplified in the handling of his case, and for the defense, strong as it could be, which he made for his client, but the verdict of the jury, the sentence of the court, the confession of the convict, and the sentiment of the people, in stentorian tones, speak the truth. While "robbery is robbery" to use the language of Anderson, on receiving the sentence from the lips of Judge Jones, a consistent record of sixty-nine years of robbery has a weighty force.

It was as if the prisoner had said, the law has no right to "rob" me of my freedom. The law, the people, do not think this way about it. And the prisoner says, "I will make no attempt to get away."

Anderson is in bad condition physically, being a sufferer from hemorrhoids. It is likely, however, he will live ten years.

Because of his age and his physical disability, possibly because he is not an ignoramus, and shows "fight" and "grit" since his incarceration in the Hall County jail, Anderson has been shown more than ordinary charity on the part of many. Many callers have been to see him and he has been supplied with books and papers to read, with special things to eat, and has been treated like a gentleman. But we are not harshly criticizing these actions on the part of the charitably inclined.

So much has been said to stir public sentiment in behalf of the poor, wayfaring stranger in jail "within our gates," that a *News* representative, looking for truth, thought it best to take a personal look at the wirey little robber, hear the tone of his voice, and get an expression of his idea.

Last Friday noon we saw Anderson in his cell at the jail.

For fifteen minutes we heard him talk. We couldn't edge in a word. We didn't want to. He had just eaten dinner, was fresh, and hadn't had an opportunity in several hours to exercise his vocal chords. He'll talk yes, he'll talk, talk the "arms off a billy goat."

Anderson rose from a chair in the cell to shake hands. "Glad to see

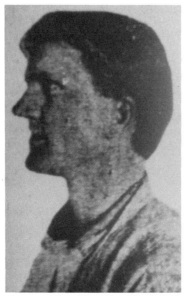 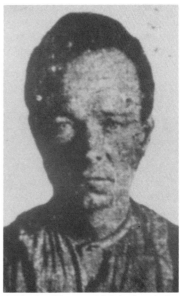

Photographs of Jim Handford *(left)* and Charley Hunter *(right)* after their capture in Lumpkin County, Georgia, on February 22, 1911, for the robbery of Southern Railway Train No. 36 on February 18, 1911. From the *Atlanta Constitution*, March 5, 1911.

you, have a seat," pointing to a chair in the hall, outside the cell. "Beg pardon for not changing shirts, but this is the only shirt I have. Pretty day we're having. Feeling pretty good, and getting on nicely."

There was sarcasm and egotism in his tones.

We didn't mention his crimes, but told him we understood he had read a good deal, and thought a good deal more, and that he was a socialist in political belief.

He talked, and told us more about socialism, and what he had said at various times during the last ten years, and what his actions had been in defense of the doctrines of the socialist party, than we had ever thought could have been in his mind.

He is considerably above the ordinary man in intellectual development. He is naturally endowed with exceptional strong intellect. He is not an educated man. He has done his own thinking, more than likely in self defense. He has coolly, calculatedly, placed himself in position, where he has been forced to plot and plan to keep his own life.

He has taken no training from his fellow man, he has received no spiritual enlightenment.

If his natural mental talents had been trained in the right channel, he would have been a power.

His brain faculties have been stronger than the fellows with whom he has worked, but for brief seasons, at various times in his career, he has come in contact with a class of leading thinkers of the age. He has heard Eugene V. Debs speak, and seen the effect of his work, and he worships at the shrine of such leaders of socialism.

He has worked on wages, and was not satisfied to do the work planned by other heads. The microbe of laziness attacked him and he was not able, day in and day out, to follow a business outline of his own making. It was easier to hold up trains and rob banks.

While he has thought, his thinking has been done by "fits and starts," and he has taken care to keep himself very well. At sixty-nine he doesn't look a year older than fifty.

His bluish grey eyes show a little speck of water and it will not hold the steady look of an honest man. He says he sees little chance in making a socialist of Sheriff Crow.

Anderson is writing a history of his life, which is to be published. He says as a conclusion to the story, which is a life of daring doings of wrong, he will make an appeal to others to avoid the errors he has made, and thereby escape the penalty he deserves. Anderson's entire life is a life of untruth, and the placing of the story of such a life in the hands of the young, to say the least, is very dangerous.[3]

Of all the news articles written about Bill Miner, this one showed the most insight. Miner's vehement denial of ever telling a lie was in itself the biggest lie of all. His insistence in stating that George Anderson was his real name, alluding to the nonexistent bank robbery in Portland, Oregon, and later his statements regarding his birthplace and early life were all deliberate fabrications. Every yarn that he knew could not be verified he embellished with half truths or falsehoods, tales that to this day have been accepted as truth. His hatred of corporations and love of socialism, as it was presented in his day, gave Miner the excuse to believe he had the right to rob those who robbed others. That Bill Miner actually believed much of what he made up is apparent.

The gentlemanly ways, evident intelligence, and personal charm of the old bandit aroused the sympathy of the people, which consequently resulted in the many favors allowed him while in jail. He became a folk hero in Georgia, in Canada, and in the northwestern United States, for there were many who not only had compassion for him but shared his dim view of big business. The difference was that Bill Miner, in his righteous anger, did more about it than just talk.

The old outlaw lied about many things, but he told the truth to Sheriff Crow about the hidden money. On March 6, after various searches, Mrs. Mary Walker of Dahlonega found $283 under a rock near town. The money was turned over to a Southern Railway agent and Mrs. Walker received 30 percent as a reward. The last bit of stolen money, $17.50, was found a week later in the Nimberwill district, where Miner had been arrested.[4]

William Pinkerton, head of the Pinkerton Detective Agency, came to Georgia on business during the first week of March. On March 5 he was interviewed by a reporter from The *Atlanta Constitution* about Bill Miner. Predicted Pinkerton astutely, "Bill Miner will get away; mark my words. That fellow's a fox, he is. You can't keep a man in a road camp who can get through brick walls."[5]

Despite Pinkerton's warning, the authorities, finding no other crimes connected to Miner, ordered his transfer to the Newton County Convict Camp in Covington. Arriving on March 15, he was immediately set to work on the road gang along with Handford and Hunter.[6]

 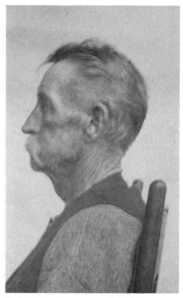

Mug shots of Bill Miner taken in Georgia in 1911. Courtesy of Pinkerton's, Inc., Van Nuys, California.

Greed for the thousand-dollar reward offered by the Southern Express Company created a dogfight in Lumpkin County between Sheriff Sargent and former Sheriff Davis. Around March 15, Davis received the three hundred dollar reward offered by the state which Sargent could not contest because, as an elected official, he was exempt from collecting it.

The railroad's reward was another matter, and Sheriff Sargent wanted one-third of it. By March 17, both men hired attorneys to fight the case. The reward had been placed in the hands of the clerk of Lumpkin County Superior Court until the dispute was settled. In early May the issue was further muddled by Walt Walters and Bob Long, who, through their attorneys, also made claim for the reward. Apparently, Davis prevailed and received the entire reward.[7]

After only three months at the Newton County Convict Camp, Bill Miner, pleading ill health and claiming that he was "all in," petitioned the Georgia State Prison Commission to transfer him to the prison farm at Milledgeville. The newspapers played up the affair, and sentimentally referred to the elderly robber as "Poor Old Bill Miner," stating that his health was broken and his nerve gone. It was reported that he had become so decrepit that he could no longer work on the public roads. On July 8, 1911, Bill was officially transferred to the newly built Milledgeville prison farm for lighter duties. The wily old outlaw was just biding his time.[8]

In 1897, during the waning era of convict slave labor in Georgia, a prison farm was built two miles west of Milledgeville. After the structure burned down, the state prison commission began erecting a new building in March 1911 three miles west of Milledgeville. The main building was a U-shaped two-story ferroconcrete building faced with brick and had two projecting cell wings. The ground floor contained the dining room, kitchen, boiler room, and guardroom. Offices, hospital space, and the first cells, to accommodate two hundred fifty convicts, were located on the second floor. It became the main prison facility in Georgia until the penitentiary at Reidsville was built in the late 1930s.

The prison farm would draw nationwide attention in 1915 when Leo Frank, an innocent man convicted of murdering a young girl who worked in his factory, was seized by a mob, dragged from the prison, and lynched. In 1924, Georgia would adopt the electric chair, and by the time the prison closed, one hundred sixty-two convicts had been executed. When the facility was being built, The *Union-*

Recorder in Milledgeville reported on March 7, 1911, that the prison was expected to meet the needs of the state for one hundred years. Bill Miner had the dubious privilege of being one of its first inmates.[9]

Shortly after Miner's transfer, he befriended twenty-one-year-old Tom Moore, who was serving a life sentence from Burke County for murder. Moore worked at the prison hospital where, as a trusty, he had been the camp druggist for two years. Moore's association with Miner would soon bring about dire consequences for the younger man.

Tom Moore had been convicted of murdering his brother, John, who was shot to death in his buggy a few miles outside Keysville, Georgia, on the night of January 17, 1907. On January 26, 1907, the *True Citizen* in Waynesboro reported:

> The two brothers A. H. and Tom Moore conducted a mercantile business at Keysville and John was a clerk for them. They have been in financial straits and the payment on insurance policies on the store which was burned last October has been held up pending investigation, this and the fact that John carried $5,000 life insurance in favor of the accused man furnishes probable motive for the crime.

Moore was arrested for the murder on January 24 and was convicted during the April 1907 term of Burke County Court. The trial transcript implies that Moore was convicted largely on public opinion because he had a mean disposition and was feared by his neighbors.[10]

Just after his conviction in March, Bill Miner told a reporter from the *Gainesville News* that he had no desire to get away, and with both a life sentence in Canada and a twenty-year sentence in Georgia hanging over him, he would give up to the inevitable. On October 17, 1911, Robert E. Davidson, chairman of the prison board, was visiting the prison farm at Milledgeville and met with Miner. At the time, Bill was working in the cotton fields and, in wry humor, told Davidson that if he had it to do over again, he would have devoted his life to inventing a machine to pick cotton.[11]

The conversation then shifted to the question of escape. Said Davidson, "Bill, when I allowed you to come here from the Newton County Camp you gave me your word that you would make no attempt to escape. Are you going to stick to the promise?"

"Sure, Mr. Davidson," the wily old bandit replied. "What ever else Old Bill may be, he is not deceitful, and keeps his word. It is easy here and I am going to stay right at this place, as I promised."[12]

At two o'clock the next morning, Bill Miner escaped.

The first news report stated that Old Bill choked night guard Bloodworth, seized the guard's gun, and fled with two other convicts. A second account reported that Miner rapped the guard over the head and made his escape with the two inmates.[13] But it was learned later that the guard had fabricated one or both of these stories to cover up his negligence.

The guardroom at the prison farm had several large peepholes through which the guards could look into the stockade to observe the prisoners. During the early hours of October 18, John B. Watts, a forty-one-year-old convict from Pulaski County who was serving twenty years for murder, peered through one of the peepholes and saw Guard Bloodworth sound asleep at a table. Watts, a small man weighing 128 pounds, was able to squeeze through one of the peepholes, lift the guard's pistol and keys, and unlock the stockade doors.

Watts then awakened Bill Miner and Tom Moore, and the three quickly slipped out the stockade door, went through the kitchen, and scaled the high fence surrounding the building, avoiding the barbed wire on top. As they were creeping from the building, the door slammed, waking the day guard. He investigated and, finding the kitchen door unlocked, sounded the alarm. Guard Bloodworth was sleeping so soundly that he did not wake up until a prisoner poked him in the ribs with a broom handle. For his carelessness, Bloodworth was discharged from his job.[14]

The prison officers immediately released the bloodhounds and easily trailed the convicts until a heavy rain fell, wiping out all tracks and scent. The search was called off and the prison officials promptly informed the Southern Railway Company of the escape. By November 19, more than four thousand identification posters with Bill Miner's photograph and description and a three hundred dollar reward offer for his capture were circulated statewide by the Southern Express Company. The Georgia State Prison Commission offered a minuscule fifty-dollar reward. By the twentieth, no sign of Old Bill or the other convicts had been found, and in desperation the Southern Railway Company engaged the services of the Pinkerton Detective Agency to aid in the search.[15]

If the extreme embarrassment that the railway company and prison commission suffered because of Miner's escape was not enough, the newspapers certainly made it worse. Headlines proclaiming "OLD BILL MINER WAS 'ALL IN,' NOW BILL MINER IS 'ALL OUT,'" "OLD FOX MAKES HIS ESCAPE," "OLD BILL MINER A LIAR AND A DIPLOMAT TO

BOOT," and "HOW DID BILL MINER MAKE HIS ESCAPE?" were bad enough, but the situation was aggravated by a comic twist. Reported the *Union Recorder* under the headline "MINER THANKS STATE OFFICIALS FOR KINDNESS":

> Old Bill Miner, the train robber, who escaped from the state prison at Milledgeville on Tuesday, and who is also wanted by the Canadian authorities, has reminded the state authorities that he is still at liberty. A note from him was received today at the offices of the prison commission thanking them for their kindness. The note read: "My Dear Sir—I write to thank you for your Kindness in puting me at Milegeville My Dear Sir don't trust prisoner don't matter how sick he is or makes out her is. Yours truly, B. Miner"[16]

The *Atlanta Constitution* published essentially the same report under the headline, "DON'T TRUST A PRISONER, WRITES OLD BILL MINER TO COMMISSION."[17]

The newspapers published photographs of the note, which was an obvious fake, intended to embarrass the authorities. The handwriting did not remotely resemble Bill Miner's, and the style was too primitive for the old fugitive.

By October 19 the newspapers began receiving conflicting reports of Bill Miner's whereabouts. A Southern Express agent at Aribi, Georgia, reported that Old Bill had been spotted there. The information had been passed to the agent by a bank cashier who said the aging outlaw entered the bank and tried to borrow a dollar and afterward was seen on a freight train heading for Jacksonville, Florida. On the same day, Miner was reported to have been captured at Jessup, Georgia, after shooting a railroad conductor.

The slippery bandit was next reported in Thomasville by a citizen who identified him through a photograph published in the *Atlanta Constitution*. The citizen, Col. J. Fondren Mitchell, stated that after Bill Miner greeted him with "Howdy," he shook hands with him, believing that the old man was a local farmer. The last report came from a Cordelle, Georgia, resident, Esom Holland. While traveling by buggy from Cordelle to Raines on the twenty-third, Holland claimed that he was stopped by Miner, who asked him politely for a ride.[18] Joked the *Atlanta Constitution:*

WHERE IS "OLD BILL" MINER?

It has become a statewide and humorous quest—the quest for "Old Bill" Miner. Where is the aged but foxy highwayman, the decrepit but agile law breaker who a few weeks ago, sick and puling, took French leave from the prison farm at Milledgeville, and has ever since been reported as among those present from a score of Georgia towns and villages and hamlets?

Who says this is an age of young men? Regard Bill! He is almost a septuagenarian. Yet with the suppleness of a kitten and the guile of a serpent he is somewhere squirming his way through Georgia, enjoying life, we don't doubt it, and quietly laughing in his sleeve at all the excitement he has kicked up. Unless they lasso Bill soon, he will go hurtling through Georgia history as one of its greatest and most facetious mysteries.[19]

Bill Miner's "hurtle through Georgia history" ended abrubtly on the night of November 3. Only then did the full story of his escape and flight come to light. Old Bill related that none of the three prisoners had planned to make an escape that night. When Watts spotted the sleeping guard, he promptly made good use of the opportunity. After stealing the guard's keys and gun, Watts awoke Miner and Moore, informing them that the doors were open, and the three convicts quickly slipped away. Walking a short distance from the prison, Miner and Moore separated from Watts who kept to the road while the other two took to the fields. Bill and his comrades were well prepared for a break, as all three had dressed in civilian clothes which they had managed to secrete in the stockade. Watts's escape was successful, but another fate awaited Miner and his young companion, Tom Moore.

Moore was considered one of the best behaved prisoners at the prison farm. At the time of his escape he was being considered for parole and the authorities were surprised and baffled by his actions. The *Atlanta Constitution* speculated on the reasons why Moore took part in the prison break:

> Moore was in search for some papers that he considered important in his case and was accompanied by Miner. Moore had a case in Augusta against some insurance company who carried the policy on his brother's life and he has had several mistrials with it. It was for this case that he was searching for papers when he and his pal were surprised at St. Clair last night. Moore hoped to reopen the case at some future date.

During Moore's trial, he claimed to have no knowledge of the existence of the insurance policy, which named him as beneficiary and which his mother had taken out on his brother's life. The papers for which he was allegedly searching would supposedly have substantiated this claim.[20] However, it is probable that Moore was bending to Bill Miner's will and control, which many other younger and less-experienced men had done. Whether Moore filled the same role as Bill's many young companions before him can only be speculated upon.

Miner and Moore made their way to the railroad tracks where they hopped a train to Augusta. Here the two fugitives spent the major portion of their freedom hiding out with Moore's friends. Two weeks later they left Augusta and headed for Moore's hometown of Keysville in Burke County. Somehow Moore had injured his knee, and Miner refused to leave him. The fugitives were forced to travel slowly as they headed south.[21]

On November 2, Miner and Moore reached the vicinity of Saint Clair and spent that night in a pasture near town. Before dawn the next morning, Miner trudged into Saint Clair and had breakfast at the home of J. W. Swint. The old bandit offered to pay for the food, but Swint refused. Bill and his host then went to Swint's store, where the fugitive purchased a three-day supply of canned goods and crackers.

As Miner was leaving town, his furtive actions attracted the attention of some of the citizens, who immediately recognized him. By the time he reached Moore, a posse of citizens was hot on his trail. They chased the two fugitives into a swamp, where the trail was lost. The sheriff's office in Waynesboro was notified by telephone, and Deputy Sheriff Samuels organized another posse and left at once for Saint Clair. After searching in vain most of the day, the lawmen returned to Waynesboro.

Meanwhile, Old Bill and his young comrade made their way through the swamp to Keysville, where they persuaded a brakeman with the Georgia and Southern Railroad to allow them to get into an empty boxcar and ride south to Midville. At 9:30 P.M. the freight train arrived at Saint Clair. A local resident, J. W. Whittle, was at the train station and overheard the brakeman ask the fugitives if they were cold. When questioned by Whittle about the occupants in the freight car, the brakeman replied they were just two white bums. Hearing the brakeman's description of the two passengers, Whittle deduced that they were the same men seen in Saint Clair that morning, so he ran to get help from two other citizens, W. H. White and L. J. Smith. Returning to the depot, they grabbed their guns, sent for another citizen, William Salter, and had the conductor hold the train.

Now surrounded, Miner and Moore were ordered to come out of the car. The fugitives made no reply, and the citizens asked the brakeman to see if the two were still in the boxcar. As the brakeman peered into the car, Miner told him, "We will come out." Old Bill clambered down and was ordered, "Get your hands up quick." He promptly raised his left hand but kept his right hand in his pocket, grasping a .32-caliber automatic. "Hands up or be killed," ordered one of the citizens. Bill Miner sensed he had no chance and reluctantly raised his right arm and surrendered.

Tom Moore had different ideas and came to the door of the boxcar with his pistol in his hand. When ordered to put up his hands, he fired into the crowd of men. Salter immediately returned fire. A bullet slammed into Moore's face and he fell back into the boxcar. By the time the men reached him, he was dead.[22]

Bill Miner was searched immediately. Found on his person were two sticks of dynamite, some fuse caps, a candle, a .32-caliber Savage automatic, and two dollars. Miner was held all night in Saint Clair. Early the next morning, Deputy Sheriff Samuels took him into custody and brought him to Waynesboro, where large crowds visited the jail to get a glimpse of the notorious outlaw.[23]

Undaunted by his capture, Old Bill Miner was as cocky as ever. Reported the *Atlanta Constitution:*

> SAYS HE'LL ESCAPE AGAIN
> He thanked Commissioner Graham for some favor done him and when Deputy Sheriff Samuels, who had charge of him, told Miner he had been looking for him all day Friday, Bill replied that he was at home, why didn't he come in. He says he was in the swamps. Miner was in the best of spirits and talked as if nothing had happened. He says he will escape again if the opportunity presents itself.[24]

On November 4, Miner was visited in his cell by a reporter from the *True Citizen*, who seems to have gotten an earful of Bill's yarns:

> He was sound asleep when we arrived, and was called twice before he was roused. He got up at once. He is about 69 years old, tall, clean shaven, and has grey hair cut close. He claims Jackson County, Kentucky as his native home, but says he went to California when quite young. That Miner is an alias, as he did not want to bring disgrace upon his family name.
> Bill says he never robbed a poor man, but has a penchant for holding up express cars, which he says is owned by rich people who can afford it.[25]

Deputy Sheriff Samuels returned Miner to Milledgeville by train on Sunday afternoon, November 5. A large crowd was at the depot to catch a glimpse of the notorious outlaw and escape artist. He was immediately turned over to Warden J. E. Smith and Supt. L. Burke, whisked into a waiting carriage, and returned to the prison farm.[26] Miner's eighteen days of freedom and glory were over. But, if judged by later events, he had captured the hearts of the public, the newspaper reporters, and some of the prison officials.

At the time of Miner's imprisonment, the Georgia prison system had no centralized penitentiary, only the prison camp in Newton County and the farm at Milledgeville. Surprisingly, Old Bill was returned to the insecure facility at Milledgeville. Miner had given the Georgia authorities fair warning that he would escape again if given an opportunity. Evidently the prison-farm officials reasoned that his age was against him and that his warning was no more than an idle boast. Besides, the first escape was a freak accident resulting from the negligence of a sleeping guard. The prison guards, however, did take the precaution of shackling him securely to his cot every night. Feeling that this was sufficient, the prison officials posted no guards at night to check on him.

During the next nine months, Bill became friendly with two other inmates, W. M. Wiggins and W. J. Widencamp from Tattnall County, who had the same idea as Miner—to escape. During this period, Widencamp's wife made several visits to see her husband at the prison farm. On one of her visits she smuggled saws past the guards and turned them over to her husband, along with one thousand three hundred dollars in cash. Widencamp, in turn, furnished Miner and Wiggins with some of the saws. On the night of June 27, 1912, the wily and determined old bandit and his two confederates made their break for freedom.[27]

During the early evening hours, Miner, Wiggins and Widencamp sawed through their shackles and then the window bars. Making a rope from their bedding, they lowered themselves from the second-story window to the ground and quickly made their way to the Oconee River. At eleven o'clock that night, the guards, while making their rounds, discovered the escape and gave the alarm. Search parties were immediately sent out, but it was a vain effort as the fugitives had put too much distance between themselves and their pursuers.[28]

On July 3 a paltry fifty dollar reward was issued by the state prison system. Commented the *Atlanta Constitution:*

The reward offered for him is but $50, and has caused many persons to say that the state authorities are not as anxious to recapture the old man as they were when he made his first escape.

Public sentiment is largely on the side of the aged criminal and the fact that he is more than three-score and ten years of age may result in the search for him being more lax than if he was 40 years younger.[29]

Whatever efforts were being made to recapture Miner were of little consequence to the old man, for at this point he had more immediate problems to deal with. After reaching the Oconee River, the three fugitives had headed south. Traveling by night and hiding during the day, the trio reached the mouth of Camp Creek on the twenty-ninth. Here they stole a boat and started down river that night.

A short distance downriver, their boat hit a snag and capsized. Widencamp drowned and Bill Miner barely escaped with his life, swallowing what seemed to him gallons of the noxious swamp water. After recuperating from the ordeal, Miner and Wiggins took to the dense swamps and soon became lost. For three days and nights they laboriously waded through the inhospitable terrain, living on nothing but blackberries. Surrounded by poisonous swamp water and stinging insects, they became half-crazed with thirst. Briars and brush shredded their clothes and sliced their bodies raw.

In the early morning hours of July 3 the two exhausted fugitives finally stumbled out of the swamp near Toomsboro. During the entire ordeal they had managed to travel only twenty miles. They stopped at the first farmhouse and begged their first solid food in five days. The farmer recognized Bill Miner and, as soon as it was possible, informed the local officers, who quickly arrested the two unresisting fugitives.

The lawmen sent a telegram at once to the prison authorities at Milledgeville, informing them of the capture. They sent an automobile to Toomsboro to pick up Miner and Wiggins. Under heavy guard, the shackled fugitives arrived in Milledgeville at 10:30 A.M. on the same day of their capture. A huge crowd of people had gathered in town to give Old Bill Miner a hero's welcome. The mob brought the automobile to a stop in front of the telegraph office. A hat was passed and a sizable amount of money was collected for Bill, and he was supplied liberally with cigars. As the automobile pulled out for the prison farm, Bill Miner waved his hat to the cheering crowd in appreciation for the honor paid him.[30]

For Old Bill Miner, it was a glorious way to end a half-century career of crime. The cheering crowd had recognized not a legendary bandit and jailbreaker, but a symbol of rebellion against a political and economic system they did not always trust.

In the South during the early years of the twentieth century, the price of the main commodity, cotton, had fallen drastically to less than five cents a pound, forcing small farmers to migrate to the cities to work for corporate factories at low wages. Those farmers who stayed and baled their cotton were charged such high freight rates by the railroad that profit was nonexistent.[31] Public resentment toward these corporations and the railroads was manifest in the welcome given Bill Miner. No outlaw before him ever received such an ovation on his final day of freedom. There is no question that Bill Miner deeply appreciated the tribute and the attention, but it was the old outlaw's last hurrah.

CHAPTER 18

Final Escape

THE sixty-five-year-old bandit finally had run out of steam. It seemed remarkable that he was in such high spirits and good humor after his harrowing ordeal in the swamps. When asked where he and the others were headed after their escape, Bill Miner stated that they were trying to reach Brunswick, Georgia, where they intended to ship out as deck hands on a freighter. When questioned about his intentions to make another escape attempt, Miner showed no signs of his former self. Without boasting or displaying his usual spirit of bravado, he remarked that it would be useless now as there were too many public roads, telephones, and automobiles to be successful. Besides, Bill wearily admitted, he was worn out.[1]

After Miner's return to the Milledgeville prison farm, signs of his former cockiness began to emerge. After adamantly refusing to give his word not to escape again, he was fitted with ankle chains. In his boastful yet captivating style, he said that he still cherished the hope of escaping a third time and making his way to Europe to rob the Paris-to-Constantinople express on the Mediterranean coast.[2]

Bill Miner may have been in high spirits, but his physical condition had deteriorated, and the feeble old bandit was allowed to tend the prison flower garden, where many of the local citizens came to watch him at work. He also finished a highly fabricated and glossed-over thirty-thousand-word autobiography, which he gave to a guard who befriended him.[3]

The rapid decline in his health was largely the result of periodic bouts of gastritis from swallowing the rancid swamp water during his last escape. Despite his failing health, Miner maintained an endearing cheerfulness. His ability to cast his charming spell over all who came in contact with him was demonstrated by an article in the *Atlanta Journal* titled, "A Friend To All," which appeared after his death:

The old Georgia State Prison Farm at Milledgeville, Georgia, site of Bill Miner's two escapes and his death on September 2, 1913. The infirmary where Miner died was on the second floor. The building is now used as a warehouse. Photographed and furnished to Mark Dugan by Roger McLeod, Georgia College Library, Milledgeville, Georgia.

> His boastful claim was that no man whom he came to know could refuse to be friends with him; and he proved this boast at the prison. He was not only a highwayman who robbed coaches and trains in every state of the union and in many foreign countries, but he also was a kindly, lovable old man, whose words were gentle, whose thoughts were humorous, whose manner was that of one who was a friend to all human kind.
> To the prison he was known as "Uncle Billy"—the most courtly, the most kindly-spoken, the most venerable man of the prison; one whom they all regard with affection and something of esteem.[4]

Around the tenth of August 1913, Bill Miner suffered a severe attack of gastritis. He knew that he was dying and agreed to tell Warden J. E. Smith the true story of his life. But even facing death, Old Bill would not or could not allow himself to admit the truth. Almost fifty years of deception and guile were ingrained in the old man, and by this time he quite possibly did not know the truth himself. Perhaps he actually believed his fanciful ramblings.

In essence, he told Warden Smith that his real name was George Anderson and that he was born in California of well-to-do parents. He claimed to have ridden with the Jesse James gang and said that during his career he had stolen more than half a million dollars. He then related his claimed adventures in Europe and Africa.

However, when he stated that he had not robbed individuals, only corporations and that he had never killed anyone during his criminal escapades, he spoke fairly truthfully. Either because of his illness or because he felt the need to be somewhat truthful, he finally admitted that his name was actually Miner. When asked if he had any living relatives, Miner told the warden that he had a sister named W. J. Wilmer living in Bellingham Bay, British Columbia.[5]

Bill Miner may have been trying to tell the truth about his sister but might have been hindered by feebleness of mind because of his illness or age. In fact, his sister Mary Jane Wellman was still living in 1913 and was listed with her husband Louis in the *Bellingham Bay, Washington, Directory* for that year. By 1916 she was listed as the widow of Louis. Her name does not appear after 1916; evidently she either died or moved a year after her husband's death.[6]

Shortly after Miner's acute attack of gastritis, a reporter from the *Atlanta Journal* interviewed him and was highly pleased to get his "true-life story." Despite his ill health, Miner could not resist putting one over on the newspaperman. He reported:

> The full story of his life, told by Bill Miner as death approached, which has just been gained by *The Journal* correspondent, is one that would thrill the most unimaginative and fill page after page of the most adventurous stories ever promised by writers of fiction.

In this account, Miner related that he was born in 1847 in Jackson County, Kentucky, as George Anderson. Here he lived a wild and free life, and, by the time he was fifteen, he was known throughout the length and breadth of the state. The article mentioned only his confinements in San Quentin and his career in Oregon, Canada, and Georgia. The reporter closed his story by saying, "This is the first full story ever published of the famous bandit's life. The record is official and authentic."[7]

This article and another published in the same issue of the *Atlanta Journal*, were essentially recapitulations of Bill's autobiography. That the press and prison officials accepted Miner's statements as fact is astonishing: the discrepancies and contradictions throughout each article were conspicuous.

After Miner made his statements to the warden, he asked that no preacher be allowed to see him as he felt religion should have no place at his deathbed. Soon after this, Old Bill lost consciousness and remained comatose. The prison physicians gave up hope and reported that the end was near. For about two weeks, the unconscious Miner struggled to hold on to life.

Around the twenty-ninth, the old fox reached way down into his bag of tricks and pulled out his last one. He rallied and regained consciousness. His strength seemed to return, and he improved so much that it appeared he would actually recover. Throughout his life, Miner had been able to charm and deceive those around him. It seemed now as if he had outwitted death itself, but finally his powers failed him. On Sunday, August 31, he suffered a relapse and again lost consciousness.[8]

For two days Bill Miner lay semicomatose, his vital signs growing weaker and weaker. The only signs of life were his sometimes-open eyes and shallow breathing. On the evening of September 2, 1913, the night watchman and several prisoners had gathered at his bedside to keep vigil. At 9:25 P.M., without a struggle or a gasp, the Grey Fox's eyes closed for eternity. Defiant to the end, Bill Miner died wearing ankle chains because he refused to give his word not to escape.

For several minutes, those gathered around him thought he had just dozed again. One of the prisoners then leaned over the bed and noticed that Bill's breathing had stopped. The prisoner then leaned farther forward, touched Miner's closed eyes, and then told the others that Old Bill Miner was dead.[9] Although Miner's quiet death was an antithesis to his turbulent life, he was finally a free man.

Miner's body was turned over to Joseph A. Moore, embalmer for the state anatomical board and owner of the local undertaking establishment in Milledgeville. Old Bill lay in state for several days while Moore attempted to obtain instructions for disposition of the body. Because of the erroneous information Bill had given to the warden, Moore was unable to contact Miner's sister. Meanwhile, hundreds of people flocked to gaze at the body of the old outlaw.[10] As a young boy, Louis Andrews, historian and resident of Milledgeville, viewed Miner's body. Vividly remembering the incident, he reflected that

FINAL ESCAPE

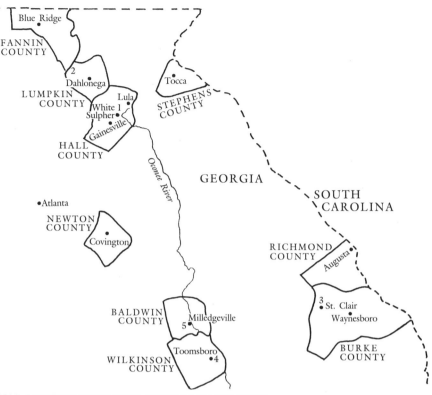

BILL MINER'S CRIMINAL CAREER IN GEORGIA, 1911–13
1. Robbery of the Southern Railway Express, February 18, 1911, Miner, Hunter, and Handford.
2. Capture of Miner, Hunter, and Handford, February 22, 1911.
3. Capture of Miner and killing of Moore, November 2, 1911, after escaping from the Milledgeville prison farm, October 18, 1911.
4. Capture of Miner and Wiggins, July 3, 1912, after escaping from the Milledgeville prison farm, June 27, 1912.
5. Bill Miner dies at the Milledgeville prison farm, September 2, 1913.

Bill Miner had good features and astutely observed that Miner looked more like a con man than a bandit.[11]

Unable to locate Miner's sister, Moore prepared the outlaw's body for burial in the city cemetery in Milledgeville.[12] Even in death Miner seemed to exercise his power of persuasion and charm: several citizens were moved to contribute money and give him a decent burial. It was agreed that Bill Miner should not be buried in the prisoners' plot, so W. W. Miller donated a burial site in Memory Hill Cemetery. Miner's burial suit of clothes was provided by Adolph Joseph, a local clothier, and Joseph Moore donated a casket and paid all funeral expenses.[13]

Meanwhile major newspapers throughout the country picked up the story of Miner's death. Many of them ran lengthy obituaries. The *Inter Ocean* in Chicago published a detailed account of his career and concluded, "For over a half a century his doings have filled columns in public press and the name Bill Miner was known to every officer, crook, trainman and penitentiary warden in the United States and Canada. His doings would seem stranger than fiction, and his bravery would put the blood and thunder dime novel to shame."[14] The romantic eulogy in the *Seattle Post-Intelligencer* explains Miner's popular appeal:

> Miner was a study in criminal psychology. A man of iron nerve and desperate courage, he never took a life in all his wild career, not even when the door of liberty would have opened before him. His course was marked by deeds of spontaneous kindness and a benevolence as reckless as his crimes. A little man, undersized and of slight build, with grizzled grey moustache and steely eyes, his life story reads stranger than fiction. He possessed a splendid self-acquired education; a wonderful faculty for studying human nature, and a tongue, wit, and brain second to none. Although exceedingly wild from the age of sixteen, he never relaxed his attentions to religion and he was as well versed on the Bible as many preachers. Apparently he had a code of morals all his own.[15]

Miner's funeral was held on the afternoon of September 8. Prominent Milledgeville citizens acted as pallbearers. The Reverend H. L. J. Williams of Saint Stephen's Episcopal Church conducted the ceremony. The much-loved old bandit was laid to rest in an unmarked grave and was virtually forgotten for fifty years.[16]

In the early 1960s, James C. Bonner, an eminent Georgia historian and history professor at Georgia College in Milledgeville, became interested in Miner's life. On October 27, 1963, Bonner published a story on Miner titled "Old West's Last Desperado" in the *Atlanta Journal and Constitution Magazine*. He based the story mainly on the statements Miner made to the warden at the Milledgeville prison farm. To his credit, Bonner probably realized that Miner's tales were mainly fictitious as he concluded, "Old Bill has at last found that

Last photograph of Bill Miner, taken at the prison farm at Milledgeville, Georgia, just before his death on September 2, 1913. This photo and articles depicting his life story were published posthumously in the *Atlanta Journal* on September 3, 1913.

Bill Miner's last laugh. Gravestone in Hill Cemetery at Milledgeville, Georgia. The tombstone was erected in late winter of 1964, and in error the year of his death was engraved as 1914 instead of the correct year, 1913. Photographed and furnished to Mark Dugan by Roger McLeod, Georgia College Library, Milledgeville, Georgia.

complete anonymity with which he sought to live his life and ply his craft."

A few weeks prior to the publication of his article, Bonner gave a talk on Bill Miner to the Milledgeville Rotary Club. After the meeting, Robert Rice, who was in the monument business, offered to donate a gravestone for Miner if Bonner would write the epitaph. Just before Christmas 1963, Rice gave Bonner's epitaph to Billy Scales of Elberton, Georgia, who cut and engraved a tombstone approximately two feet by two feet in size.

These proceedings came to the attention of the prisoners in the Georgia State Penitentiary near Reidsville. In an act of solidarity they collected their small change in the amount of thirty-five dollars and forwarded it to Bonner to help pay for the stone. The money was given to the Heart Fund, since the tombstone was donated. In the latter part of February 1964, Rice had the tombstone erected with the help of Joe Moore, who pointed out the exact location of the grave.[17]

The complete anonymity that Miner had sought was gone now, but one cannot help wonder whether Old Bill Miner, bandit and confidence man *extraordinaire*, did not have the last laugh on those who would seek to unearth his life and his legend. The stone reads:

BILL MINER
THE LAST OF THE FAMOUS
WESTERN BANDITS BORN 1843
DIED IN THE MILLEDGEVILLE
STATE PRISON SEPT 2, 1914

Not surprisingly, the date of birth was wrong, because of Bill's countless untruthful yarns. But somehow the year of his death had also been engraved incorrectly as 1914. Though probably the stonecutter's error, it was almost as if the old bandit had reached from his grave to confuse and outwit his pursuers one last time.

EPILOGUE

Folk Hero or Social Bandit?

The Man

"IF his natural mental talents had been trained in the right channel, he would have been a power." Thus wrote the anonymous reporter for the *Gainesville News* two years before Bill Miner's death. These words remain Bill Miner's most fitting epitaph.[1] They also raise intriguing questions. Why were his talents not trained in the right direction? Why did he become a bandit? Was Bill Miner's real power a symbolic one—as a folk hero? How does he fit into the ethos of the western outlaw? Lastly, was he a so-called social bandit?

It is very difficult to say why Bill Miner became a bandit. However, by looking at Miner's background and the circumstances in which he grew to manhood we can find a few clues. He was, of course, a product of his social and family environment. Like many young men who fall into crime, he came of age in a single-parent family. After the age of ten he grew up without a father and the restraining influences that a father might have exercised upon him. As a youth, and later as an adult, he was independent, reckless, and irresponsible, and it seems clear that his widowed mother could not control him. Harriet Miner, like many pioneers before and after her, brought her family west for a new start. There, a whole new set of social factors worked their influence upon Bill Miner. We can only wonder whether he would have become a professional bandit had his mother not brought him to California, but certain facts suggest otherwise.

Of the movement west, C. L. Sonnichsen has written: "The number of those who shed their old selves and started afresh in a new environment ran into the thousands. The West was our national escape hatch."[2] Athough the Miner family came west for a fresh start, many others who trekked westward did not "shed their old selves" and start anew. To the West's various cattle and mining frontiers

EPILOGUE: FOLK HERO OR SOCIAL BANDIT?

flocked reckless wanderers and misfits from all over the world, many motivated by lust for money and adventure. In these wide open, flush gold camps and cattle towns, fortunes might be made at a swing of a pick, the shake of a washpan, or a flip of a card. For the reckless adventurer who did not find his fortune in the West, it was not a huge step to cross the line and become a highway robber or a cattle thief. Society was in flux, and the proliferation of brash young males without the settling influences of women, family, and established community resulted in extremely high crime rates and an extraordinary level of violence.

Historians debate whether the rates of theft and and robbery in frontier communities were high when compared with those of today.[3] But when it comes to crimes of violence—assaults, shootings, cutting scrapes, and homicides—there is substantial evidence that the Old West was far more violent than our modern society. Roger McGrath's exhaustive study shows that the boom camp of Bodie, California, had a homicide rate in the 1870s eleven times greater than our nation's 1990 rate.[4] Other studies confirm these findings. In 1855, California's homicide rate was sixteen times the current national rate.[5] Between 1870 and 1875, San Diego, California, experienced a homicide rate eleven times the current (1990) national rate.[6] The homicide rate of San Francisco in 1850 was almost five times the the modern U.S. rate.[7]

Bill Miner grew to adult manhood amid such violence. In the mining camps and rural regions of California in the 1860s, almost all men carried firearms for protection. Many writers have demonstrated how the manly virtue of defense of one's honor could easily lead to bloodshed over trivial matters.[8] Too, Americans in the frontier era were expected to solve personal and social problems themselves; the government was not expected to curb crime.[9] Thus men were accustomed to acting on their own behalf, with deadly force if necessary.

Guns became part of Bill Miner's life at an early age, and he carried them throughout his years on the frontier and even as an old man. His crimes were always committed in sparsely settled frontier or rural regions, which afforded isolation and protection from pursuers. As George Hendricks has commented in his study of the western badman, "It is small wonder that in company with all this prodigal vice on the Western frontier and with the protection afforded by nature, the outlaw was strongly influenced to do wrong. The habitat of the West presented a powerful incentive to the outlaw to depredate."[10]

Bill Miner clearly resented authority. From the time he deserted from the army in 1863 until his dying days as a prison inmate and escapee, he demonstrated an inability to be restrained by law or convention. He had no affinity for the grinding labor of the hard-rock miner and surely was unhappy with the great social and economic gap between miner and mine owner. He seems to have harbored strong resentment against the rich, from his days as a young laborer at Yankee Jims to his later years, when he boasted that he robbed only corporations.

Thus we are presented with a man who was raised fatherless on the mining frontier; who grew to manhood in an atmosphere where violence was accepted and even exalted; who resented all forms of authority; who resented the the social and financial disparity between mine owner and laborer; and who thoroughly absorbed the rough frontier ethic of quick, easy money and self-redress with the six-gun. Once he had embarked on his career of banditry, he was motivated primarily by greed and secondarily by thirst for adventure. Too, he was motivated by a quest for freedom from the dismal labor of the hard rock miner. It is the ultimate irony of Bill Miner's life, and the quintessential moral of his story, that this thirst for freedom brought him a lifetime behind prison bars.

The Myth

In legend, the westerner becomes an outlaw when he attempts to right some wrong or when he exacts vengeance upon those who have oppressed him. The best examples of this myth are Jesse James, supposedly made an outlaw by Unionists after the Civil War, and Billy the Kid, purportedly outlawed after he sought revenge on those who killed his friends in the Lincoln County War. No such myth surrounds the genesis of Bill Miner's outlaw career. The reasons for his banditry that can be reliably identified have already been set forth.

Legends usually spring up almost immediately after an outlaw's demise. Joaquin Murrieta, California's celebrated "Marauder of the Mines," who was slain in 1853, was the subject of a partly fictional, partly factual biography published only a year after his death. This spawned many imitations and eventually, by 1932, Murrieta was immortalized by Walter Noble Burns as "The Robin Hood of El Dorado," a description about as far from the truth as can be conjured up. As a result, Murrieta became America's most famous Hispanic outlaw, but at the same time the legends manufactured by these writers have made it almost impossible for the historian to separate the real man from the mythical one.

Robert N. Mullin has demonstrated that Billy the Kid was not widely known outside New Mexico during his lifetime.[11] Shortly after his death he was featured in several dime novels, which launched an avalanche of literature, culminating in 1926 when Walter Noble Burns made him internationally famous in his immensely popular and factually inaccurate *Saga of Billy the Kid*. Like Murrieta, Burns portrayed the Kid as a western Robin Hood, a flagrantly false characterization.

A more recent example of outlaw mythmaking is that of Robert LeRoy Parker, better known as Butch Cassidy. Prior to 1969 he was well known mainly to old-timers of the Rocky Mountain region and to western history buffs. But in that year the enormously successful film *Butch Cassidy and the Sundance Kid* catapulted his name into every American household and firmly secured his niche along with Jesse James and Billy the Kid as one of the Old West's three most famous outlaws.

Bill Miner's legend, on the other hand, sprang up during his lifetime, especially toward the end of his career. Unlike those of Jesse James, Billy the Kid, Butch Cassidy, and Joaquin Murrieta, it was largely self-created, the product of his own wild yarns. But there was enough fact behind the legend to make the public believe what he said. His personal magnetism proved particularly attractive. By the early 1900s, Bill Miner was an old man, a curiosity. He carried a gun but harmed no one in Canada or Georgia. His sense of humor, his daring, his prison-breaking skill, and his colorful past captivated the public in two countries. He seemed not a threat to society but instead a good-humored rogue who thumbed his nose at authority and took his punishment with grace, confident that he would never remain long in the clutches of the law.

As any student of Jesse James or Billy the Kid can relate, the gap between their legends and the truth is a wide one. For the fact remains that no matter how valiant, how colorful, or how loyal Jesse James and Billy the Kid were portrayed, history shows them to have been violent, dangerous, remorseless men who deserve recognition but certainly not adulation. This is not entirely true of Bill Miner. For his legend is none too far removed from the fact. He was valiant, he was colorful, he boldly flouted the law, he never killed anyone, and except for his early years of banditry, he robbed only railroads and express companies. No outlaw is deserving of public adulation, but Bill Miner is certainly a better candidate for it than Jesse James or Billy the Kid. In many ways he was like Butch Cassidy and stage robber Black Bart (Charles E. Boles)—a good-natured bandit who avoided killing.

But there was, of course, a dark side to Bill Miner's character which the legend ignores, just as the legends of all western outlaws ignore their protaganists' dark sides. As Joseph G. Rosa has observed in his study of western gunfighters:

> The image of the "good" bad man as a young Robin Hood became well established soon after the close of the Civil War. The old-time novelist often treated the bad man with considerable sympathy and, aware that no one is all good or all bad, found sufficient reason to excuse his faults. Evidence about the actual nature of the Western bad man disproves many of the "kind to animals, women and children" characteristics attributed to him by the eulogizers. A more realistic approach places greater stress on the qualities of greed and arrogance that made the average bad man a taker rather than a giver.[12]

Bill Miner, though kind to women and children, was certainly a taker and not a giver. While his mother suffered in poverty and ill health in Sacramento, he lived the high life in Michigan. While the dupe Charlie Cooper went into Stockton on an errand, Bill and Alkali Jim gave him the slip and made off with Cooper's share of their booty. As an old man, Bill claimed he never robbed a workingman, but he conveniently forgot his early holdups in 1866 and 1871, when he robbed several workingmen, including teamster Porter and stage driver Bill Cuttler. Miner inveigled numerous youths into careers of crime, and may have preyed on some of them sexually. His bisexuality seems to have been prompted by circumstance and convenience, and coupled with his use of opium, it is evident of a hedonistic and opportunistic nature. Although he never killed, Bill was hardly nonviolent. In 1871 he tried to gun down Officer Mitch Bellew in San Jose and attempted to shoot the San Francisco policemen who captured him a few days later; in 1879 he participated in the savage prison beating of Austin Smith; in Colorado, it is thought that Miner shot Sheriff Bronaugh and his posseman, Sam Goodaker, while the victims slept.

Much of Bill Miner's legend he created himself. Yet he did so not out of a sense of posterity—one cannot imagine him giving a fig what historians might think of him. Instead, he seems to have taken great pleasure in spinning yarns for newspapermen and in pulling the wool over their eyes. Too, he may have wished to spare his sisters the pain of his notoriety. Although the "facts" he fed the press were untrue, the general fabric of what he said was accurate: he was a gentlemen bandit, he was kind to children, he did shun killing, he did often succeed in outwitting the law, and, in his later career, he did rob only corporations.

The Social Bandit Concept

In more recent years historians have turned to an analytical model to explain and define the western outlaw. This concept, the social bandit, was developed by British historian Eric Hobsbawm to explain certain movements of peasant brigandage in Europe, India, Asia, and South America from the Middle Ages until modern times. Whether this theory can be adequately transplanted in an American setting is subject to debate.

Hobsbawm writes: "Social banditry, a universal and virtually unchanging phenomenon, is little more than endemic peasant protest against oppression and poverty, a cry for vengeance on the rich and the oppressors, a vague dream of some curb upon them, a righting of individual wrongs."[13] Hobsbawm sees social banditry as a social movement, primarily rural in nature. "The point about social bandits is that they are peasant outlaws whom the lord and state regard as criminals, but who remain within peasant society, and are considered by their people as heroes, as champions, avengers, fighters for justice, perhaps even leaders of liberation, and in any case as men to be admired, helped, and supported."[14]

Hobsbawm defines three types of social bandits: the "noble robber," or Robin Hood; the primitive rebel; and the terrorist avenger. At first blush, Bill Miner would appear to fit perfectly the model of the "noble robber" category of social bandit. He was a popular outlaw, a bandit who never killed, who was kind to women and children, who robbed the rich. The public loved him, and the railroads and express companies despised him. But a closer inspection not only reveals problems in attempting to fit Bill Miner into the social bandit concept, it also reveals problems with the social banditry theory itself when the theory is applied to western outlaws.

Bill Miner did not come from the peasant class. He came from the middle class; his father was a prosperous landholder. The historical West—that safety valve of cheap land rich in natural resources, where a poor man could live free and prosper—is the antithesis of the European peasant society which Hobsbawm sees as having spawned movements of social banditry. It was that very European peasant society which, after all, fired and fueled the great emigration to America. With the exception of the Hispanic experience, there was no peasant class in the Old West. The western movement and social banditry are a contradiction in terms.

The most enduring symbol of the Old West, and its quintessential folk hero, is not the western outlaw, but rather the cowboy. It was this highly mobile hero on horseback who captured the nation's imagination. Thus it is no coincidence that a large number of the western outlaws who have become folk heroes were cowboys, among them Billy the Kid, Clay Allison, Butch Cassidy, Black Jack Ketchum, Bill Doolin, Sam Bass, and John Wesley Hardin. The American cowboy was not Hobsbawm's unarmed, meek peasant who was tied to the land and subjugated by his lord. On the contrary, the typical cowboy was wild, free, and usually well armed—such were the types of men who took these dangerous, thankless, and low-paying jobs.

Bill Miner fits neither the cowboy-outlaw or the social bandit mold. He did work at times as a cowhand and ranch laborer. But he was not a traditional cowboy bandit, for only rarely did he take to the saddle. In California with Alkali Jim, he traveled by foot, train, and buggy. In Colorado with Billy LeRoy, he again moved about by foot and by train, not on horseback. During his later career in Canada and Georgia, he used the same modes of transportation. One cannot help wonder whether Miner may have been more successful in eluding lawmen had he relied more often upon a good horse. Either way, he does not fit the image of the elusive bandit on horseback.

Hobsbawm's vision of the social bandit is twofold. First, the social bandit is perceived by the public to be a rebel or a Robin Hood. Second, the social bandit is in fact a rebel or a Robin Hood. Hobsbawm claims that "in one sense banditry is a rather primitive form of organized social protest."[15] Speaking of the noble robber–Robin Hood image, Hobsbawm describes it in detail—he is the victim of injustice, he rights wrongs, he takes from the rich and gives to the poor, he kills only in self-defense—and declares that "the facts largely confirm the image" and that "genuine Robin Hoods have been known," without providing any proof for such startling conclusions.[16] Hobsbawm further believes that bandits "will almost certainly try to conform to the Robin Hood stereotype in some respects," that is, they do good to gain public sympathy.[17]

However, as many western writers and historians have repeatedly pointed out, the good outlaw of myth never existed in the Old West. Jesse James, the Youngers, the Daltons, Billy the Kid, and their compadres were bad men who wreaked havoc on society. Kent Ladd Steckmesser has said it best: "The outlaw hero, from Robin Hood to Sam Bass, is a thoroughly folkloric product. His concern for the poor, his exemplary character, his cleverness, his 'betrayal' by a traitor are all aspects of legend rather than of history."[18]

No historian has yet identified a movement of social banditry as a cause of American crime. The idea of a broad-based movement of noble robbers and primitive rebels in the Old West seems far fetched at best. America's great social rebels of the nineteenth century were writers, poets, suffragettes, reformers, and labor agitators. To suggest that western bandits fall into this category is most unpersuasive. One needs to search very deeply to find a social or political agenda behind bank, train, or stage robbery.

The causes of violent crime on the frontier, as today, were complex and ranged from the personal to the societal. As Clare V. McKenna has pointed out, "Hobsbawm's ideas are thought-provoking, but he seems to ignore the fact that men turn to crime for a multiplicity of reasons."[19] On the American frontier, social banditry as Hobsbawm defines it appears to have been neither a cause of crime nor a social movement. No evidence has been introduced to show a movement of the rural western poor to engage in a primitive revolt or banditry against the rich or the oppressors. Certainly there were men like Bill Miner who did hate the rich, who did prey upon corporations, and who shrewdly engendered public support by claiming to be noble robbers. And certainly there were many western outlaws who were publicly idolized and aided during their lifetimes and a smaller number who became genuine folk heroes. But a social movement of noble robbers and primitive rebels? No such scenario is reflected in the history of the American West.

Perhaps recognizing the weaknesses of Hobsbawm's social banditry theory, several western historians have defined social bandits only in terms of how the public perceives them. Richard Maxwell Brown describes the western social bandit as "the notable breaker of the law who has, paradoxically, widespread approval among the law-abiding members of society."[20] Writes Robert M. Utley in his recent biography of Billy the Kid, "The test is not whether the social bandit, like Robin Hood or Jesse James, robbed from the rich and gave to the poor, but rather whether people thought he did and thus accorded him the status of a folk hero."[21]

Richard White has defined social bandits in terms that are in some ways similar to Hobsbawm's: "What separates social bandits from ordinary criminals . . . is the existence of large numbers of other people who aid them but who are only technically implicated in their crimes. . . . When such people exist in large enough numbers to make an area a haven for a particular group of outlaws, then social banditry exists."[22] This analysis incorporates much of Hobsbawm's concept of the peasant bandit, who receives succor and support from the peasantry. Says Hobsbawm, "This relation between the ordinary peasant and the rebel, outlaw, and robber is what makes social banditry interesting and significant. It also distinguishes it from . . . mere freebooters ('common robbers')."[23]

However, the fact that certain bandits achieve popularity and receive support does not mean, ipso facto, that there is a social movement afoot. As Anton Blok has pointed out, "In a sense, all bandits are social in so far as they, like all human beings, are linked to other people by various ties."[24] Although Blok referred to Sicilian bandits, his comments on social banditry apply equally to western outlaws: "Given the specific conditions of outlawry, bandits have to rely very strongly on other people. It is important to appreciate that all outlaws and robbers require protection in order to operate as bandits and to survive at all."[25] There are some exceptions to this, of course, mainly lone bandits such as California stage robber Charles E. Boles, alias Black Bart, who posed as a respectable mining man and never revealed to anyone that he was a highwayman. Yet none of the western badmen who have been suggested as social bandits were lone outlaws; all received support and protection in greater or lesser degrees.

The James brothers, Younger brothers, Billy the Kid, Sam Bass, Bill Doolin, the Dalton boys, Joaquin Murrieta, and Tiburcio Vasquez have all been identified by various writers as social bandits.[26] Although the James-Younger band did receive rather extensive actual and moral support in Missouri, the support received by many of the others named above was minor in comparison. Indeed, Billy the Kid and pal Dave Rudabaugh barely escaped a lynch mob at Las Vegas,

New Mexico Territory, in 1880; only the courage of their captor, Pat Garrett, saved their lives. A few months later, still in custody, the Kid was threatened by mobs at Rincon and Las Cruces, New Mexico Territory. Sam Bass was slain by Texas lawmen before he had a chance to receive much public support. He was little known outside Texas during his lifetime and achieved renown only after his death when "The Ballad of Sam Bass" secured his niche in legend. The Dalton boys, whose family had once lived near Coffeyville, Kansas, met their fate in 1892 at the hands of their former neighbors, who seemingly failed to recognize the outlaws' social bandit status. When the Daltons attempted to rob two banks in Coffeyville simultaneously, the peaceable townfolk annihilated the gang in one of America's most dramatic real-life morality plays. When Bill Doolin was captured and brought to the jail at Guthrie, Oklahoma Territory, in 1896, the hero of the hour was not the notorious robber but rather the man who captured him, Bill Tilghman, one of the great lawmen of the Old West. In California, bandit chieftain Tiburcio Vasquez received a great deal of succor from the Hispanic community, but his career was marked by repeated instances of his preying on Hispanics and fellow Hispanic gang members.[27]

White's analysis of social banditry seems to ignore the fact that some bandits are popular for political reasons, such as Jesse James, the Confederates' hero, or for economic reasons, such as Bill Doolin or Billy the Kid, who bought protection by sharing stolen cattle and loot with local ranchers; or for reasons related to their personalities, such as Butch Cassidy and Bill Miner, who were personally popular because of their gentlemanly and good-humored natures. Other bandits captured the westerner's imagination for a more basic reason. Rural life in the Old West was often dull and colorless. The days were usually spent in backbreaking labor, with entertainment rare and newspapers and books scarce. Outlaws and the rumors and stories of their exploits brought color and excitement into otherwise drab lives. It must be emphasized that none of these reasons for the existence of popular bandits is an indication of a social movement.

The popular appeal of the western outlaw is the same whether he is viewed as a social bandit or a folk hero. Indeed, the analyses of White's American social bandit and Steckmesser's western folk hero are almost identical. Says White of the social bandit's appeal: "The portrait of the outlaw as a strong man righting his own wrongs and taking his own revenge had a deep appeal to a society concerned with the place of masculinity and masculine virtues in a newly industrialized and seemingly effete order."[28] Steckmesser, in explaining the appeal of western folk heroes, writes that they "personify traits which Americans have always admired. Courage, self-reliance, and physical prowess have usually been rated high on the scale. These traits may seem anachronistic in a settled and industrialized society. Indeed, much of the heroes' appeal seems to be connected with a sentimental nostalgia for the freedom of a vanished frontier."[29]

The fact remains that no recorded examples of Robin Hoods or primitive bandit-rebels in the Old West have yet come to light. Each western bandit, famous or forgotten, upon close examination reveals himself as a predatory criminal. Some criminals were braver than others, some more colorful, some more daring, some more gentlemanly, some more elusive, some more successful. Nonetheless, they were all what Hobsbawm calls "common robbers," only some were less common than others. And simply because some of them became popular with the public does not transform them into social bandits, noble robbers, or primitive rebels. The social bandits seen by Hobsbawm, White, and other writers are merely folk heroes in analytical garb.

Thus the western social bandit, stripped of his analytical cloak, turns out to be a simple folk hero. Perhaps there were true social bandits in Europe or Asia or South America, but in the Old West there were no Robin Hoods, no primitive rebels—only folk heroes. Hobsbawm's social bandit concept carries with it connotations of goodness, selflessness, and political rebelliousness, which are wholly out of place in defining the likes of a Jesse James, a Billy the Kid, or a Bill Miner. Thus the term "social bandit" is a confusing and misleading one when applied to western outlaws and perhaps should be replaced with a more fitting term, such as "folk bandit" or "popular bandit." For that is all the western social bandit was: a popular bandit, a folk hero. This concept—that of the popular bandit—does indeed fit Bill Miner, just as it fits Jesse James, Butch Cassidy, Billy the Kid, and Sam Bass.

The popular bandit–heroic outlaw is a mythic image which exists far beyond the borders of the American West. Joseph Campbell has demonstrated how myths are remarkably similar from culture to culture and consist of universal themes. Of the mythic hero, whom he calls, "the hero with a thousand faces," Campbell concludes that "there is a certain typical hero sequence of actions which can be detected in stories from all over the world and from many periods of history."[30] Likewise, Steckmesser has traced the similarities between the Robin Hood legend and the myth of the good outlaw of the West: "The similarities between Robin Hood and the American outlaws are clearly owing to the uniformity of folk belief across the centuries."[31] Too, Hobsbawm's studies have found mythic Robin Hood characters in different cultures throughout the world.

It seems clear that modern man has a basic need for the outlaw hero. Humans by nature yearn to be free, and modern man has an innate, albeit often subconscious, skepticism of government, laws, and those controls that would bind him. The man who rebels against these controls symbolizes and acts out this subconscious distrust. Thus the outlaw as social rebel remains one of mankind's most compelling and enduring symbols.

Chronology

1810: Joseph Miner (father) born in New London, Connecticut.
1816: Harriet Jane Miner (mother) born in New York.
Mid-1830s: Joseph and Harriet Miner married.
1834: Harriet R. Miner (sister) born in Connecticut.
1836: Miners moved to Vevay Township, Ingham County, Michigan.
November 21, 1840: Henry C. Miner (brother) born.
May 17, 1843: Mary Jane Miner (sister) born.
December 27, 1846: Ezra Allan (Bill) Miner born.
1852: Miners move to Clinton, Michigan.
April 1, 1853: Joseph Benjamin Miner (brother) born.
November 1, 1856: Joseph Miner dies of brain disease.
1859–1860: Miner land sold and all of Miner family, except Henry, move to Yankee Jims, Placer County, California.
June 25, 1863: William Miner and James Keller steal twenty-two head of horses in Los Angeles County. They were caught on July 31, and Miner and Keller were indicted for grand larceny on September 18. Miner was released on one thousand dollars bail the same day. On December 5, Keller's case was dismissed and apparently so was Miner's.
April 26, 1864: Bill Miner joins Union army in Sacramento.
July 22, 1864: Bill Miner deserts at Camp Union, California.
August 5, 1864: Henry C. Miner dies of chronic dysentery at De Valls Bluff, Arkansas while in Union army.
Early December 1865: Miner commits first proven crime, robs employer of three hundred dollars but is let off because of his youth.
December 28, 1865: Miner steals horse from livery stable at Newcastle. Robs merchant at Auburn of ninety dollars' worth of clothing and a gold watch.
January 4, 1866: Miner steals horse from livery stable in Forest Hill.
January 19, 1866: Miner and John Sinclair hire two horses in San Francisco and Miner trades them near Georgetown.

January 22, 1866: Miner and Sinclair rob a man named Porter of eighty dollars in San Joaquin County.
January 23, 1866: Miner and Sinclair captured at Woodbridge.
February 22, 1866: Miner and Sinclair caught trying to escape from jail in Stockton.
April 3, 1866: Miner convicted in San Joaquin County of Porter robbery and sentenced to three years at San Quentin. Sinclair also sentenced to three years.
April 5, 1866: Miner enters San Quentin as convict No. 3248.
June 9, 1866: Miner released from prison to stand trial in Placer County for theft of the two horses.
June 29, 1866: Miner convicted, two years added to his term.
July 3, 1866: Miner is returned to San Quentin as No. 3313.
July 12, 1870: Miner released from San Quentin.
Early January 1871: Miner and Alkali Jim Harrington burglarize homes in San Jose.
January 17, 1871: Miner and Harrington likely robbed stage at Angels Camp.
January 23, 1871: Miner, Harrington, and Charlie Cooper rob stage of twenty-six hundred dollars near San Andreas, Calaveras County.
January 27, 1871: Miner and Harrington in shootout with officer in San Jose; both escape.
February 5, 1871: Miner arrested in San Francisco shortly after arrest of Harrington and Cooper.
March 5, 1871: Miner and Harrington attempt to escape jail in Calaveras County.
June 22, 1871: Miner and Harrington convicted and sentenced in Calaveras County to ten years at San Quentin. Cooper turns states' evidence.
June 28, 1871: Miner enters San Quentin for third term as No. 4902.
March 21, 1872: Miner and Harrington given new trial in Calaveras County. Each receives thirteen-year term.
March 30, 1872: Miner returned to San Quentin for fourth term as No. 5206.
June 15, 1872: Miner's remaining brother, nineteen-year-old Ben Miner, commits suicide in Truckee, California.
May 7, 1874: Miner attempts escape at San Quentin, sentenced to nine days in the dungeon, twenty lashes, and loss of all credit time.
August 13, 1879: Miner sentenced to twelve lashes for beating another prisoner.

July 14, 1880: Miner released from San Quentin.

Mid-September 1880: In Colorado, Miner teams up with Billy LeRoy.

September 23, 1880: Miner and LeRoy rob Sanderson stage of fifty dollars near Ohio City.

October 7, 1880: Miner and LeRoy rob Sanderson stage of one hundred dollars at Slumgullion Pass.

October 14, 1880: Miner and LeRoy rob Sanderson stage of four thousand dollars between Alamosa and Del Norte. Miner and LeRoy split up at Pueblo; Miner heads for his hometown of Onondaga, Michigan, where he poses as a rich mining man from California and becomes engaged to the daughter of one of the leading citizens.

January 1881: Running out of funds, Miner leaves Onondaga on pretense that his mother is ill. Leaves for Colorado with Stanton T. Jones.

February 3, 1881: Miner, Jones, and stage employee Charles Dingman rob Sanderson stage of only ten dollars near Del Norte. Dingman caught and convicted.

April 18, 1881: Miner, Jones, and James East steal three horses near Saguache.

April 23, 1881: Miner and confederates likely rifle mail pouches on the stage from Uncompahgre to Barnum.

April 27, 1881: Miner and confederates steal saddle from Sam Goodaker in Saguache County and are trailed and captured on the twenty-eighth. Miner and Jones manage to escape after wounding Goodaker and Sheriff W. A. Bronaugh; they likely hid out at the mines in Leadville owned by Miner's sister and brother-in-law. They later made their way to Tuolumne County, California.

November 7, 1881: Miner, Jones, Bill Miller, and James Crum rob the Sonora-Milton stage of three thousand seven hundred dollars near Sonora.

December 3–4, 1881: Crum, Miller and Miner captured near Sacramento. Jones flees California and is never caught.

December 19, 1881: All three bandits convicted in Tuolumne County. Miner receives twenty-five years at San Quentin.

December 21, 1881: Miner enters San Quentin for fifth term as No. 10191.

April 17, 1884: Miner attempts lone escape but is immediately apprehended. Sentenced to one day in the dungeon and loss of all credit time.

September 23, 1886: Miner leads a prison mutiny and loses all credit time previously earned.

April 5, 1887: Miner helps put out fire in the prison's door-and-sash factory but does not regain lost credits.

May 19, 1889: Miner's throat is slashed by another convict, Bill Hicks, but the wound is not serious.

November 29, 1892: Miner and Joseph Marshall attempt to escape. Marshall is shot and killed; Miner is wounded in the face.

February 1901: Miner's mother dies.

June 17, 1901: Miner released from prison after serving almost twenty years. Leaves California for Samish Flats, Washington, where he works as superintendent of an oyster bed for approximately two years.

September 19, 1903: Miner, ex-prison chum Gay Harshman, and seventeen-year-old Charles Hoehn attempt but fail to rob the Oregon Railway and Navigation Express train near Clarnie, Oregon.

September 23, 1903: Miner and associates again attempt but fail to rob express train near Portland. In the fracas, Harshman is shot in the head and Miner and Hoehn escape. Miner returns to his job on the oyster beds until he hears of Harshman's confession and Hoehn's arrest on October 7.

October 9, 1903: Miner escapes to Canada with help of ex-prison mate and smuggler Jake Terry; settles in Princeton, British Columbia, where he is well liked and respected; joins Terry in smuggling operations along border.

October 27, 1903: Pinkerton Detective Agency issues reward for Bill Miner; poster notes that Miner is bisexual.

September 10, 1904: Miner, Terry, and Shorty Dunn rob a Canadian Pacific train at Mission Junction. The first train robbery in Canada, it is planned by Terry, formerly a railroad engineer. The take is seven thousand dollars in money and gold plus three hundred thousand dollars in bonds and securities.

October 2, 1905: Miner and Terry rob a Great Northern train of thirty six thousand dollars near Seattle, Washington. Spoils probably hidden in nearby woods.

May 9, 1906: Miner, Dunn, and Louis Colquhoun hold up a Canadian Pacific train at Ducks. The take is only $15.50.

May 14, 1906: Miner and associates captured near Douglas Lake. Dunn wounded in leg.

June 1, 1906: All three bandits tried and convicted at Kamloops. Miner sentenced to life imprisonment.

June 2, 1906: Miner, Dunn, and Colquhoun delivered to penitentiary at New Westminster, near Vancouver.

August 8, 1907: Terry is dead. Miner is allowed to escape as part of a deal with prison authorities and the Canadian Pacific Railway for the return of three hundred thousand dollars in securities. Miner picks up the buried loot near Seattle and goes to Denver, Colorado; there he lives a fashionable life until his money runs out (in 1910).

Spring 1910: Miner goes to Michigan, meets Charlie Hunter. The two make their way south, working in coal mines and sawmills. In October at a sawmill in Virginia, they meet Jim Handford and plan a train robbery.

February 18, 1911: Miner, Hunter, and Handford rob a Southern Railway train at White Sulphur Springs, Georgia. The take is a little over two thousand two hundred dollars.

February 22, 1911: All three bandits captured in northern Georgia.

March 3, 1911: All three bandits convicted; Miner sentenced to twenty years' imprisonment. He is sixty-four years old.

March 15, 1911: Miner delivered to Newton County Convict Camp to work on road gang.

July 8, 1911: Pleading ill health, Miner is transferred to Milledgeville prison farm for lighter duties.

October 18, 1911: Miner, John Watts, and Tom Moore escape from prison farm. Miner and Moore remain together and make their way to Augusta, where they hide out for two weeks before heading toward Keysville.

November 3, 1911: Miner captured and Moore killed in a shootout at Saint Clair. Miner is returned to Milledgeville on November 5.

June 27, 1912: Miner makes his second escape, with W. M. Wiggins and W. J. Widencamp. They head down the Oconee River in a stolen boat that capsizes. Widencamp drowns. Miner nearly drowns, swallowing large amounts of rancid, poisonous swamp water. Wiggins and Miner remain lost.

July 3, 1912: The two fugitives find their way out of the swamp at Toomsboro, only twenty miles from the prison, and are recaptured immediately. As Miner is being returned to Milledgeville, his automobile is stopped by a large crowd of people who cheer and give him money and cigars.

August 10, 1913: As a result of ingesting rancid water, Miner suffers gastritis. During a severe attack, he becomes comatose. On August

29 he regains consciousness and becomes stronger. On August 31 he again loses consciousness.

September 2, 1913: Bill Miner dies at age sixty-six; he is the only prisoner for whom all funeral expenses were paid by the citizens of Milledgeville.

February 1964: James C. Bonner, Georgia historian, has tombstone erected on Bill Miner's grave.

Appendix
Synopsis and Photographs from the Motion Picture
*The Grey Fox**

**Courtesy Mercury Pictures, Inc.
Vancouver, British Columbia, Canada**

*(All rights in and to the picture and the title
The Grey Fox are owned by Grey Fox Pictures, Inc.)

The Grey Fox: A Commentary

THE *Grey Fox* is a film about a train robber and his exploits. In this day and age, we expect a film of this type to be action packed, full of violent and bloody scenes. The moviegoer is in for a surprise and a pleasant one at that. Not only is violence absent, but the four-letter expletives that pepper modern films are also nonexistent. This film subtly blends history and fiction in a manner that leaves the historical value of the film intact. And who knows whether some of the fiction could not have been fact, as some of Bill Miner's life is obscure.

Beyond the tasteful presentation of this film and the completely breathtaking shots of the scenery in the Pacific Northwest and British Columbia, the most important point of *The Grey Fox* is the characterization of Miner himself. Richard Farnsworth's portrayal of the wily old bandit is perfect. Farnsworth *is* Bill Miner. The ability of Director-Coproducer Phillip Borsos to give to the public a true and accurate picture of Miner gives this film a notable quality. The audience is captivated by Miner and feels his ability to influence others. By the end of the film, the viewer is wishing him well, as did the people in Canada and in Georgia.

The enchantment begins in the very first scene of the film, in which Miner has been released from San Quentin in 1901 and is traveling by railroad to his sister's home in Washington state. Miner and a traveling salesman are discussing the industrial progress of the country, which Miner has not been a part of for almost twenty years. The salesman asks Miner what line of work he is in, and Miner replies that he is between jobs at present. The salesman then asks him what his profession is and Miner matter-of-factly, with just a touch of pride in his voice, answers, "I rob stagecoaches."

This film is a classic and has been selected as one of the ten best films ever produced in Canada. Although the authors are not professional film critics, we can truthfully say that everyone who is fortunate enough to see *The Grey Fox* will be captivated by this charming film.

We thank Mercury Pictures, Inc., Vancouver, B.C., Canada, for allowing us to include the film poster and synopsis of *The Grey Fox* in these pages.

The Grey Fox Synopsis

On June 17, 1901, after 33 years in San Quentin Prison, Bill Miner was released into the Twentieth Century.

Poster advertising the movie *The Grey Fox*. Courtesy of Mercury Pictures, Inc., Vancouver, B.C., Canada.

The Grey Fox is based on the history and folklore of Bill Miner. He was a gentleman, worldly-wise, dignified, and courageous; he was also of the great bandits of his time and is still a legend in the Pacific Northwest.

After an exciting life as a highwayman and robber of stagecoaches in the southwestern United States, Miner was captured tried and convicted. After spending half a lifetime in prison, he was released at the age of 60. At the time of a subsequent arrest, a newspaper account noted: "He claims to be 60, looks like a man of 50, and moves like one of 30."

The Grey Fox tells the story of Miner's life, from the time of his release to that final arrest.

After leaving San Quentin, Bill Miner made his way to Washington state, to his sister Jenny and her husband's homestead, where he tried to settle into a "normal" family life. He got a job picking oysters but it was no kind of life for a man of Miner's independent and adventurous nature and it didn't last long. Despite Jenny's pleas, Miner left to make his own way, a nineteenth century man alone in a twentieth century world.

Miner soon discovered that there were no stagecoaches left to rob, but one evening he attended a screening of the 1903 classic *The Great Train Robbery,* and a new career was born. Unfortunately, Miner quickly discovered that robbing stagecoaches and trains were very different occupations. His first train robbery was a messy bungle, forcing his gang to escape and separate in the woods, leaving Miner on his own again.

Miner managed to elude the law all the way into Canada, where he changed his name to George Edwards and took a job at a barrel factory on the Pacific Coast of British Columbia. He predictably became restless at the job but he did make the acquantaince of one Shorty Dunn, a naive, nervous, but gutsy and loyal man, who became the Grey Fox's new accomplice.

On one September evening in 1904 Miner and Shorty made their move. The Canadian Pacific Railway Transcontinental Express No. 56 was stopped near Mission, British Columbia and held up by three men who escaped with over $7,000 in gold dust and currency. It was the first train robbery in Canada and Bill Miner's entry into Canadian folklore.

With the law at their heels, including members of the British Columbia Provincial Police, Pinkerton agents from the U.S., and a special detachment of the Northwest Mounted Police, Miner and Shorty fled to the city of Kamloops, B.C. where Miner's old friend, Jack Budd, himself not above a scheme of two, agreed to hide them in his hotel in exchange for a little labour at his newly acquired gold mine—won in a game of cards.

Miner and Shorty quickly settled into Kamloops and found a third partner in Louis Colquhoun. Miner's softspoken, easy charm quickly won him the respect of the town, and most importantly of the local police sergeant, Constable Fernie, who saw Miner as a man of civility, culture and humour.

A quiet and seemingly safe, temporary haven from the law wasn't the only thing Miner found in Kamloops. There he met his match in the fiery Kate Flynn, a photographer "recording injustice with a camera" who fled the social constrictions of turn of the century Chicago to seek an independent life in the West. Their attraction was immediate and mutual and soon Miner began to have regrets about the temporary nature of his stay in Kamloops.

The messy business Miner left behind him in Washington was catching up with him. Detective Seavey, a special Pinkerton Agent, was sent to British Columbia to track down Miner and when he arrived in Kamloops at the local office of the Northwest Mounted Police, he demanded their full cooperation in the search for Miner. Detective Seavey's precise description of Miner alerted the N.W.M.P. to the possibility that the courly newcomer to Kamloops, George Edwards, was the man Seavey wanted.

Although ambitious, the now Constable Fernie didn't want to be the one to arrest Miner, so he tried to warn Miner through Kate. Kate didn't have to tell Miner, he knew that the law was close at hand; after making plans with Kate to meet in Chicago, he, Shorty and Louis left Kamloops.

Now on the run from the law, Miner and his colleagues tried another robbery outside Kamloops. This time they weren't so lucky, making off with only $15 and a bottle of liver pills. They headed east, posing as prospectors, trying to stay ahead of the Mounties, but they were outnumbered, and were soon surrounded and apprehended.

The Mounties and Detective Seavey of Pinkerton's were triumphant, but the scene outside the police station in Kamloops was not a joyous one the day of their arrest. For Bill Miner had already become a legend in the area and people admired, rather than feared, the courtly gentleman train robber.

Notes

INTRODUCTION

1. *Atlanta Journal,* September 3, 1913. The photograph of Bill Miner was eight and one-half inches wide, which, according to newspaper configurations, is equal to four columns.

CHAPTER 1

1. Frank W. Anderson, *Bill Miner . . . Stagecoach and Train Robber,* 13. Colin Rickards, "Bill Miner: 50 Years a Hold-up Man," *The English Westerners Brand Book* 8, no. 2 (January 1966): 9. James C. Bonner, "Old West's Last Desperado," *Atlanta Journal and Constitution Magazine,* October 27, 1963. Ed Kirby, "Bill Miner—The Grey Fox," *Quarterly of the National Association and Center for Outlaw And Lawman History* 10, no. 1 (Summer 1985): 3, 4. Various prison records that show the discrepancies regarding Miner's birthplace will be reported in notes in later chapters.
2. John Boessenecker, *Badge and Buckshot,* 159.
3. 1850 Ingham County, Michigan, Census, 45.
4. *Ingham County Pioneer Families* 1:149, 4:229. *Bellingham Herald,* October 12, 1903. Bill Miner's sister, Mary Jane Wellman, was living in Whatcom, Washington, at this time and gave his name as A. E. or Allen Miner.
5. 1850 Ingham County, Michigan, Census, 45. Harriet R. Miner, age sixteen, is listed as living in the Joseph Miner household. Samuel W. Durant, *History of Ingham and Eaton Counties, Michigan,* 305. *Ingham County Pioneer Families* 1:149. Joseph Miner's brothers and sisters were Orrin (b. 1800), Lyman (b. 1817), Ezra A. (b. 1821), William (b. 1826), James, Betsy Mack, Hannah, Emily, and Mary Jane. The marriage of Joseph and Harriet Miner is not recorded in Arnold Records of Births, Marriages, and Deaths in the City Clerk's Office in New London, Connecticut, or in the Town Hall in Groton, Connecticut.
6. Lenawee County, Michigan, Probate File No. 1472 D-225, *Estate of Henry C. Miner, Mary J. Miner, Ezra A. Miner, and Joseph B. Miner, minors.*
7. Durant, 305. *Early Land Transfers, Ingham County, Michigan, 1835–1853* 1:124; 2:8, 154; 3:15.
8. *Early Land Transfers, Ingham County, Michigan, 1835–1853,* 3:125, 132. 1850 Ingham County, Michigan, Census, 40, 96. 1850 Livingston County, Michigan, Census, 944. Lenawee County Probate File No. 1472 D-225. The probate records show that the Miners owned village lots 9 and 12 in block 10 according to Brown's Plat of the Village of Clinton.

9. Lenawee County Probate File No. 1472 D-225. War of the Rebellion, Dependent Pension Claim No. 219247 of Harriet J. Miner for the death of her son Henry C. Miner.

10. Genevieve S. Reilly, ed., *The Clinton Story, 1825–1958*, pp. 3, 6, and 11; *The Clinton High School Re-Union, Quarter Centennial Anniversary, 1860–1885*, 26.

11. War of the Rebellion, Dependent Pension Claim No. 219247.

12. Lenawee County Probate File No. 1472 D-225.

13. War of the Rebellion, Dependent Pension Claim No. 219247. 1860 Placer County, California Census, 235. Pardon File No. 1687, William Allen Miner. In the file is a letter dated September 29, 1867, from C. A. Tweed of Auburn, California, a personal friend of the Miners, to Governor F. F. Low in Sacramento supporting a pardon for Bill Miner. In this letter, Tweed stated that "Mrs. Miner is an old resident of Yankee Jims having lived there about eight years. . . . she is a widow, is poor."

14. *History of Placer County, California, with Illustrations and Biographical Sketches of Its Prominent Men and Pioneers*, 399, 400.

15. Rickards, 8, no. 2:9, 12. Letter from Doris Parker-Coons, County of Placer Historical Museum, Auburn, California, to author Mark Dugan, July 26, 1984.

16. *Record of Service of Michigan Volunteers in the Civil War 1861–1865*, 109. 1850, Livingston County, Michigan, Census, 944. Frank Miner apparently was the son of Ezra A. Miner, brother of Joseph Miner. Although Frank Miner claimed he was nineteen when he enlisted, the census shows he would have been fifteen in 1864. Muster Roll and Returns, Company I, 12th Regiment Michigan Infantry, Henry C. Miner. War of the Rebellion, Dependent Pension Claim No. 219247. Harriet Miner applied for the pension in December 1874 and it was granted September 15, 1879.

17. War of the Rebellion, Dependent Pension Claim No. 219247.

18. *Muster Roll and Descriptive List, Company L, 2nd Regiment of California Cavalry Volunteers*, April 26, 1864. Brig. Gen. Richard H. Orton, ed. and comp., *Records of California Men in the War of the Rebellion, 1861–1867*, 171, 182. Muster Roll and Returns, Company L, 2nd Regiment California Cavalry, William A. Miner.

CHAPTER 2

1. Pardon File No. 1687, William Allen Miner.

2. Erwin G. Gudde, *California Gold Camps*, 378.

3. Ralph Mann, *After the Gold Rush: Society in Grass Valley and Nevada City, California, 1849–1870*, 3, 139–42, 148.

4. *Dahlonega Nugget*, March 3, 1911. *Gainesville News*, March 1, 1911.

5. Anderson, 13, 14. Rickards, 8, No. 2: 9. Bonner, "Old West's Last Desperado." Kirby, 4.

6. File Nos. 637 and 638, Los Angeles County Court of Sessions Case Nos. 308, 310, James Keller, and 309, 311, William Miner, Indictments for Grand Larceny. Register of Actions, Book No. 1, Case Nos. 1–332, Court of Sessions Case No. 311. *Daily Alta California*, August 7, 1863. *Los Angeles Star*, December 12, 1863.

7. *Stockton Daily Evening Herald*, March 12, 1866.

8. *Placer Herald*, December 30, 1865. *Auburn Stars and Stripes*, January 3, 1866.

NOTES

Stockton Daily Evening Herald, March 12, 1866, February 7, 1971. *People of the State of California vs. A. Miner,* Placer County Circuit Court Case No. 594, Grand Larceny.

9. *People of the State of California vs. A. Miner,* Placer County Circuit Court Case Nos. 592 and 594, Grand Larceny. San Quentin Prison Register, Convict No. 3249, John Sainclair [*sic*], F3653–5 (VB1113). *Stockton Daily Evening Herald,* March 12, 1866, February 7, 1871. *Stockton Daily Independent,* January 24, 1866. Pardon File No. 1687, William Allen Miner.

10. *Stockton Daily Evening Herald,* March 12, 1866, February 7, 1871. *Stockton Daily Independent,* January 24, 25, 1866.

11. *Stockton Daily Independent,* January 25, 1866. *Stockton Daily Evening Herald,* January 31, 1866.

12. *Stockton Daily Evening Herald,* February 22, 1866. *Stockton Daily Independent,* February 23, 1866.

13. *Stockton Daily Evening Herald,* March 10, 12, 24, April 2, 1866. *Stockton Daily Independent,* January 25, 1866. Pardon File No. 1913, John Sinclair.

14. *Stockton Daily Evening Herald,* March 10, 12, 21, April 3, 1866. *Stockton Daily Independent,* April 4, 1866. People of the State of California vs. A. Miner.

15. Pardon File No. 4772, William A. Miner.

16. *Stockton Daily Independent,* April 4, 1866. San Quentin Prison Register, Convict No. 3248, William A. Miner, F3653–5 (VB1113).

17. San Quentin Prison Register, Convict No. 3249, John Sainclair [*sic*], Convict No. 4038, William St.Clair [*sic*], F3653–5 (VB1113), Convict No. 6683, John St.Clair [*sic*], F3653–6. As William St.Clair he entered San Quentin for the second time on February 9, 1869, for burglary in San Francisco and was discharged November 6, 1871. He began his third term as John St.Clair on September 20, 1875, for grand larceny in San Francisco and was released April 13, 1878.

18. John Boessenecker, "Buckshot for Bill Miner," *True West* (August 1988): 20–24.

19. *Placer Herald,* February 6, 1858.

20. Anderson, pp. 14, 15. Martin Robbin, *The Bad and the Lonely,* p. 190.

21. *Alameda County Gazette* (San Leandro), July 31, 1869.

22. Kenneth Lamott, *Chronicles of San Quentin,* 116–17, 120–22. Lawrence M. Friedman and Robert V. Percival, *The Roots of Justice: Crime and Punishment in Alameda County, California 1870–1910,* 295.

23. Gresham M. Sykes, "The Pains of Imprisonment," in David M. Peterson and Charles W. Thomas, eds. *Corrections: Problems and Prospects,* 58.

24. John Gagnon and William Simon, "The Social Meaning of Prison Homosexuality," in Peterson and Thomas, *Corrections: Problems and Prospects,* 104.

25. Pinkerton National Detective Agency reward poster for the arrest of Bill Miner for the train robbery of September 23, 1903. Copy furnished to author by Robert Olson of Pico Rivera, California, who is in possession of original poster.

26. *Placer Herald,* June 9, 16, 30, 1866. San Quentin Prison Register, Convict No. 3248, William A. Miner, Convict No. 3313, William A. Miner, F3653–5 (VB1113).

27. San Quentin Prison Register, Convict No. 3313, William A. Miner, F3653–5 (VB1113). Pardon File No. 1687, William Allen Miner.

CHAPTER 3

1. San Quentin Prison Register, Convict No. 2735, William Waverly; Convict No. 3224, James W. Clark; Convict No. 4122, William Harrington, F3653–6 (VB113). *Stockton Daily Evening Herald,* February 6, 1871. James B. Hume and Jno. N. Thacker, *Wells Fargo & Co's. Robbers Record,* 35.
2. *San Jose Daily Patriot,* January 27, 1871.
3. *Calaveras Chronicle* (Mokelumne Hill), January 21, 1871.
4. *Stockton Daily Evening Herald,* February 6, 1871. (b) *The San Francisco Call,* February 5, 1871.
5. Hume and Thacker, 86. San Quentin Prison Register, Convict No. 4301, George Robertson, F3653–6 (VB113). *Calaveras Chronicle,* February 11, 1871. Edward Byram. San Francisco Police Record Book No. 3, 56.
6. *Stockton Daily Evening Herald,* February 6, 1871. *San Francisco Call,* February 5, 1871. *San Francisco Bulletin,* February 11, 1871.
7. *Stockton Daily Evening Herald,* January 23, February 6, 1871. *Stockton Daily Independent,* January 24, 1871. *Calaveras Chronicle,* January 28, 1871. *San Francisco Call,* February 5, 1871.
8. William A. Pinkerton, *Train Robberies and Train Robbers,* 48.
9. *Stockton Daily Evening Herald,* February 6, 1871. *Stockton Daily Independent,* February 7, 1871. *San Francisco Call,* February 5, 1871. *San Francisco Bulletin,* February 11, 1871.
10. *San Jose Daily Patriot,* January 27, 1871. *San Jose Daily Independent,* January 28, 1871. *San Francisco Call,* February 5, 1871.
11. *Stockton Daily Evening Herald,* February 6, 1871. *Stockton Daily Independent,* February 7, 1871. *San Francisco Call,* February 5, 1871. *San Jose Daily Patriot,* February 1, 1871. *Redwood City Gazette,* February 3, 1871.
12. *Stockton Daily Evening Herald,* February 6, 1871. *San Francisco Call,* February 5, 1871. Edward Byram. San Francisco Police Record Book No. 3, 56.
13. *San Francisco Call,* February 7, 1871.
14. *Stockton Daily Evening Herald,* February 7, 1871. *Stockton Daily Independent,* February 7, 1871. *Calaveras Chronicle,* February 11, 1871. *San Francisco Bulletin,* February 11, 1871.
15. *Calaveras Chronicle,* February 26, 1871.
16. Ibid., March 11, 1871.
17. Pardon File No. 3565, William A. Miner: Letter from Attorney Wesley K. Boucher, Mokulumne Hill, California, to Governor William Irwin, Sacramento, California, October 8, 1878.
18. *People vs William Miner and James Harrington,* Calaveras County Criminal Docket Book No. 1, 29; Cooper's name does not appear on the docket. San Francisco Police Record Book No. 3, 56.
19. Hume and Thacker, 78, 86. San Quentin Prison Register, Convict No. 6430, Charles Williamson; Convict No. 10051, Charles Cooper, F3653–6 (VB113). On January 15, 1875, Cooper and Sol ("Ned") Allen robbed a stage from Lone Pine to Bakersfield in Kern County. They were captured immediately, and Cooper received a taste of his own medicine when Allen turned state's evidence against him and was released. Tried in Kern County, Cooper was sentenced to ten years' imprisonment and began his second term at San Quentin March 13, 1875, as convict

NOTES 229

No. 6430. Less than two months after his discharge on August 6, 1881, Cooper was convicted in San Francisco for grand larceny, sentenced to four years, and returned to San Quentin September 19 as convict No. 10051. Nothing is known of Cooper after his discharge on September 19, 1884.

20. *People vs William Miner and James Harrington*, 29. Pardon File No. 3565, William A. Miner: Letter from Attorney Wesley K. Boucher, Mokulumne Hill, California, to Governor William Irwin, Sacramento, California, October 8, 1878. *Calaveras Chronicle*, June 24, 1871. *San Francisco Bulletin*, November 11, 1871.

CHAPTER 4

1. San Quentin Prison Register, Convict No. 4902, William A. Miner, and convict No. 4903, James Harrington, F3653–6 (VB113).

2. Pardon File No. 3565, William A. Miner. San Quentin Prison Register, Convict No. 4902, William A. Miner and Convict No. 4903, James Harrington, F3653–6 (VB113). *San Francisco Bulletin*, November 11, 1871.

3. *Calaveras Chronicle*, February 17, 1872.

4. *People vs William Miner and James Harrington*, 29. Pardon File No. 3565, William A. Miner: Letter from Attorney Wesley K. Boucher, Mokulumne Hill, California, to Governor William Irwin, Sacramento, California, October 8, 1878.

5. San Quentin Prison Register, Convict No. 4902, William A. Miner, and convict No. 4903, James Harrington, F3653–6 (VB113).

6. San Quentin Prison Register, Convict No. 4903, James Harrington, F3653–6 (VB113). Hume and Thacker, 35.

7. John Irwin, *The Felon*, 84.

8. Record of Punishment, San Quentin Prison, 32.

9. Pardon File No. 3565, William A. Miner: Letters from A. C. McAllister, Captain of the Yard at San Quentin Penitentiary, and James A. Johnson, Lieutenant Governor of California, to Governor George Perkins, Sacramento, California, January 17, 1880.

10. Pardon File No. 3565, William A. Miner: various letters in file.

11. *The Clinton High School Re-Union*, 4. On May 14, 1885, in response to an invitation to attend an 1885 reunion of her Union High School class in Clinton, Michigan, Mary Jane Wellman wrote a long letter from Lyndon, Washington Territory, to a friend and former classmate, Mrs. Mary Hause, which was printed in full in this rare book. In the letter, Mary Jane Wellman vividly described her life in Colorado and made this quip about leaving California: "After shaking the dust of California from our feet (a difficult matter, as California dust is as tenacious as memories of school days), we moved to Colorado." Understandably, she made no mention of Bill Miner in the letter.

12. Pardon File No. 3565, William A. Miner, and Pardon File No. 3102, William A. Miner: various letters in files. War of the Rebellion, Dependent Pension Claim No. 219247.

13. *Truckee Republican*, June 18, 1872.

14. Sacramento City Directory, 1870, 215; 1871, 317. *Sacramento Daily Bee*, June 17, 1872.

15. Pardon File No. 3565, William A. Miner.

16. *San Francisco Chronicle*, September 18, 1879. *Marin County Journal*, September 18, 1879. State Board of Prison Directors, Minutes, vol. 1, p. 118.

17. San Quentin Prison Register, Convict No. 4902, William A. Miner, F3653–6 (VB113).

CHAPTER 5

1. Mark Dugan, *Bandit Years: A Gathering of Wolves*, 14–15. The complete history of Miner's actions in Colorado is also contained in this book. *Denver Republican*, May 24, 1881.
2. *Denver Republican*, May 24, 1881.
3. The life history of Billy LeRoy is on pp. 26–45 in Dugan, *Bandit Years*.
4. *The Denver Republican*, May 24, 1881, April 5, 1882. *Denver Tribune*, January 15, 1881.
5. *Colorado Chieftain*, September 30, 1880. *Denver Republican*, May 24, 1881. *Denver Tribune*, January 15, 1881. RG 21, U.S. District Court, Pueblo, Colorado, U.S. vs. William LeRoy, Case File No. 17. The government claimed the value as one hundred dollars instead of fifty dollars.
6. *Colorado Chieftain*, September 30, 1880.
7. *Denver Republican*, May 24, 1881.
8. *Denver Republican*, May 24, 1881. *Denver Tribune*, January 15, 1881. RG 21, U.S. District Court, Pueblo, Colorado, U.S. vs. William LeRoy, Case File No. 18.
9. *Denver Republican*, May 24, 1881. *Daily News* (Denver), October 15, 1880. RG 21, U.S. District Court, Pueblo, Colorado, *U.S. vs. William LeRoy*, Case File No. 19.
10. *Daily News*, October 15, 1880. *Denver Republican*, May 24, 1881. *Denver Tribune*, January 15, 1881. RG 21, U.S. District Court, Pueblo, Colorado, U.S. vs. William LeRoy, Case File No. 19.
11. *Denver Republican*, May 24, 1881, April 5, 1882.
12. *Denver Republican*, May 24, 1881. *New York Sun*, March 7, 1883(?), *Dawson Scrapbook* 18:465. *Denver Republican*, October 21, 1911, *Dawson Scrapbook* 18:469. *Washington Post*, March 26, 1911, *Dawson Scrapbook* 18:467. *Daily Alta California*, March 8, 1886.

CHAPTER 6

1. Durant, 291–294. *Pioneer History of Ingham County*, 681–714.
2. *Dawson Scrapbook* 18: 465, 467, 469. *Daily Alta California*, March 8, 1886.
3. Durant, 294. *Pioneer History of Ingham County*, 686, 687, 712. Michigan Department of Health Certificate of Death, Jennie Louise [Willis] Boucher, Local File No. 7.
4. The following local historians in Onondaga and descendants of Jennie Willis Boucher, who also knew her, confirmed this story on taped interviews: Isabelle Moyer of Onondaga, June 29, 30, July 7, 1990; Nadine Bodell of Onondaga, July 7, 1990; Joseph Boucher of Jackson, Michigan, grandson of Jennie, June 29, 1990; Robert Corwin of Jackson, Michigan, great-nephew of Jennie, July 7, 1990.
5. *Dawson Scrapbook* 18: 465, 467, 469. *Daily Alta California*, March 8, 1886. *Leslie Local Republican*, October 1880–April, 1881. A complete search of this newspaper, which contained the local news from Onondaga, failed to uncover anything regarding Miner's visit. Taped interviews with Isabelle Moyer of Onondaga, June 29, 30, July 7, 1990. Durant, p. 294.

6. Michigan Department of Health Certificate of Death, Jennie Louise [Willis] Boucher, Local File No. 7. *Jackson Citizen Patriot,* September 19, 1945.
7. *Atlanta Constitution,* March 5, 1911.
8. *Dawson Scrapbook* 18: 465, 467. Letter: Janet Thompson, Reference Librarian, Ohio Historical Society, Columbus, to author, October 24, 1984. There is no record of Stanton T. Jones in either the Ohio Penitentiary Records from 1870 on or in the Chillicothe Jail Register from 1881 to 1892.

CHAPTER 7

1. *Description and History of Convicts in United States Penitentiary at Laramie City, Wyoming Territory,* Convict No. 106, Charles B. Dingman. Ellen F. Walrath, "Stagecoach Holdups in the San Luis Valley," *Colorado Magazine* 14, no. 1 (June 1937): 30–31. RG 204, Application for Pardon, Charles B. Dingman, Case File J-138. Colorado State Penitentiary Records, Inmate No. 338, Cyrus B. Dingman.
2. *San Juan Prospector,* February 5, 26, 1881. Walrath, "Stagecoach Holdups in the San Luis Valley," 30–31. *Dawson Scrapbook* 18:465, 467. The article on p. 467 says the robbery was committed in early spring 1881.
3. *San Juan Prospector,* February 26, 1881. RG 204, Application for Pardon, Charles B. Dingman, Case File J-138.
4. RG 21, U.S. District Court, Del Norte, Colorado, U.S. vs Chas. B. Dingman, Case File No. 9. *San Juan Prospector,* September 17, 1881, September 24, 1881. RG 204, Application for Pardon, Charles B. Dingman, Case File J-138.
5. *Description and History of Convicts in United States Penitentiary at Laramie City, Wyoming Territory,* Convict No. 106, Charles B. Dingman.
6. RG 204, Application for Pardon, Charles B. Dingman, Case File J-138.
7. *San Juan Prospector,* February 26, 1881.
8. *Dawson Scrapbook* 18:467.
9. District Court Record 1875–1884, County of Saguache, Colorado, May 25, 1881, p. 80: *The People vs. James East, Stanton T. Jones, and William A. Morgan,* Case Nos. 20, 21.
10. *Denver Republican,* April 29, 1881. *Daily News,* April 29, 1881.
11. *San Juan Prospector,* April 30, 1881; *Dawson Scrapbook* 18:465.
12. District Court Record 1875–1884, County of Saguache, Colorado, May 25, 1881, pp. 80, 81, 85; June 7, 1882, p. 268: *The People vs James East, Stanton T. Jones, and William A. Morgan,* Case Nos. 20, 21. Judges Docket Book 1875–1894, County of Saguache, Colorado, June 7, 1882, p. 62: *The People vs. James East, Stanton T. Jones, and William A. Morgan. Saguache Chronicle,* May 27, 1881; Colorado State Penitentiary Records, Inmate No. 575, James East.
13. Hume and Thacker, 51–52. *Placer Herald,* September 25, 1880. *Placer Argus,* September 25, 1880.
14. Rickards, 10–12.
15. Anderson, 22. Hume and Thacker, 52. Letter: Margaret Costales, Assistant Librarian, Public Library, Silver City, New Mexico, to author Mark Dugan, July 14, 1987: "After researching our microfilm library of newspapers for the period from February through November 1881, which included past issues of the *Silver City Enterprise,* the *Grant County Herald,* and the *New Southwest,* I was unable to discover any information relating to a stagecoach robbery taking place on the route between Silver City and Deming, New Mexico, during that time."

16. *Denver Republican,* April 5, 1882.
17. *Dawson Scrapbook* 18:465. Taped interviews with Isabelle Moyer of Onondaga, June 29, 30, July 7, 1990.

CHAPTER 8

1. *Sacramento Daily Record-Union,* December 8, 1881. Pardon File No. 5250, William A. Miller. Hume and Thacker, 52.
2. *Sacramento Daily Record-Union,* December 17, 18, 1866. San Quentin Prison Register, F 3653–6 (VB 113), Convict No. 10192, James Crum; F 3653–5 (VB 113), Convict No. 4271, Benjamin Frazee. Pardon File No. 3850, James Crum. *San Francisco Chronicle,* August 10, 1882, February 17, 18, 1883.
3. *Sacramento Daily Record-Union,* December 8, 1881. *Sacramento Daily Bee,* December 8, 9, 1881. *Stockton Daily Independent,* December 10, 1881. *New York Sun,* March 7, 1883(?), *Dawson Scrapbook* 18:465.
4. *Sacramento Daily Record-Union,* May 14, 1870. *Daily Territorial Enterprise* (Virginia City, Nevada), December 8, 1870, April 16, 1871. San Quentin Prison Register, F 3653–6 (VB 113), Convict No. 10190, William A. Miller. Pardon File No. 5250, William A. Miller.
5. *Stockton Daily Independent,* November 8, 1881. *Sacramento Daily Record-Union,* November 8, 1881. *San Francisco Chronicle,* November 8, 1881.
6. *Stockton Daily Independent,* November 8, 1881.
7. Ibid., December 7, 9, 10, 1881; Undated Oakland, California, newspaper clipping, James B. Hume Scrapbook.
8. *Dawson Scrapbook* 18:465. *Atlanta Constitution,* March 5, 1911.
9. *Daily Alta California,* March 8, 1886.
10. Undated Oakland, California, newspaper clipping, James B. Hume Scrapbook.
11. *Dawson Scrapbook* 18: 465. Wells, Fargo & Company reward circular for the Sonora stage robbers issued by Special Officer James B. Hume, December 6, 1881. Undated Oakland, California, newspaper clipping, James B. Hume Scrapbook. *Stockton Daily Independent,* December 7, 10, 1881. *Daily Alta California,* March 8, 1886.
12. *Stockton Daily Independent,* December 7, 10, 1881. *San Francisco Chronicle,* December 10, 1881.
13. *Sacramento Daily Record-Union,* December 8, 1881.
14. *Stockton Daily Independent,* December 10, 1881. *Sacramento Daily Record-Union,* December 8, 1881. *Sacramento Daily Bee,* December 8, 1881. *Daily Alta California,* March 8, 1886. Undated Oakland, California, newspaper clipping, James B. Hume Scrapbook.
15. *Sacramento Daily Record-Union,* December 8, 1881. *San Francisco Chronicle,* December 10, 1881. *Sacramento Daily Bee,* December 8, 1881.
16. *Stockton Daily Independent,* December 10, 11, 1881. *Sacramento Daily Bee,* December 9, 1881. *San Francisco Chronicle,* December 10, 1881. San Quentin Prison Register, F 3653–6 (VB 113), Convict No. 10203, Benj. F. Frazee.
17. Wells, Fargo & Company reward circular for the Sonora stage robbers. Rickards, p. 11. *The Shoulder Strap,* Official Journal of the British Columbia Police Force, 10th ed. (September 1943): 41. Letter: R. E. Pittman, Records Super-

NOTES 233

visor, Colorado Department of Corrections, Colorado Springs, Colorado, to author Mark Dugan, June 15, 1984. The Colorado Department of Corrections has no record of Stanton T. Jones's being incarcerated in the Colorado State Penitentiary. Letter: Janet Thompson, Reference Librarian, Ohio Historical Society, Columbus, Ohio to author Mark Dugan, October 24, 1984. There is no record of Stanton T. Jones in either the Ohio Penitentiary Records from 1870 or the Chillicothe Jail Register from 1881 through 1892.

18. Pardon File No. 3850, James Crum. Pardon File No. 5250, William A. Miller.

CHAPTER 9

1. Pardon File No. 5250, William A. Miller. San Quentin Prison Register, F 3653–6 (VB 113), Convict No. 10190 William A. Miller, Convict No. 10191 William A. Miner, Convict No. 10192 James Crum. *Calaveras Weekly Citizen*, December 24, 1881.

2. Pardon File No. 3850, James Crum. San Quentin Prison Register, F 3653–6 (VB 113), Convict No. 10203, Benj. F. Frazee.

3. Folsom Prison Register, F 3654–1 (VB 115), Convict No. 460, William A. Miller. Pardon File No. 5250, William A. Miller.

4. San Quentin Prison Register, F 3653–6 (VB 113), Convict No. 10191, William A. Miner.

5. *Dawson Scrapbook* 18:465; Letter: Charles Aull to S. D. Brastow, November 27, 1882.

6. Prison Minutes, San Quentin Penitentiary, 1:294.

7. *San Francisco Call*, April 18, 1884. Prison Minutes, San Quentin Penitentiary, 2:68. Record of Punishment, San Quentin Prison, p. 124. Hume and Thacker, 52.

8. *San Francisco Examiner*, September 25, 1886.

9. Lamott, 143–44. *San Francisco Examiner*, September 24, 25, 1886, May 21, 1889. Prison Minutes, San Quentin Penitentiary, 2:395, 396.

10. Prison Minutes, San Quentin Penitentiary, 2:428, 429.

11. Prison Minutes, San Quentin Penitentiary, 3:74.

12. *San Francisco Examiner*, March 24, 1889.

13. *San Francisco Examiner*, May 21, 1889. Anderson, 46. A description of Miner taken from the Pinkerton files stated that Miner had two scars on his neck. *Atlanta Constitution*, October 19, 1911.

14. Prison Minutes, San Quentin Penitentiary, 3:336.

15. *San Francisco Call*, November 30, 1892. *San Francisco Examiner*, November 30, 1892. *San Francisco Chronicle*, November 30, 1892.

16. *San Francisco Examiner*, November 30, 1892

17. Prison Minutes, San Quentin Penitentiary, 4:319, 320.

18. *Marin County Tocsin*, December 10, 1892.

19. Ibid., December 15, 1892.

20. Prison Minutes, San Quentin Penitentiary, 5:277, 278.

21. Pardon File No. 4772, William A. Miner.

22. Prison Minutes, San Quentin Penitentiary, 5:418, 456, 6:88, 134. Pardon File No. 4772, William A. Miner.

23. Prison Minutes, San Quentin Penitentiary, 6:173, 245, 246.

24. San Quentin Prison Register, F 3653–6 (VB 113), Convict No. 10191, William A. Miner.

CHAPTER 10

1. War of the Rebellion, Dependent Pension Claim No. 219247.
2. The *Clinton High School Re-Union*, 7. *Morning Oregonian* (Portland), October 11, 12, 1903. *Bellingham Herald*, October 12, 1903.
3. *Seattle Post-Intelligencer*, October 5, 1905. There is a detailed life history of Jake Terry in *Tales Never Told around the Campfire* by Mark Dugan.
4. Rickards, 8, 2:11.
5. *Morning Oregonian*, October 12, 13, 1903.
6. *Oregon Daily Journal* (Portland), October 16, 1903.
7. *Morning Oregonian*, October 7, 1903.
8. *Morning Oregonian*, October 13, 1903. *Oregon Daily Journal*, October 16, 1903.
9. *Morning Oregonian*, October 14, 1903. This is the sole existing account of what transpired during the attempted robbery reported by Harshman.
10. *Morning Oregonian*, October 12, 13, 1903. *Oregon Daily Journal*, October 16, 1903. *Bellingham Herald*, September 24, 1903.
11. *Bellingham Reveille*, September 24, 1903. *Oregon Daily Journal*, September 24, 25, 26, October 12, 1903. *Morning Oregonian*, October 12, 1903. *Mount Vernon Argus*, October 16, 1903.
12. *Oregon Daily Journal*, September 24, 1903.
13. Ibid., September 25, 26, 1903.
14. *Morning Oregonian*, October 9, 12, 1903. *Oregon Daily Journal*, October 12, 1903.
15. *Morning Oregonian*, October 12, 1903. *Oregon Daily Journal*, October 12, 1903. *Bellingham Herald*, October 12, 1903.
16. *Morning Oregonian*, October 7, 9, 1903.
17. *Morning Oregonian*, October 11, 12, 13, 1903. *Oregon Daily Journal*, October 12, 1903. *Bellingham Herald*, October 12, 1903. *Mount Vernon Argus*, October 16, 1903.
18. *Morning Oregonian*, October 11, 12, 1903. *Bellingham Herald*, October 12, 1903.
19. *Morning Oregonian*, October 11, 12, 13, 1903. *Oregon Daily Journal*, October 12, 1903. *Bellingham Herald*, October 12, 1903.
20. *Oregon Journal*, October 17, 1903. *Morning Oregonian*, November 11, 1903.
21. Pinkerton National Detective Agency reward poster, October 27, 1903.
22. *Morning Oregonian*, November 14, 25, 1903. Oregon State Penitentiary Great Register 5 (1894–1910): 168, 169. Oregon State Archives, Salem.
23. Oregon State Penitentiary Great Register 5 (1894–1910): 168, 169. Oregon State Penitentiary Case Files, Convict No. 4792, Charles Hoehn. Oregon State Penitentiary, Salem. Secretary of State: Record of Pardons, Remissions and Commutations 1 (1904–1911): 229, Charles Hoehn, Oregon State Archives, Salem.
24. Oregon State Penitentiary Great Register 5 (1894–1910): 168, 169. Oregon State Penitentiary Case Files, Convict No. 4796, Gay Harshman.
25. See note 7 above.

CHAPTER 11

1. Anderson, 29, 30.
2. Anderson, p. 30. *The Shoulder Strap,* 10th ed., 43.
3. RG 73, New Westminster Convict Register, 1878–1934, Accession V-84-85/329, p. 147. RG 73, Accession: V-84-85/329, Roman Catholic Chaplains Register, 1878–1919, 7. Anderson, 3.
4. See note 3 of chapter 10.
5. *Bellingham Herald,* August 9, 1907.
6. *Seattle Post-Intelligencer,* July 6, 1907. *Bellingham Herald,* July 5, August 9, 1907.
7. *The Shoulder Strap,* 10th ed., 42. Although Miner, Dunn, and Terry were never brought to trial for this robbery, nor was Terry's name linked to the holdup, later events and newspapers connect Terry with the crime.
8. Anderson, 5, 7.
9. *Seattle Post-Intelligencer,* October 5, 1905. Jack Parberry, as told to Colin Rickards, "Lawman of the Old Northwest," *The West,* (November, 1968), 49–50.
10. Anderson, 7, 9. Rickards, Colin, "Bill Miner: 50 Years A Hold-Up Man." *The English Westerners Brand Book,* 8:3 (April, 1966):1. "C.P.R. Train Hold-up. First Train Hold-up in Canada. Bill Miner," Conversation with Andrew Herbert Mitchell, 31 January 1944. *Seattle Post-Intelligencer,* October 5, 1905. Bruce Wishart, "Bill Miner: The Canadian Years," *True West* (January 1990): 28.
11. Anderson, 9–11. *The Shoulder Strap,* 10th ed., 42.
12. Anderson, 30–31. *The Shoulder Strap,* 10th ed., 42.
13. "A New Side Of Bill Miner's Character" by Mrs. Maisie A. C. Armytage-Moore, 8 July 1943, Additional Manuscript 54, vol. 13, File M206, Bill Miner.
14. *Seattle Post-Intelligencer,* October 5, 1905.
15. Anderson, 31.
16. *Seattle Post-Intelligencer,* October 6, 1905.
17. Ibid., July 6, 1907.
18. Ibid., October 3, 4, 5, 6; November 30, 1905.
19. Ibid., October 5, 1905.
20. Ibid., October 3, 4, 5, 6, November 30, 1905.
21. Ibid., October 3, 1905.
22. Ibid., October 5, 6, 1905.
23. Ibid., November 30, 1905.
24. Ibid., October 3, November 30, 1905.

CHAPTER 12

1. Roy Franklin Jones, *Boundary Town,* 252, 262. *Bellingham Herald,* July 5, August 9, 1907. See note 3 of Chapter 10.
2. RG 73, New Westminster Convict Register, 1878–1934, p. 147. Anderson, 31.
3. *The Shoulder Strap,* 7th ed., (February 1942): 50.
4. Richard W. Markov, August 20, 1972, "A Decade of Enforcement, The Chinese Exclusion and Whatcom County, 1890 to 1900," unpublished manuscript, 1–4, 9–11. Roland L. DeLorme, "The United States Bureau of Customs and Smuggling on Puget Sound, 1851 to 1913," *Prologue, Journal of the National Archives* 5, no. 2 (Summer 1973): 84.

5. Anderson, 31. Rickards, 8, 3:2. (c) *The Shoulder Strap*, 10th ed., 42, 7th ed., 50.
6. *Royal Canadian Mounted Police Quarterly* 14, no. 2 (October 1948): 88. Anderson, 33–34. Rickards, 2. *The Shoulder Strap*, 10th ed., 42.
7. Anderson, 36–38, 58–60.
8. *Report of the Royal North-West Mounted Police, 1906*, Sessional Paper No. 28, 17.
9. *Report of the Royal North-West Mounted Police, 1906*, 17–18. Anderson, 37, 61, 62.
10. *Report of the Royal North-West Mounted Police, 1906*, 18.
11. Ibid., *Royal Canadian Mounted Police Quarterly* 88–89.
12. *Report of the Royal North-West Mounted Police, 1906*, 18–19; Anderson, 38–40. Rickards, 2. Wishart, 32.
13. *Report of the Royal North-West Mounted Police, 1906*, 18–19; *The Shoulder Strap*, 10th ed., 43. Anderson, 38–41.
14. "A New Side Of Bill Miner's Character." Anderson, 40–41. Wishart, 32.
15. RG 73, New Westminster Convict Register, 1878–1934, 147. Anderson, 41.

CHAPTER 13

1. Anderson, 42–48. F. W. Lindsay, *The Outlaws*, 46. *Montreal Gazette*, February 12, 18, March 3, 1909.
2. *Bellingham Herald*, July 5, August 9, 1907.
3. Ibid., July 5, 1907.
4. Ibid., August 9, 1907.
5. Anderson, 46–48. *Bellingham Herald*, July 5, August 9, 1907. *Atlanta Constitution*, February 28, March 3, 1911. *Atlanta Georgian and News*, February 28, 1911.
6. Anderson, 44–46. Rickards, 8, 3:3. *Bellingham Herald*, August 9, 1907. *Seattle Post-Intelligencer*, August 9, 1907.
7. *The Seattle Post-Intelligencer*, August 13, 15, 1907.
8. Robbin, pp. 214–16.
9. Anderson, pp. 47–48. *Montreal Gazette*, January 29, March 3, 1909.
10. Anderson, 47–48. *Montreal Gazette*, February 12, 1909.
11. *Montreal Gazette*, February 18, 1909.
12. Ibid., March 3, 1909. Lindsay, 46–47; Anderson, 47–48.

CHAPTER 14

1. Anderson, 48.
2. *Atlanta Constitution*, February 28, March 3, 1911. *Atlanta Georgian and News*, February 28, 1911.
3. Anderson, 44–45. RG 13, C2, Microfilm Reel No. M1797, File 8001, Correspondence regarding the release of William Dunn from the British Columbia Penitentiary on May 25, 1915. *The Shoulder Strap*, 15th ed. (April 1946): 69–71.
4. Anderson, 45. RG 73, New Westminster Convict Register, 1878–1934, 47.
5. Anderson, 49. Rickards, 3. *The Shoulder Strap*, 10th ed., 45.
6. *Morning Oregonian*, December 8, 10, 1908. *Oregon Daily Journal*, December 8, 9, 10, 1908.
7. Cecil Clark, *B.C. Provincial Police Stories*, 98–99; Colin Rickards, "Bill Miner: 50 Years a Holdup Man," *Real West* (October 1970), 53. *The Shoulder Strap*, 7th ed., 51–58.
8. *Seattle Post-Intelligencer*, August 12, 1907.

9. *Bellingham Herald,* July 5, 1907. see note 3 of chapter 10.
10. *Seattle Post-Intellingencer,* September 4, 1913.
11. Letter: J. M. Everly of Snoqualmie, Washington, to Robert Olson of Pico Rivera, California, February 6, 1971; furnished to author Mark Dugan by Robert Olson of Pico Rivera, California.
12. *Atlanta Journal,* September 3, 1913.
13. *Denver Republican,* October 21, 1911. *Atlanta Constitution,* March 3, 1911.

CHAPTER 15

1. *Gainesville News,* March 1, 1911. *Atlanta Journal,* February 24, 1911. The State vs. George Anderson (Bill Miner alias George Anderson): Robbery; Hall Superior Court; Special Term 1911. When first questioned regarding his association with Miner, Charley Hunter said he met Miner in Michigan; later, during the trial, he said it was Pennsylvania. The reason behind this was Hunter's insistence that his family never find out about his participation in the train robbery.
2. Pardon Files, Jim Handford, Georgia Department of Archives and History, Atlanta.
3. *Atlanta Constitution,* March 5, 1911. *The State vs. George Anderson.*
4. *Dahlonega Nugget,* February 24, 1911. *Atlanta Constitution,* March 5, 1911.
5. *Atlanta Journal,* February 6, 1911.
6. *Atlanta Georgian and News,* February 20, 1911. *Dahlonega Nugget,* February 24, 1911. *Gainesville News,* March 1, 1911. *Atlanta Constitution,* March 5, 1911.
7. *Atlanta Journal,* February 18, 19, 1911. *Atlanta Constitution,* February 19, 1911.
8. *Atlanta Journal,* February 18, 1911. *Atlanta Constitution,* February 19, 1911. *Atlanta Georgian and News,* February 18, 1911. *The State vs. George Anderson.*
9. *Atlanta Journal,* February 18, 1911. Series of newspaper clippings regarding train robberies throughout the south furnished to author by Dave Murray, Inverness, Scotland, United Kingdom. Bill Miner has often been incorrectly credited with committing Georgia's first train robbery.
10. *Atlanta Journal,* February 18, 19, 1911. *Atlanta Constitution,* February 19, 1911. *Atlanta Georgian and News,* February 18, 20, 1911. *Gainesville News,* February 22, 1911.
11. *Atlanta Journal,* February 24, March 4, 1911. *Dahlonega Nugget,* February 24, 1911. The State vs. George Anderson.
12. *Gainesville News,* February 22, 1911. *Atlanta Constitution,* March 5, 1911. *Dahlonega Nugget,* February 24, 1911. *The State vs. George Anderson.*
13. *Atlanta Journal,* February 26, 1911.
14. *The State vs George Anderson. Atlanta Journal,* February 26, 1911. *Gainesville News,* February 22, 1911.
15. *Atlanta Journal,* February 23, 1911. *Atlanta Constitution,* February 23, 1911. *Atlanta Georgian and News,* February 23, 1911.

CHAPTER 16

1. *Atlanta Journal,* February 23, 1911.
2. *Dahlonega Nugget,* March 3, 1911.
3. Ibid., September 15, 1911. Letter: James C. Bonner, Jr., of Decatur, Georgia, to author Mark Dugan, January 25, 1988. The meerschaum pipe Miner gave to A. E. Watson was identified and obtained by Dr. James C. Bonner sometime in

the 1960s. After Dr. Bonner's death on January 22, 1982, the pipe came into the possession of his son, James C. Bonner, Jr. On December 17, 1987, Mr. Bonner gave the pipe to the author Mark Dugan.

4. *Atlanta Journal*, February 24, 26, 1911. *Atlanta Constitution*, February 25, 1911. *Dahlonega Nugget*, March 3, 1911. *The State vs George Anderson*.

5. *Gainesville News*, March 1, 1911.

6. Ibid., March 1, 1911. *Atlanta Journal*, February 24, 1911.

7. *Atlanta Journal*, February 24, 1911.

8. Hall County Superior Court Minute Book N, 1909–1912, 345. *Gainesville News*, March 1, 1911.

9. *Atlanta Georgian and News*, February 28, 1911. *Atlanta Constitution*, February 28, 1911. Anderson, 46.

10. *Sacramento Daily Bee*, February 27, 1911.

11. *Atlanta Georgian and News*, February 28, 1911. *Atlanta Constitution*, February 28, 1911.

12. *Atlanta Journal*, March 2, 1911.

13. *Atlanta Georgian and News*, March 2, 1911. *Atlanta Constitution*, March 3, 1911.

14. *Atlanta Constitution*, March 3, 1911.

15. *Dahlonega Nugget*, March 10, 1911.

16. *Gainesville News*, March 8, 1911.

17. *Atlanta Constitution*, March 5, 1911.

18. *The State vs George Anderson*.

19. *Atlanta Journal*, March 4, 1911. *Atlanta Constitution*, March 4, 5, 1911. Hall County Superior Court Minute Book N, 1909–1912, 347–48.

20. *Atlanta Constitution*, March 5, 1911.

CHAPTER 17

1. RG 21-3-27, Central Register of Convicts, vol. 7. A thorough search of the Governor's Proclamation Books revealed that no proclamation or reward was ever issued for Hunter.

2. Pardon Files, Jim Handford. RG 21-3-27.

3. *Gainesville News*, March 15, 1911.

4. *Atlanta Georgian and News*, March 6, 1911. *Dahlonega Nugget*, March 10, 24, 1911.

5. *Atlanta Constitution*, March 6, 1911.

6. *Gainesville News*, March 22, 1911. RG 21-3-27.

7. *Dahlonega Nugget*, March 17, April 18, May 5, 1911. Letter: Bob Davis, Jasper, Georgia, to author Mark Dugan, June 11, 1984. Davis, a Georgia historian and researcher, wrote that through his research he had received the information that former Sheriff Davis had collected the reward.

8. *Atlanta Journal*, October 17, 1911. *Gainesville News*, September 13, 1911. RG 21-3-27.

9. National Register of Historic Places Nomination Form, Old State Prison Building, Milledgeville, Baldwin County, Georgia, May 16, 1978. The old prison is now in the National Register of Historic Sites. *Macon Telegraph and News*, January 22, 1986. Furnished to author, Mark Dugan, by Marvin E. Joyce, Human Resource Manager, Forstmann & Co., Milledgeville, Georgia. On December 18,

NOTES   239

1987, Joyce conducted the author through the entire old prison building, which is now owned by Forstmann & Co. I saw the room where Miner died, the block of cells where he was incarcerated, and the dining room where fading and peeling convict artwork adorns the walls.

10. *Atlanta Constitution,* October 18, 1911. *True Citizen,* January 19, 26, April 6, 1907. Letter: Bob Davis, Jasper, Georgia, to author Mark Dugan, December 24, 1984. Davis reviewed the trial transcript of Tom Moore and furnished this information.
11. *Gainesville News,* March 8, 1911. *Atlanta Journal,* October 19, 1911.
12. *Union Recorder,* October 24, 1911.
13. *Atlanta Journal,* October 17, 1911. *Gainesville News,* October 18, 1911.
14. *Atlanta Journal,* October 19, 1911. *Union Recorder,* October 24, 1911. *True Citizen,* October 21, 1911.
15. *Atlanta Constitution,* October 19, 20, 21, 1911. *Union Recorder,* October 24, 1911.
16. *Atlanta Journal,* October 17, 19, 1911. *Atlanta Constitution,* October 19, 1911. *Union Recorder,* October 24, 1911.
17. *Atlanta Constitution,* October 20, 1911.
18. Ibid., October 20, 21, 24, 26, 1911. *Atlanta Journal,* October 20, 1911.
19. *Atlanta Constitution,* October 30, 1911.
20. Ibid., October 18, November 5, 1911. See note 10 above.
21. *True Citizen,* November 4, 1911.
22. *True Citizen,* November 4, 1911. *Union Recorder,* November 7, 1911. *Gainesville News,* November 8, 1911.
23. *True Citizen,* November 4, 1911. *Gainesville News,* November 8, 1911.
24. *Atlanta Constitution,* November 5, 1911.
25. *True Citizen,* November 4, 1911.
26. *Union Recorder,* November 7, 1911.
27. Ibid., July 2, 9, 1912.
28. Ibid., July 2, 9, 1912. *Atlanta Constitution,* July 3, 1912.
29. *Atlanta Constitution,* July 3, 1912.
30. *Union Recorder,* July 9, 1912. *Atlanta Journal,* July 3, 1912. *Atlanta Constitution,* July 4, 1912.
31. Harry Golden, *A Little Girl Is Dead,* 26–27. In this documented story of the murder of fourteen-year old Mary Phagan and the subsequent lynching of Leo Frank, Golden gives an accurate view of the economic conditions in Georgia in 1913.

CHAPTER 18

1. *Atlanta Journal,* July 3, 1912. *Atlanta Constitution,* July 4, 1912. *Union Recorder,* July 9, 1912.
2. *Atlanta Journal, September 3, 1913.*
3. Bonner, "Old West's Last Desperado."
4. *Atlanta Journal,* September 3, 1913.
5. Ibid., September 3, 1913.
6. *Bellingham Bay, Washington, Directory,* 1913–1917.
7. *Atlanta Journal,* September 3, 1913.
8. Ibid., September 2, 3, 1913.

9. Ibid., September 3, 1913.
10. *Milledgeville News,* September 5, 1913.
11. Taped interview with Louis Andrews of Milledgeville, Georgia, July 17, 1984.
12. *Milledgeville News,* September 12, 1913.
13. Taped interview with Louis Andrews. Taped interview with Mickey Couey of Milledgeville, Georgia, July 17, 1984. Couey is the funeral director at Moore's Funeral Home and was given the information regarding Miner's funeral by Joseph Moore before his death.
14. *Inter Ocean* (Chicago, Illinois), November 16, 1913.
15. *Seattle Post-Intelligencer,* September 4, 1913.
16. *Milledgeville News,* September 12, 1913.
17. Taped interview with Robert Rice of Atlanta, Georgia, August 21, 1984.

EPILOGUE

1. *Gainesville News,* March 15, 1911.
2. C. L. Sonnichsen, *Outlaw: Bill Mitchell alias Baldy Russell,* 1.
3. For evidence of low frontier robbery rates, see Roger McGrath, *Gunfighters, Highwaymen, and Vigilantes,* 248–49. For an opposite view, see John Boessenecker, "Stage Robbers and Banditry: Myth v. Fact," *The Californians* 5, no. 2 (March–April 1987): 32–35.
4. McGrath, 254.
5. Boessenecker, *Badge and Buckshot,* 15. Hubert Howe Bancroft, *Popular Tribunals,* 131.
6. Claire V. McKenna, "Crime in California," *Pacific Historical Review* 55, (May 1986): 295.
7. Kevin J. Mullen, *Let Justice Be Done: Crime and Politics in Early San Francisco,* 297–98.
8. McGrath, 255. Richard Maxwell Brown, *Strain of Violence: Historical Studies of American Violence and Vigilantism,* 237–87. W. Eugene Hollon, *Frontier Violence: Another Look,* 106–23.
9. Mullen, *Let Justice Be Done,* 74. Kevin J. Mullen, "Founding the San Francisco Police Department," *Pacific Historian* 27, no. 3, (Fall 1983): 12. Frank Richard Prassel, *The Western Peace Officer: A Legacy of Law and Order,* 30.
10. George D. Hendricks, *The Bad Man of the West,* 28.
11. Robert N. Mullin and Charles E. Welch, Jr., "Billy the Kid: The Making of a Hero," *Western Folklore* 32, no. 2 (April 1973): 106–7.
12. Joseph G. Rosa, *The Gunfighter: Man or Myth?* 41–42.
13. Eric J. Hobsbawm, *Primitive Rebels: Studies in Archaic Forms of Social Movement in the 19th and 20th Centuries,* 5.
14. Eric J. Hobsbawm, *Bandits,* 13.
15. Hobsbawm, *Primitive Rebels,* 13.
16. Hobsbawm, *Bandits,* 34–36.
17. Hobsbawm, *Primitive Rebels,* 19.
18. Kent Ladd Steckmesser, "Robin Hood and the American Outlaw," *Journal of American Folklore* 79 (April–June 1966): 354.
19. Claire V. McKenna, "Banditry in California, 1850–1880: Myth and Reality," *Brand Book Number Eight,* San Diego Corral of Westerners (1987), 46.

20. Richard Maxwell Brown in the foreword to Paul I. Wellman, *A Dynasty of Western Outlaws*, 5–6.

21. Robert M. Utley, *Billy the Kid: A Short and Violent Life*, 200.

22. Richard White, "Outlaw Gangs of the Middle Border: American Social Bandits," *Western Historical Quarterly* 12, (October 1981), 389.

23. Hobsbawm, *Bandits*, 13–14.

24. Anton Blok, "The Peasant and the Brigand: Social Banditry Reconsidered," *Comparative Studies in Society and History* 14, (1972): 497.

25. Ibid., 498.

26. White, 387; Brown, 16; Utley, 200; Pedro Castillo and Albert Camarillo, *Furia y Murete: Los Bandidos Chicanos*, 1–51.

27. For Joaquin Murrieta and Tiburcio Vasquez as social bandits, see Castillo and Camarillo, 1–51. For an opposite view, see McKenna, "Banditry in California," 45–46, and John Boessenecker, "Social Banditry's Righteous Rebels vs. Common Criminals," *The Californians* 5, no. 6 (November–December 1987): 36–37.

28. White, 406.

29. Kent Ladd Steckmesser, *Western Hero in History and Legend*, 255.

30. Joseph Campbell, *Power of Myth*, 136.

31. Steckmesser, "Robin Hood and the American Outlaw," 354.

Bibliography

BOOKS

Adams, Mrs. Franc L., comp and ed. *Pioneer History of Ingham County.* Lansing, Mich.: Wyncoop Hollenbeck Crawford Co., 1923.

Anderson, Frank W. *Bill Miner . . . Stagecoach and Train Robber.* Surrey, British Columbia: Heritage House Publishing Co., 1982.

Bancroft, Hubert Howe. *Popular Tribunals.* San Francisco: The History Co., 1887.

Bellingham Bay, Washington Directory, 1913–1917. Bellingham Public Library, Bellingham, Washington.

Billy LeRoy, the Colorado Bandit: Or, The King of American Highwaymen. New York: Richard K. Fox, 1881.

Boggs, Mae Bacon. *My Playhouse Was a Concord Coach.* Oakland, Calif.: Howell-North Press, 1942.

Boessenecker, John. *Badge and Buckshot: Lawlessness in Old California.* Norman: University of Oklahoma Press, 1988.

Brown, Richard Maxwell. *Strain of Violence: Historical Studies of American Violence and Vigilantism.* New York: Oxford University Press, 1975.

Campbell, Joseph. *The Power of Myth.* New York: Doubleday, 1988.

Castillo, Pedro, and Albert Camarillo. *Furia y Murete: Los Bandidos Chicanos.* Los Angeles: Aztlan Publications, 1973.

Clark, Cecil. *B.C. Provincial Police Stories.* Surrey, British Columbia: Heritage House Publishing Co., 1986.

The Clinton High School Re-Union, Quarter Centennial Anniversary, 1860–1885. Clinton, Michigan: Program Committee, 1885. Collection of Ruth Hoover, Clinton, Michigan.

Cowles, Albert Eugene. *Past and Present of the City of Lansing and Ingham County, Michigan.* Lansing: Michigan Historical Publishing Association, 1905(?).

Dugan, Mark. *Bandit Years: A Gathering Of Wolves.* Santa Fe, N.M.: Sunstone Press, 1987.

———. *Tales Never Told around the Campfire.* Athens: Ohio University Press, 1991.

Durant, Samuel W. *History of Ingham and Eaton Counties, Michigan, with Illustrations and Biographical Sketches of Their Prominent Men and Pioneers.* Philadelphia: D. W. Ensign, 1880.

Early Land Transfers, Ingham County, Michigan, 1835–1853. Vols. 1–3. Lansing: Michigan State Library, 1947.

Friedman, Lawrence M., and Robert V. Percival. *The Roots Of Justice: Crime and Punishment in Alameda County, California 1870–1910.* Chapel Hill: University of North Carolina Press, 1981.

Golden, Harry. *A Little Girl Is Dead.* New York: Avon Books, 1967.

Gudde, Erwin G. *California Gold Camps.* Berkeley: University of California Press, 1975.

Kendricks, George D. *The Bad Man of the West.* New York: Ace Books, 1942; reprint 1959.

History of Placer County, California, with Illustrations and Biographical Sketches of Its Prominent Men And Pioneers. Oakland, Calif.: Thompson and West, 1882.

Hobsbawm, Eric J. *Bandits.* Englewood Cliffs, N.J.: Prentice-Hall, 1969.

———. *Primitive Rebels: Studies in Archaic Forms of Social Movement in the 19th and 20th Centuries.* New York: W. W. Norton, 1959; reprint 1965.

Hollon, W. Eugene. *Frontier Violence: Another Look.* New York: Oxford University Press, 1974.

Horan, James D. *The Pinkertons.* New York: Bonanza Books, 1967.

———, and Paul Sann. *Pictorial History of the Wild West.* New York: Crown Publishers, 1954.

———, and Howard Swigget, *The Pinkerton Story.* New York: G. P. Putnam's Sons, 1951.

Hume, James B., and Jno. N. Thacker. *Wells Fargo & Co's. Robbers Record.* San Francisco: H. S. Crocker, 1884.

Illustrated History of Skagit and Snohomish Counties, Their People, Their Commerce, and Their Resources. N.p., Interstate, 1906.

Ingham County Pioneer Families. Comp. by George L. Hammell. Vols. 1 and 4. Michigan State Library, Lansing.

Irwin, John. *The Felon.* Englewood Cliffs, N.J.: Prentice-Hall, 1970.

Johnson, Dorothy M. *Western Badmen.* New York: Dodd, Mead, 1970.

Jones, Roy Franklin. *Boundary Town.* Vancouver, Wash.: Fleet Printing, 1958.

Lamott, Kenneth. *Chronicles of San Quentin.* New York: David McKay, 1961.

Lindsay, F. W. *The Outlaws.* Quesnel, British Columbia: N.p., 1963.

McGrath, Roger. *Gunfighters, Highwaymen and Vigilantes.* Berkeley: University of California Press, 1984.

McLoughlin, Denis. *Wild & Wooley.* Garden City, New York: Doubleday, 1975.

Mann, Ralph. *After the Gold Rush: Society in Grass Valley and Nevada City, California, 1849–1870.* Stanford, Calif: Stanford University Press, 1982.

Mullen, Kevin J. *Let Justice Be Done: Crime and Politics in Early San Francisco.* Reno and Las Vegas: University of Nevada Press, 1989.

Orton, Brig. Gen. Richard H., ed. and comp. *Records of California Men in the War of the Rebellion, 1861–1867.* Sacramento, Calif.: State Office, State Printing, 1890.

Patterson, T. W. *Outlaws of Western Canada.* Langly, British Columbia: Mr. Paperback, 1974.

Peterson, David M., and Charles W. Thomas, eds. *Corrections: Problems and Prospects*. Englewood Cliffs, N.J.: Prentice-Hall, 1975.
Pinkerton, William A. *Train Robberies and Train Robbers*. Fort Davis, Tex.: Frontier Book Co., 1968.
Prassel, Frank Richard. *The Western Peace Officer: A Legacy of Law and Order.* Norman: University of Oklahoma Press, 1972.
Quiett, Glenn Chesney. *Pay Dirt*. Lincoln, Neb.: Johnsen Publishing Co., 1971.
Record of Service of Michigan Volunteers in the Civil War 1861–1865. Published by the authority of the Senate and House of Representatives of the Michigan Legislature under the direction of Brig. Gen. Geo. H. Brown, Adjutant General. Michigan State University Library, Lansing.
Reilly, Genevieve S., ed. *The Clinton Story, 1825–1958*. N.p.: The Woman's Club, 1958.
Report of the Royal North-West Mounted Police, 1906, Sessional Paper No. 28. S. E. Dawson, Printer to the King's Most Excellent Majesty, 1907. Public Archives of Canada, Ottawa, Ontario.
Robbin, Martin. *The Band and the Lonely*. Toronto, Ontario: James Lorimer and Co., 1976.
Rosa, Joseph G. *The Gunfighter: Man or Myth?* Norman: University of Oklahoma Press, 1969.
Sacramento City Directory, 1870, 1871, 1872. California State Library, California Room, Sacramento.
Sonnichsen, C. L. *Outlaw: Bill Mitchell alias Baldy Russell*. New York: Ballantine Books, 1974.
Steckmesser, Kent Ladd. *The Western Hero in History and Legend*. Norman: University of Oklahoma Press, 1965.
Utley, Robert M. *Billy the Kid: A Short and Violent Life*. Lincoln: University of Nebraska Press, 1989.
Wellman, Paul I. *A Dynasty of Western Outlaws*. Lincoln: University of Nebraska Press, 1961; reprint 1986.

ARTICLES AND PERIODICALS

Blok, Anton. "The Peasant and the Brigand: Social Banditry Reconsidered," *Comparative Studies in Society and History* 14 (1972).
Boessenecker, John. "Buckshot for Bill Miner," *True West* (August 1988).
―――. "Social Banditry's Righteous Rebels vs. Common Criminals," *The Californians* 5, no. 6 (November–December 1987).
―――, "Stage Robbers and Banditry: Myth v. Fact," *The Californians* 5, no. 2 (March–April 1987).
DeLorme, Roland L. "The United States Bureau of Customs and Smuggling on Puget Sound, 1851 to 1913," *Prologue, Journal of The National Archives*, Summer 1973, 5, no. 2.
Kirby, Ed. "Bill Miner—The Grey Fox," *Quarterly of the National Association and Center for Outlaw and Lawman History* 10, no. 1 (Summer, 1985).
McKenna, Clare V. "Banditry in California, 1850–1880: Myth and Reality," *Brand Book Number Eight*, San Diego Corral of Westerners, 1987.

———. "Crime in California," *Pacific Historical Review* 55 (May 1986).
Mullen, Kevin J. "Founding the San Francisco Police Department," *Pacific Historian* 27, no. 3 (Fall 1983).
Mullin, Robert N., and Charles E. Welch, Jr. "Billy the Kid: The Making of a Hero," *Western Folklore*, 32, no. 2 (April 1973).
Parberry, Jack, as told to Colin Rickards. "Lawman of the Old Northwest," *The West* (November 1968).
Pawley, Eugene. "He Out-robbed Jesse James," *Badman Annual* (1971).
Rasch, Phillip J. "Re: Billy LeRoy," Los Angeles Westerners Corral *Branding Iron* no. 36 (December 1956).
Rickards, Colin. "Bill Miner: 50 Years a Hold-Up Man." *The English Westerners Brand Book*, 8, no. 2 (January 1966) and no. 3 (April 1966).
———. "Bill Miner: 50 Years a Holdup Man," *Real West* (October 1970).
Royal Canadian Mounted Police Quarterly 14, no. 2 (October 1948).
The Shoulder Strap, Official Journal of the British Columbia Police Force, 7th ed. (February 1942), 10th ed. (September 1943), 15th ed. (April 1946).
Steckmesser, Kent Ladd. "Robin Hood and the American Outlaw," *Journal of American Folklore* 79 (April–June 1966).
Walrath, Ellen F. "Stagecoach Holdups in the San Luis Valley," *Colorado Magazine* 14, no. 1 (June 1937).
White, Richard. "Outlaw Gangs of the Middle Border: American Social Bandits," *Western Historical Quarterly* 12 (October 1981).
Wishart, Bruce. "Bill Miner: The Canadian Years," *True West* (January 1990).

UNPUBLISHED MATERIALS

City Archives, Vancouver, British Columbia. "A New Side of Bill Miner's Character," by Mrs. Maisie A. C. Armatyge-Moore, 8 July 1943, Additional Manuscript 54, vol. 13, File M206, Bill Miner.
City Archives, Vancouver, British Columbia. "C.P.R. Train Hold-up. First Train Hold-up in Canada. Bill Miner." Conversation with Andrew Herbert Mitchell, 31 January 1944.
Mark Dugan's Collection. "Del Norte, Its Past and Present." Unpublished brochure furnished to author by Clara Vickers of Del Norte, Colorado.
Western Washington University, Bellingham. Richard W. Markov, August 20, 1972, "A Decade of Enforcement, The Chinese Exclusion And Whatcom County, 1890 to 1900," unpublished manuscript, 1–4, 9–11.

PUBLIC DOCUMENTS

California State Archives, Sacramento. Folsom Prison Register, F3654–1 (VB115).
California State Archives, Sacramento. Governor's Pardon Files, San Quentin and Folsom Penitentiaries.
California State Archives, Sacramento. *Muster Roll and Descriptive List, Company L, 2nd Regiment of California Cavalry Volunteers,* April 26, 1864. Bin 3519-5, Civil War Volunteers, Military Record Group.
California State Archives, Sacramento. Prison Minutes. San Quentin Penitentiary.

BIBLIOGRAPHY 247

California State Archives, Sacramento. San Quentin Prison, Record of Punishment.
California State Archives, Sacramento. San Quentin Prison Registers.
Colorado Department of Corrections, Canon City. Colorado State Penitentiary Records.
Colorado Historical Society, Denver. *Dawson Scrapbook*. Vol. 18.
Federal Archives and Records Center, Denver, Colorado. RG 21, U.S. District Court, Del Norte, Colorado, Case File No. 9, *U.S. vs Charles B. Dingman*.
Federal Archives and Records Center, Denver, Colorado. RG 21, U.S. District Court, Pueblo, Colorado, Case File Nos. 17–19, *U.S. vs William LeRoy*.
Georgia Department of Archives and History, Atlanta. Pardon Files, Jim Hanford.
Georgia Department of Archives and History, Atlanta. RG 21-3-27, Central Register of Convicts, vol. 7.
Hall County Courthouse, Gainesville, Georgia. Hall County Superior Court Minute Book N, 1909–1912, *The State vs. George Anderson*, 347–48.
Hall County Courthouse, Gainesville, Georgia. *The State vs. George Anderson (Bill Miner alias George Anderson)*: Robbery; Hall Superior Court; Special Term 1911.
Ingham County Clerk's Office, Mason, Michigan. Michigan Department of Health Certificate of Death, Jennie Louise [Willis] Boucher, Local File No. 7.
Ingham County, Michigan. Census Population Schedules, 1850.
Lenawee County Probate Court, Adrian, Michigan. Lenawee County, Michigan, Probate File No. 1472 D-225, *Estate of Joseph Miner*.
Los Angeles County Clerk, Record Center, Los Angeles, California. File Nos. 637 and 638, Los Angeles County Court of Sessions Case Nos. 308, 310, James Keller, and 309, 311, William Miner, Indictments for Grand Larceny.
Los Angeles County Clerk, Record Center, Los Angeles, California. Register of Actions, Book No. 1, Case Nos. 1–332, Court of Sessions, Los Angeles County, Case No. 311, William Miner.
National Archives, Washington, D.C. RG 204, Application for Pardon, Charles B. Dingman, Case File J-138.
National Archives, Washington, D.C. Muster Roll and Returns, Company I, 12th Regiment Michigan Infantry.
National Archives, Washington, D.C. Muster Roll and Returns, Company L, 2nd Regiment California Cavalry.
National Archives, Washington, D.C. War of the Rebellion, Dependent Pension Claim No. 219247 of Harriet Miner for the death of her son Henry C. Miner.
Office of the Clerk and Recorder, San Andreas, California. *People vs. William Miner and James Harrington*, Calaveras County Criminal Docket Book No. 1.
Oregon State Archives, Salem. Oregon State Penitentiary Great Register 5 (1894–1910).

Oregon State Archives, Salem. Secretary of State: Record of Pardons, Remissions and Commutations 1 (1904–1911).
Oregon State Penitentiary, Salem. Oregon State Penitentiary Case Files.
Placer County, California. Census Population Schedules, 1860.
Placer County Clerk's Office, Auburn, California. *People of the State of California vs. A. Miner,* Placer County Circuit Court Case Nos. 592 and 594, Grand Larceny.
Public Archives of Canada, Ottawa, Ontario. RG 13, C2, Microfilm Reel No. 1797, File 8001, British Columbia Penitentiary.
Public Archives of Canada, Ottawa, Ontario. RG 73, New Westminster Convict Register, 1878–1934, Accession: V-84–85/329.
Public Archives of Canada, Ottawa, Ontario. RG 73, Roman Catholic Chaplins Register, 1878–1919, Accession: V-84–85/329.
Saguache County Courthouse, Saguache, Colorado. District Court Record 1875–1884, County of Saguache, Colorado, *The People vs. James East, Stanton T. Jones, and William A. Morgan,* Case Nos. 20 and 21.
Saguache County Courthouse, Saguache, Colorado. Judges Docket Book 1875–1894, County of Saguache, Colorado, *The People vs. James East, Stanton T. Jones, and William A. Morgan.*
Wells Fargo Bank History Department, San Francisco, California. Letter: Charles Aull to S. D. Brastow, November 27, 1882.
Wyoming State Archives, Museum and Historical Department, Cheyenne. *Description and History of Convicts in United States Penitentiary at Laramie City, Wyoming Territory.*

NEWSPAPERS

CALIFORNIA

Alameda County Gazette.
Auburn Stars and Stripes.
Calaveras Chronicle. (Mokelumne Hill).
Calaveras Weekly Citizen.
Daily Alta California.
Los Angeles Star.
Marin County Journal.
Marin County Tocsin.
Placer Argus.
Placer Herald (Auburn).
Redwood City Gazette.
Sacramento Daily Bee.
Sacramento Daily Record-Union.
San Francisco Bulletin.
San Francisco Call.
San Francisco Chronicle.
San Francisco Examiner.
San Jose Daily Independent.
San Jose Daily Patriot.

Stockton Daily Evening Herald.
Stockton Daily Independent.
Truckee Republican.

COLORADO

Colorado Chieftain.
Daily News (Denver).
Denver Republican.
Denver Tribune.
Saguache Chronicle.
San Juan Prospector.

GEORGIA

Atlanta Constitution.
Atlanta Georgian and News.
Atlanta Journal.
Atlanta Journal and Constitution Magazine.
Dahlonega Nugget.
Gainesville News.
Milledgeville News.
True Citizen (Waynesboro).
Union Recorder.

ILLINOIS

Inter Ocean (Chicago).

MICHIGAN

Jackson Citizen Patriot.
Leslie Local Republican.

NEVADA

Daily Territorial Enterprise (Virginia City).

OREGON

Morning Oregonian (Portland).
Oregon Daily Journal.

WASHINGTON

Bellingham Herald.
Bellingham Reveille.
Mount Vernon Argus.
Seattle Post-Intelligencer.

CANADA

Montreal Gazette.

CORRESPONDENCE

James C. Bonner, Jr., Decatur, Georgia.
Colorado Department of Corrections, Colorado Springs. R. E. Pittman.
Bob Davis, Jasper, Georgia.
Mark Dugan's Collection. Letter, J. M. Everly of Snoqualmie, Washington, to Robert Olson of Pico Rivera, California, February 6, 1971; furnished to author by Robert Olson.
Ruth Hoover, Clinton, Michigan.
Ingham County Courthouse, Mason, Michigan. Judge of the Probate Office.
Ohio Historical Society, Columbus. Janet Thompson.
Placer County Historical Museum, Auburn, California.
Public Library, Silver City, New Mexico. Margaret Costales.

INTERVIEWS

Taped interview with Louis Andrews of Milledgeville, Georgia, July 17, 1984.
Taped interview with Mickey Couey of Milledgeville, Georgia, July 17, 1984.
Taped interview with Robert Rice of Atlanta, Georgia, August 21, 1984.
Taped interview with Joseph Boucher of Jackson, Michigan, June 29, 1990.
Taped interview with Isabelle Moyer of Onondaga, Michigan, June 29 and 30, and July 7, 1990.
Taped interview with Nadine Bodell of Onondaga, Michigan, July 7, 1990.
Taped interview with Robert Corwin of Jackson, Michigan, July 7, 1990.

PRIVATE COLLECTIONS

John Boessenecker Collection. Edward Byram. San Francisco Police Record Book No. 3.
John Boessenecker Collection. Wells, Fargo & Company reward circular for the Sonora stage robbers issued by Special Officer James B. Hume, December 6, 1881.
Robert Olson Collection. Pinkerton National Detective Agency reward poster for the arrest of Bill Miner for the train robbery of September 23, 1903.
Wells, Fargo Bank History Department, San Francisco, California. James B. Hume Scrapbook.

Index

Abbott, Bill, 109
Adams, Thomas, 6
Adrian, Mich., 5
Alamosa, Colo., 47, 54–55
Alexander, W. A. (prison guard), 86–91
Allen ("Dad"), 133
Allison, Clay, 206
Alpine, Colo., 45
Alvitre, Lucio, 13
Anacortes, Wash., 99–100
Anderson, George (alias Bill Miner), 3, 155, 164, 168–70, 173, 176–77, 179, 193
Anderson, William (alias Bill Miner), 3, 64, 69, 70, 75
Andrews, Louis, 194
Angels Camp, Calif., 25, 69
Aribi, Ga., 184
Arlington, William (police officer), 69, 73–75
Armstrong, Lew (sheriff), 59
Armytage-Moore, Maisie A. C., 111, 130–31
Arthur, Chester A. (U.S. president), 56
Ashcroft, B.C., 151
Ashley, Samuel, 57, 60
Aspen Grove, B.C., 105, 118, 133
Atlanta, Ga., 158
Atwood (deputy sheriff), 68
Aubrey, Victor, 66
Auburn, Calif., 6, 11, 14–15, 23

Augusta, Ga., 185–86
Aull, Charles (prison captain), 69, 72–75, 77–79, 81–82
Aylesworth (minister of justice), 143–47

Bald Mountain, B.C., 105
Baldwin (justice), 17
Ballard, Wash., 114
Banff, B.C., 124
Bank robbery (Portland, Oreg., 1908), 150–51
Banshee Station (Colo.), 47
Barclay, James (judge), 33
Barnum, Colo., 57
Barrett, Ollie, 96–98
Bass, Sam, 206–10
Beaman, Fernando C. (judge), 5
Bellew, Mitch (police officer), 25, 30–31, 204
Bellingham, Wash., 93, 113
Benedrum, Joseph, 47
Benyon, Jim, 125
Biedecker (sheriff), 98
Billy the Kid, 202–204, 206–10
Birlem, J. F. (prison captain), 88–90
Bitter Lake, Wash., 117
Bloodworth (prison guard), 183
Blue Ridge, Ga., 156
Bodie, Calif., 201
Boles, Charles E. ("Black Bart"), 80, 204, 208

Bonner, James C., 196–98
Borden, R. L. (member of Parliament), 143, 146–47
Boucher, Joseph Edward, 52
Boucher, Wesley K. (district attorney), 33–35, 37, 40
Bourke, Catherine, 135, 141
Bourke, D. D. (deputy warden), 138, 141–47, 149
Bow, Wash., 93, 98–99
Bowen, Jack ("Black Jack"), 79
Bowers, W. J. (attorney general), 172
Bowling Green, Ky., 3
Bradley, Charles D. (judge), 60
Brastow, S. D. (Wells, Fargo agent), 32, 79
Brewster, Russel, 4
Briar Patch, Ga., 161
Bridal Veil, Oreg., 98
Brighton, Calif., 29
Bronaugh, W. A. (sheriff), 59–60, 63, 204
Brown, James (constable), 69
Brown, Joseph M. (Georgia governor), 161
Browning, J. T. (constable), 124, 126, 128
Bruffey, E. C., 52, 173, 175
Brunswick, Ga., 191
Bryant, Frank (sergeant), 151
Bryden, Robert, 96, 98
Budd, George (alias Bill Miner), 3, 155
Budd, Jack, 105, 111, 118
Budd, James H. (California governor), 18–19, 91–92, 155
Buena Vista, Colo., 45
Buford, Ga., 160
Bullock (sheriff), 66
Bullock, R. E. (detective), 136–37, 144–45
Bureau (solicitor general), 143–44

Burke, L. (prison superintendent), 188
Burkee, C. W. (detective), 161
Burrard Inlet, B.C., 140
Burrell, Martin (member of Parliament), 147
Butler, Isaac, 4
Butte, Mont., 153
Byers, J. C. (district attorney), 18
Byram, Edward (detective), 31

Cacheville (Yolo), Calif., 72
Calgary, Alb., 118
California Bill (alias Bill Miner), 3, 44, 63
Callin, J., 119–21
Cameron, Robert (U.S. postal inspector), 55–56
Campbell's Meadow, B.C., 123, 126
Camp Douglass, Utah, 10
Camp Relief, Utah, 10
Camp Union, Calif., 10
Canon City, Colo., 44, 54, 60
Cantril, Sim (U.S. marshal), 56
Capetown, South Africa, 63
Carmichael, Pete, 161
Carpenter, L. Cass (U.S. postal inspector), 48, 63
Casad, Martin R. (detective), 69, 71
Cassidy, Butch (Robert LeRoy Parker), 203–204, 206, 209–10
Caulder (railroad engineer), 114
Chamberlain, George E. (Oregon governor), 103
Chapin, Levi, 4
Chapperon Lake, B.C., 125
Chehalis, Wash., 117
Chicago, Ill., 5, 48
Chillicothe, Ohio, 53, 72
Chilliwack, B.C., 107
Chinese Camp, Calif., 69, 72
Clark, Frank, 48
Clark, Frank ("Big Frank"), 79

INDEX

Clark, George, 138
Clarnie, Oreg., 95
Cleland (judge), 103
Clinton, Mich., 5, 8–9
Coalmont, B.C., 105
Cochrane (district attorney), 88
Coffeyville, Kans., 209
Colfax, Calif., 14, 61
Collins, John C. (alias Patterson), 65–66, 78
Colorado Springs, Colo., 40, 44, 57
Colquhoun, Louis, 118–34, 150
Colusa, Calif., 36
Conklin (jailer), 17
Cooper, Charles, 25–33, 204, 228–29 n. 19
Corbett, Oreg., 95–96
Cordelle, Ga., 184
Corner (colonel), 3
Couch, Charley H. *See* Handford, Jim
Coulson, B. D., 150
Covington, Ga., 176
Crane, Mark, 166
Crow, W. A. (sheriff), 170, 173–74, 177, 179–80
Crowley, Patrick (police chief), 31–32
Crum, James ("Jim"), 53, 65–78
Cummings, William, 66
Cunningham, Thomas (sheriff), 68, 72, 75, 86
Curtin, John, 70
Cuttler, William, 26–29, 204

Dahlonega, Ga., 156–58, 161–66, 180
Dalton boys, 207–209
Davidson, James, 46
Davidson, Robert E. (prison board chairman), 182
Davies, B. R., 111
Davis, Jim, 162–63, 168, 181

Davis, Joe, 162–63
Dawson (inspector), 136, 142, 144–47
Debs, Eugene V., 177
Decker, Isaac (constable), 151
Del Norte, Colo., 47–48, 54–56, 59
Deming, N.Mex., 63
Denver, Colo., 44, 53, 55–56, 61, 153–54
Detroit, Mich., 5, 49, 155
De Valls Bluff, Ark., 8
Devlin (prison director), 92
Dickerson (county treasurer), 14
Dingman, Abbie, 54
Dingman, Charles B. ("Swede"), 54–57, 61
Dingman, William, 54
Doolin, Bill, 206, 208–209
Dorris, H. C. ("Hank"), 55
Dorsey, Charles (alias Charley Thorn), 65–66, 78
Douglas Lake, B.C., 105, 118, 123, 125–26
Doyle, John (prison guard), 138
Ducks, Albert, 130
Ducks (Monte Creek), B.C., 119–23, 151
Dufficy (justice), 88–89
Duncan, H. M. (detective), 161
Duncan, R. H., 166
Dunn, William J. ("Shorty"), 105–34, 137, 149–50
Durant, Dr., 84
Dye, James (Pinkerton superintendent), 111

Earley, W. H., 161
East, James, 57–61, 76
Eden, Edward (coroner), 86
Edgar (prison captain), 92
Edwards, George (alias Bill Miner), 3, 105, 111, 118, 125–26, 128, 134, 153
Elberton, Ga., 198

Elgin (reverend), 166
Elliot, Charles, 82
Ellis, Henry (police captain), 31
Elston, John, 15
English, Buck, 79
Equality Colony, Wash., 94
Evans, William, 82
Everett, Wash., 101
Everly, J. M., 153

Fairbain, Andy (corporal), 150
Fant, David, 158–60, 68, 174
Fellows, H. (judge), 23
Fenning, James, 101
Fernie, William L. (constable), 121–25, 128
Folsom, Calif., 66
Folsom Prison (Calif.), 78–79
Forest Hill, Calif., 15, 18, 23
Fort Garland, Colo., 48
Frank, Leo, 181
Frankie, Alfred, 114–15
Frazee, Ben, 65–66, 71–75, 78
Freeman (deputy sheriff), 31
Freeman, Harry, 108–109
French Camp, Calif., 16
Frulock, W. R., 98
Fulkerth (sheriff), 69
Fulton (attorney general), 128

Gainesville, Ga., 156–58, 160–61, 167–68, 172
Galt, Calif., 32
Garrett, Pat, 209
Georgetown, Calif., 16
Georgetown (Seattle), Wash., 151
Gibbs, Roland, 114–15
Gibson, Peter ("Scotty"), 42
Gifford, Ont., 118
Gilliard, B. P., 168, 173–75, 177
Ginton (detective), 32
Glick, Soloman, 97

Goble, Oreg., 94–95
Goodacre, Sam, 59–60, 204
Gordon (mayor), 128
Government Island, Wash., 95–96, 98
Grafton, Calif., 66
Graham (member of Parliament), 146
Graham (prison commissioner), 187
Grell, J. William. *See* Dunn, William J.
Griffin, Dwight, 66
Gunnison, Colo., 45, 57

Hale, William (prison warden), 86–91
Hall, Hewlette (attorney general), 172
Hallett, Moses (judge), 56
Handford, Jim (Charley H. Couch), 155–70, 173–76
Haney, Bill, 151
Haney, Dave, 151
Hanie, Tom (detective), 160, 166
Hardin, John Wesley, 206
Harrington, James ("Alkali Jim"), 24–36, 204, 206
Harshman, Z. G. ("Gay"), 94–104
Hathaway, Allen, 5
Hausbrough, Jack, 45
Hays, Jack, 83
Hester, Robert (constable), 13
Heyman, Gus, 41
Hickman's Store (Calif.), 26, 32
Hicks, Bill, 83–84
Hockaday, J. B., 166–67
Hoehn, Charles, 94–103
Holland, Esom, 184
Hook (sheriff), 17
Hope Pass (trail) (B.C.), 107, 111
Hot Springs, Colo., 59
Hume, James B. (Wells, Fargo detective), 61, 72, 75

INDEX

Hunter, Charley (Charles Turner), 155–70, 173–76, 237 n. 1
Hunter, Wilson, 46

Interbay, Wash., 114
Ione, Calif., 29, 32
Ione Valley (Calif.), 29
Irving, P. A. E. (justice), 128–29
Irwin, William (Calif. governor), 36–37

Jackson, Calif., 29, 32
Jackson, Ky., 3
Jackson, Mich., 8, 49
Jacksonville, Fla., 184
Jacksonville, Oreg., 66
James, Jesse, 165, 171, 193, 202–204, 207–10
James, Jim (alias Bill Miner), 3, 101
James brothers, 208
James-Younger band, 208
Jessup, Ga., 184
Johnson, Abel, 151
Johnson, Edward L. (U.S. attorney), 56
Johnson, G. A. (constable), 150
Johnson, James A. (Calif., lt. governor), 37, 40
Johnson, Rufus, 158
Johnson's ferry (Calif.), 16
Jones, Billy (detective), 31
Jones, J. B. (judge), 170, 173, 175, 177
Jones, Stanton T., 53–60, 63–72, 75–77
Jordon, Joseph, 112
Joseph, Adolph, 196
Julette (railroad fireman), 114–16

Kamloops, B.C., 119, 124, 126, 128, 130, 135
Karcher (police chief), 69, 73

Keiser, John, 40
Keisler, John, 41
Keller, James, 13
Kelly (prison warden), 128
Kendall, Elbert, 162
Ketchum ("Black Jack"), 206
Keysville, Ga., 182, 186
Kirkland, Wash., 114
Knoxville, Tenn., 156
Korner, Fred, 97

Lake City, Colo., 46
Landers, B. B. (U.S. marshal), 161
Landers, B. C., 112
Lane, Thomas (constable), 69
Langmaid, Orrin (police chief), 69
Lansing, Mich., 49
Lanton, Bradford, 140
La Porte City, Iowa, 54
Laramie, Wyo., 56
Las Cruces, N.Mex., 209
Las Vegas, N.Mex., 208–209
Lathrop, Tom (sheriff), 31
Laurier, Sir Wilford (prime minister), 147–48
Lawrence, J., 151
Leadville, Colo., 40, 44, 57, 64
Lee (police officer), 69, 73
LeRoy, Billy (Arthur Pond), 44–48, 61, 206
Levy, J., 25
Levy, Julius, 174
Lewis, Thomas (police officer), 18
Linday, Gus, 152
Lindenstrut, Bessie, 174
Little, W. A. (sheriff), 160
Livermore, Calif., 72
Long, Joseph (deputy sheriff), 16–17, 19, 32
Long, Robert, 163, 181
Los Angeles, Calif., 3, 13
Louisville, Kans., 54

Low, Fredrick (Calif. governor), 11, 23
Luck, John (alias Bill Miner), 3, 155, 164
Lula, Ga., 158

McAfee, Mrs., 158
McAllister, A. C. (prison superintendent), 36–37, 40, 80
McCabe (deputy sheriff), 69, 75
McClusky, Albert F., 138, 151
McCoy, Henry (sheriff), 69, 72–73
McCracken, Mrs. J., 158
McGregor, A., 128
McIntosh (chief constable), 136, 146
McIntyre, Alex D., 128, 135–36, 144
Mack, Henry, 82
McKenzie (prison instructor), 146
McLean (deputy attorney general), 128
McNeil, Alex (prison guard), 138, 149
McQuaid, George (sheriff), 68, 72, 75
McQuarry, A. L., 121, 128
Markle, Chris, 82
Marshal, Charles, 36
Marshall, Joseph, 84–90
Matthews, Lee (Wells, Fargo agent), 32
May, Waldo, 5
Mayfield (Palo Alto), Calif., 31
Medina, Wash., 114
Meighen (member of Parliament), 144
Merritt, B.C., 119
Midville, Ga., 186
Milledgeville, Ga., 63, 181–82, 188–89, 194–98
Milledgeville prison farm (Ga.), 63, 153, 181, 188, 191
Miller, William A., 65–79
Miller, William B., 159, 168, 174
Miller, W. W., 196
Milton, Calif., 66, 68
Milwaukee, Wis., 105
Miner, Allen E. (derivative of Bill Miner's true name), 99
Miner, Ezra (grandfather), 4
Miner, Ezra A. (uncle), 4
Miner, Ezra Allen (given name of Bill Miner). *See* Miner, William Allen
Miner, Frank (cousin), 7
Miner, Harriet Jane (mother), 4–7, 11, 23, 40, 42, 84, 93, 200
Miner, Harriet R. (sister), 4–5, 84, 93
Miner, Henry Clay (brother), 4–5, 7, 11
Miner, Joseph (father), 4–5
Miner, Joseph Benjamin ("Ben") (brother), 5–6, 40–42
Miner, Lyman (uncle), 5
Miner, Mary Jane (sister), 4–6, 40, 44, 57, 84, 91, 93, 99–100, 193
Miner, Orrin (uncle), 5
Miner, William (uncle), 4
Miner, William Allen ("Bill"): aliases of, 3, 8, 44, 49, 53, 57, 60, 64, 69–70, 75–76, 94, 99, 101, 105, 111, 118, 125–26, 128, 134, 153, 155, 164, 168–70, 173, 176–77, 179, 193; arrest and captures of, 16–17, 31–32, 59–60, 73–77, 121–28, 161–64, 187–90; birth of, 4; bisexuality of, 22–23, 50, 61, 94, 101, 186, 204; chronology, 213–18; death of, 194; description and characteristics of, 9, 20, 40, 49, 79, 94, 101, 171, 194–96; drug use of, 119, 204; early life of, 5–11; escapes of, 17–18, 33, 35–36, 61–64, 79–80, 84–88, 98–104,

INDEX

110–13, 138–48, 172–73, 182–90; first crimes of, 12–16; funeral of, 195–96; gunfights of, 30–31, 60, 126, 187; imprisonments of, 19–23, 35–40, 42–43, 78–93, 134–38, 165–72, 176–82, 188–94; legends and folklore of, 3–4, 13, 29, 61–63, 150–51, 184, 187, 189–90, 192–94, 199; military service of, 9–10; noncriminal activities of, 10, 44, 57, 64, 94–95, 98, 105, 111–12, 118–19, 149–54; other crimes of, 12–16, 25–26, 57–59, 106; personality profile and habits of, 10–12, 24, 29, 52, 79–83, 91–92, 101, 106, 111–12, 119, 135, 141, 153–56, 165–66, 168–70, 172–79, 181–82, 184–85, 187, 191–92, 196–98, 200–206; rewards for, 25, 74, 101–102, 111–12, 128–29, 139, 160–61, 181, 183, 188–89; romances of, 49–53, 69–71, 154; as social bandit, 205–11; stage robberies of, 24–29, 44–48, 54–55, 57–58, 65–72; tombstone of, 198–99; train robberies of, 94–98, 105–10, 113–17, 119–21, 155–61; trials of, 17–19, 33–36, 78, 128–34, 173–75; wounds of, 83–86
Minster, Henry W. (Pinkerton detective), 166, 171
Mission Junction (Mission City), B.C., 108–109, 137
Mitchell, Herb, 109–10
Mitchell, J. Fondren, 184
Modesto, Calif., 66
Mokelumne Hill, Calif., 26, 32–33
Mooney, Walter T., 158–59
Moore, A. H., 182
Moore, John, 182

Moore, Joseph A., 194–96
Moore, Tom, 182–87
Moore's Flat, Calif., 66
Morgan, George (alias Bill Miner), 3, 155
Morgan, William A. (alias Bill Miner), 3, 49, 57, 60, 76, 94, 99–101
Morley, B. C., 124
Mormon Slough, Calif., 25
Morrill, J., 128
Mount Vernon, Wash., 94, 99–100
Mundorf, John, 68
Murray, John, 68
Murray, G. R., 136
Murrays Creek (Calif.), 26
Murrieta, Joaquin, 202–203, 208
Myers, Jerome (police officer), 16–17, 32

Nehalem, Oreg., 95
Nevins, James (Pinkerton superintendent), 98–100
Newcastle, Calif., 14–15, 18, 23
Newhall, H. H., 150
Newhall, Roger, 150
New London, Conn., 4
Newton County Convict Camp (Ga.), 176, 180–81, 188
New Westminster, B.C., 130, 133, 135, 140–41
New Westminster Penitentiary (B.C.), 130, 134–40
Nicola Valley, B.C., 111, 141
Nimberwill district (Ga.), 163, 180
Norman, W. B. (judge), 35

Oakland, Calif., 16–17, 71–73
Oconee River (Ga.), 160, 188–89
Ohio City, Colo., 45
Onondaga, Mich., 4, 48–53, 64
Ootsa, B.C., 150

Osgood, G. L., 68
Ottawa, Ont., 142–43
Ouray, Colo., 57

Page, Frank (congressman), 61
Parberry, Jack, 109
Parlin's Ranch (Parlin), Colo., 44–46
Partee (special agent), 160
Patton, Warren, 45
Pelham, Dr. J. E., 22, 37
Perkins, George (Calif. governor), 37
Petaluma, Calif., 15
Peters, C. R. (corporal), 123–24, 126, 128
Pinkerton, William, 29, 180
Pitkin, Colo., 45
Pittman, Dr., 60
Plumb, A. B. (senator), 56
Pocket, the (Calif.), 66, 72
Pond, Arthur. *See* LeRoy, Billy
Pond, Silas. *See* Potter, Silas
Poole, Alonzo W. (sheriff), 11, 18
Porter (ranch hand), 16–17
Portland, Oreg., 95–101, 105, 108, 113, 136, 150, 179
Port Townsend, Wash., 118
Potter, Sam (Silas Pond), 48
Princeton, B.C., 105–106, 111, 119
Pueblo, Colo., 48
Pumyea, Peter (police captain), 69, 71–72

Quilchena, B.C., 125–26

Radcliffe, A., 121
Rahm, Henry (sheriff), 68, 73
Raines, Ga., 184
Ramsey, W. J., 167
Rancho El Tejon (Calif.), 3
Reddy, Ned (prison captain), 81–82
Redwood City, Calif., 31

Reidsville, Ga., 181, 198
Reno, Nev., 61
Rice, Robert, 198
Rincon, N.Mex., 209
Rio de Janeiro, Brazil, 63
Risbel (sheriff), 99
Roberts, Alonzo, 118–19
Robertson, George. *See* Cooper, Charles
Robin Hood, 206, 208, 210–11
Robinson, Burton, 4
Robinson, Robert (captain), 9
Rooney (judge), 78
Roper (captain), 10
Rosehill, B.C., 119
Rough and Ready, Calif., 65
Royal, Neb., 155
Rudabaugh, Dave, 208–209

Sacramento, Calif., 9, 25, 29, 42, 65, 73–75, 85, 204
Sacramento River (Calif.), 73
Sadler, O. M. (detective), 161
Saguache, Colo., 57, 60
Saint Clair, Ga., 185–87
Salem, Oreg., 103
Salter, William, 186–87
Salt Lake City, Utah, 41
Salton Sea (Calif.), 3
Samish Bay (Wash.), 94, 99
Samish Flats, Wash., 93, 98–99
Samuels (deputy sheriff), 186–88
San Andreas, Calif., 26, 29, 33, 35
San Diego, Calif., 3–4, 201
San Francisco, Calif., 15–16, 30–32, 61, 66, 72, 84, 118, 201, 204
San Joaquin River (Calif.), 16
San Jose, Calif., 25, 30–31, 204
San Luis Valley (Colo.), 47, 57
San Mateo, Calif., 31
San Quentin Prison (Calif.), 19–24, 35–40, 42–43, 78–92
Sapperton, B.C., 133–34

INDEX 259

Sargent, John F. (sheriff), 156–58, 162–63, 168, 181
Scales, Billy, 198
Schisler family, 105
Scott, Nathaniel J., 108–10
Seattle, Wash., 106, 113–14, 117, 137, 151–52
Sellinger (detective), 30–32
Shaver, Ham, 176
Shirley, C. H., 158–59
Shirley, Paul (prison warden), 81
Shoebotham, T. M. (sergeant), 124, 126, 128
Short, James ("Lem"), 114, 117
Silver City, N.Mex., 63
Silver Cliff, Colo., 44
Silverdale, B.C., 108–109
Simikameen, B.C., 141
Sims, George E. (judge), 168
Sinclair, John, 15–20, 227n. 17
Slumgullion Pass, Colo., 46
Smith, A. H., 14
Smith, A. T., 42
Smith, Austin, 42, 204
Smith, G. W. (jailer), 33
Smith, J. E. (warden), 188, 192–94
Smith, L. J., 186
Smith, Peter, 82
Smith (railroad superintendent), 177
Snoqualmie, Wash., 153
Sonntag (prison director), 82
Sonora, Calif., 66, 69–70, 75, 78
Spauldin, Freeman, 4
Spokane, Wash., 115
Stanton, J. H., 136
Stark, Jackson, 151
Stevens, Frank, 41–42
Stevenson, H. F., 96
Stewart, J. C. (corporal), 123, 125–26, 128
Stockton, Calif., 15–18, 26, 29–30, 32, 75, 204

Stone, Appelton W. (detective), 30–32
Stoneman, George (Calif. governor), 78
Storey, William (sheriff), 98–101
Stout, George, 55
Stringham, Clark, 66–68
Sumas, Wash., 93, 111, 113, 118, 137
Swint, J. W., 186

Tabuteau, J. H. (constable), 123, 125
Tacoma, Wash., 98
Tatsa River Forks (B.C.), 150
Taylor, J. D. (member of Parliament), 143, 145–46
Tehama, Calif., 66
Telkwa, B.C., 150
Terrell, H. A. (detective), 160
Terrell, W. F. (detective), 160
Terry, Jake ("Cowboy Jake"), 93–94, 104–18, 136–37, 144–45, 152
Thacker, John (Wells, Fargo detective), 61, 69, 72, 73, 75
Thomas, P. G. (sergeant), 123, 125
Thomasville, Ga., 184
Thompson, Henry, 82
Thompson, Howard (district attorney), 174
Thorburn, W. M., 121
Thorn, Abbot G. (deputy sheriff), 32
Thorn, Ben (sheriff), 25, 33, 34–35, 68
Thornton, C. T. (warden), 176
Tibbits (judge), 33
Tilden, Ill., 57
Tilghman, Bill, 209
Tipton family, 156
Tobert, Bill, 156
Toccoa, Ga., 170
Todhunter, William, 66, 72–75
Toomsboro, Ga., 189
Train robbery (Ducks, B.C., 1909), 151

Troutdale, Oreg., 96
Truckee, Calif., 40–42
Turner, Charles. *See* Hunter, Charley
Tweed, C. A. (district attorney), 11, 23
Tyler, G. W., 32, 34, 37

Uncompaghre, Colo., 57
Underhill, H. B. (judge), 18

Vancouver, B.C., 107–108, 110, 140–41
Van Riper, Pomroy, 51
Vasquez, Tiburcio, 208–209
Vejar, Ricardo, 13
Venables Station (Colo.), 54
Vevay Township, Mich., 4–5, 49
Victoria, B.C., 136

Wagon Wheel Gap, Colo., 47, 55, 59
Wainwright, James C., 5
Walker (constable), 31
Walker, Mary, 180
Walters, Walt, 162–63, 181
Washington, Calif., 75
Waters (prison guard), 86–90
Watson, A. E., 156, 166
Watts, John B., 183–85
Waynesboro, Ga., 182, 186–87
Wellman, Louis, 40, 44, 57, 93, 193
Wellman, Mary Jane. *See* Miner, Mary Jane
Wells, Thomas, 57, 60
Whatcom (Bellingham), Wash., 93, 99, 105, 118

Wheelan, John, 36
White, Harry, 45–46
White, W. H., 186
Whitesail, B.C., 150
White Sulphur Springs, Ga., 158, 167
Whitlock (deputy sheriff), 31
Whittle, J. W., 186
Whonock, B.C., 111
Whyte, J. C. (warden), 136, 142, 144
Widencamp, W. J., 188–89
Wiedner, Cicero (city marshal), 55
Wiggins, W. M., 188–89
Wilcox, John, 82
Wilcox, P. P. (U.S. marshal), 55
Williams, H. L. J. (reverend), 196
Williams, John (constable), 69
Williams, Mose, 176
Williams, Professor and Mrs. O. C., 5
Williams (sheriff), 140
Willis, Henry S., 50–51
Willis, Jane Goodfellow, 50
Willis, Jennie Louise, 50–52, 64
Wilson, J. J. (sergeant), 123–26, 128, 136, 144–45
Wilson, Morris, 82
Winding Stairs Gap, Ga., 156, 161
Woodbridge, Calif., 16, 32
Woodland, Calif., 66, 72–73
Woods, Walter John, 138
Wright, George (brigadier general), 3

Yankee Jims, Calif., 6–7, 10–12, 14–15, 202
Young, F. McB. (judge), 150
Younger brothers, 207–208